Reasoning About Parallel Architectures

William W. Collier
International Business Machines Corporation
Poughkeepsie, New York

Prentice-Hall International, Inc.

This edition may be sold only in those countries to which it is consigned by Prentice-Hall International. It is not to be re-exported and it is not for sale in the U.S.A., Mexico, or Canada.

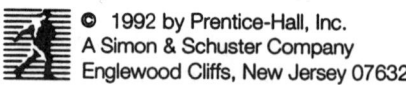
© 1992 by Prentice-Hall, Inc.
A Simon & Schuster Company
Englewood Cliffs, New Jersey 07632

All rights reserved. No part of this book may be reproduced, in any form or by any means, without permission in writing from the publisher.

Printed in the United States of America

10 9 8 7 6 5 4 3 2 1

ISBN 0-13-766098-7

Prentice-Hall International (UK) Limited, *London*
Prentice-Hall of Australia Pty. Limited, *Sydney*
Prentice-Hall Canada Inc., *Toronto*
Prentice-Hall Hispanoamericana, S.A., *Mexico*
Prentice-Hall of India Private Limited, *New Delhi*
Prentice-Hall of Japan, Inc., *Tokyo*
Simon & Schuster Asia Pte. Ltd., *Singapore*
Editora Prentice-Hall do Brasil, Ltda., *Rio de Janeiro*
Prentice-Hall, Inc., *Englewood Cliffs, New Jersey*

To **Yasuko**

Everything that is possible happens;
only what happens is possible.

"The Castle" by *Franz Kafka*

Contents

Foreword   *xv*

Preface   *xvii*

Acknowledgments   *xix*

1 Seeing Architecture Failures   1

    A Program to Test for a Violation of the Architecture Consisting of the Rules of Computation, Write Order, and Read Order   2

    A Program to Test for a Violation of the Architecture Consisting of the Rules of Computation, Write Order, Read Order, and Write Atomicity   6

    Conclusion   9

    Problems   10

    References   11

2 History   13

    Order Rules   13

Atomicity Rules   15

Intuitions About Instantaneous Write Operations   16

Applications   19

> Below the Machine Interface, 20
> At the Machine Interface, 20
> Higher Level Languages, 21
> Software Systems, 21

Preview   22

Problem   23

References   23

3 Basics   25

Sets   25

Factorials   25

Graphs   26

Problems   29

Reference   29

4 The Model   31

Building Models   31

Goals for a Model of Architectures   31

The Essence of a Multiprocessing System   32

A Model of a Multiprocessing System   33

> Executions, 33
> Events, 34
> The Value of an Event, 34
> Architectures, 35
> Transition Templates, 36

The Value of the Graph Set Structure as a Model of Time   37

Problems   38

5 The Rule of Computation   39

Computation Subrules   39

    The Statement-Read-Write Subrule (SRW), 40
    The Compute-Write-Read Subrule (CWR), 40
    The Compute-Read-Write Subrule (CRW), 41
    The Compute-Write-Write Subrule (CWW), 42

Creating the Graph Set for CMP   42

Problems   48

6 The Rules of Program Order   52

The Rule of Uniprocessor-Write-Read Order (UWR)   53

The Rule of Uniprocessor-Read-Write Order (URW)   54

The Rule of Uniprocessor-Write-Write Order (UWW)   55

The Rule of Uniprocessor Order (UPO)   57

The Rule of Program Order (PO)   57

The Rule of Write Order (WO)   60

The Rule of Read Order (RO)   62

The Rule of Program Order by Store (POS)   64

The Rule of Write Order by Store (WOS)   66

Problems   66

7 The Rules of Atomicity   70

Seeing the Failure of a Set of Events to Occur Instantaneously   70

The General Rule of Atomicity   71

    The Rule of Statement Atomicity (SA), 71
    The Rule of Write Atomicity (WA), 72
    The Rule of Read Atomicity (RA), 72

A Convenient Notation   72

Relationships between SA, WA, and RA   73

    An Execution Showing a Failure to Be Statement Atomic (Theorem A25), 73

An Execution Showing a Failure to Be Write Atomic (Adapted from Theorem A38), 75

An Execution Showing a Failure to Be Read Atomic (Theorem A32), 77

Arcs Labeled $<_{RA}$, $<_{WA}$, and $<_{SA}$ 78

Problems   80

8 The Rules of Synchronization   82

The Rule of Write Synchronization (WS)   83

An Execution Exhibiting a Failure to Be Write Synchronized (Theorem A39), 84

The Rule of Consistency (CON)   85

An Execution Exhibiting a Failure to Be Consistent (Theorem A35), 86

The Rule of Read Synchronization (RS)   87

An Execution Exhibiting a Failure to Be Read Synchronized (Theorem A41), 87

Problems   89

9 The Rules of Intrastatement Order   90

The Rule of Absolute Write Canonical Order (AWC)   90

A Violation of Atomicity?, 91

An Execution Exhibiting a Failure to Be Absolute Write Canonically Ordered (Theorem A43), 91

The Rule of Absolute Read Canonical Order (ARC)   92

An Execution Exhibiting a Failure to Be Absolute Read Canonically Ordered (Theorem A46), 93

The Rule of Relative Write Canonical Order (RWC)   94

An Execution Exhibiting a Failure to Be Relative Write Canonically Ordered (Theorem A45), 95

The Rule of Relative Read Canonical Order (RRC)   96

An Execution Exhibiting a Failure to Be Relative Read Canonically Ordered (Theorem A48), 97

Problem   98

10 The Structure of Architectures   99

The Architectures an Execution Does/Does Not Obey   99

The Executions That Do/Do Not Obey
a Given Architecture 100

Sets of Rules versus Sets of Executions 101

The Graph of Rules X,Y such that $X \Rightarrow Y$ 101

The Unique Importance of the Rule of Computation 101

The Product of Architectures 102

Problem 102

11 Out-of-Order Read Operations 103

A Simple Example of Indistinguishable Architectures 103

Out-of-Order Reads on a Multiprocessor 104

Transition Templates 104

Proof of Lemma 11.1 105

Warp Architectures 107

Problems 109

References 109

12 Write Synchronized Is Write Atomic 110

A Fundamental Result on Storage Hierarchies 110

Discussion of Part I of the Proof 113

Part I of the Proof, 114

Discussion of Part II of the Proof 115

Part II of the Proof, 116

Conclusion of the Proof 116

A Small Generalization 117

Write Synchronized Is Write Atomic 117

The Problem with Read Synchronization 118

A Source of Performance Improvement 119

Problems 120

13 Ring-shaped Systems — 121

A Ring-shaped System   121

Ring Architecture 1: Not Consistent   122

Execution 1, 122
Execution 2, 123
Execution 3, 123

Ring Architecture 2: Write Atomic   124

Execution 4, 124

Ring Architecture 3: Write Synchronized   125

Execution 5, 126

Ring Architecture 4: Program Ordered by Store   127

Execution 6, 127

Problems   128

References   128

14 A Model of a Shared Memory Multiprocessor — 129

A Typical Shared Memory Multiprocessor   129

The MP Model   130

Shortcuts   131

Architecture Rules in the MP Model   132

The Rule of Write Atomicity, 132
The Rule of Write Synchronization, 133
The Order Rules, 133
The Rule of Computation, 133

Transition Templates   133

An Execution Showing Interactions Between Processors   135

A Write Synchronized Execution, 135
Deadlock and Livelock, 136

Phantom Events   137

The Relaxation of Censier and Feautrier   138

The Analogue of Lemma 12.5 in the MP Model   140

Problems   141

15 Future Work   143

The Limits on Disobeying Rules   143

Conditional Rules   144

Rules on Global Events versus Rules on All Events   145

Problems   146

Appendix A Distinguishable Architectures   148

Appendix B A Program to Assist with Lemma 12.5   195

Appendix C Problems and Solutions   202

Appendix D Problems to Test a Machine for a Failure to Obey Its Architecture   220

Index   229

Foreword

Despite the many, many books on computer architecture already on the market, there is still disagreement about the meaning of the word "architecture." Does it refer to the rules about how a system operates, or does it refer to the organization and implementation of an actual computer?

In a practical sense the definition hardly matters. The work-a-day issue most often addressed is how to ensure that a computer appears to obey program order when, in fact, it violates program order in pursuit of improved performance. Complex cache structures and high speed data management algorithms are developed in the pursuit of greater speed. Yet always the question hangs in the air: can a programmer detect the difference between what was planned and what was implemented? Every design group dedicates people to the task of ensuring that the implementation does not violate the architecture. People are assigned to test an implementation. Reviews are conducted. Analyses of new implementation techniques are made. Technical leaders who, through skill and experience, have attained the status of project "guru", are called on to give their stamp of approval. Consequently, the topics of preserving data integrity and cache coherency get thoroughly examined. Yet despite all the efforts, there has never been a practical method for ensuring that all "windows" of possible violations have been closed.

For as long as I have known Bill Collier, he has been striving to develop a language, a symbolism to describe computer architecture. The goals have been to think clearly and to reason exactly. Different architectures can be examined for detectable differences. Deviations between an architecture and its implementation can be deduced. The design process becomes less an art and more a science.

I have seen this work in action. Beginning in 1986 Brad Frey and Ray Pedersen proposed a technique for fetching operands out of sequence under certain conditions. The conditions appeared to guarantee that the out-of-sequence execution would be invisible to the user. There were countless discussions and blackboard exercises, but still no certainty that all the "windows" had been closed. Hearing of the problem, Collier defined models of both the new and the original architecture and showed them to be indistinguishable (see Chap 11).

There are limits to the value of this approach. A proof on paper of the logical equivalence of two architectures does not guarantee that an implementation is error-free. No theorem eliminates the need for new ideas or substitutes for experience. No mathematical statement can usefully describe a physical machine.

On the other hand, no matter how good or how bad a highway, having a map is better than not having a map. Knowing even just a handful of certainties makes it easier to design a machine, to test it, and to write programs for it.

This book opens up a new field in computer architecture. It is not easy. Really new approaches rarely are. But based on what I have seen, mastery of the material is well worth the effort required.

Marie L. Wieck
International Business Machines Corporation

Preface

Computers obey rules, such as the requirements to execute instructions in order or to make changes to the value of an operand appear to occur instantaneously throughout a system. Rules govern the behavior of a computer and determine what answers a computer can calculate. Simple programs, ones consisting only of assignment statements, can reveal the failure of a computer to obey the rules governing its behavior. Chapter 1 shows how.

Two computers are distinguishable if there is a program which can compute an answer on one of the computers which it provably cannot calculate on the other computer. Otherwise, every answer calculable on one computer is calculable on the other and then the computers are called indistinguishable. Suppose a slow computer with a simple interface can be redesigned to run faster, but with a more complex internal structure. If the new computer is indistinguishable from the original computer, then the new computer can be presented to a customer as being both simple and fast. The history of computer architecture, presented in Chap. 2, is one of increasingly sophisticated understanding of the factors that make computers distinguishable or indistinguishable.

The rules of behavior for early computers were simple. There was only one processor. It executed every instruction in a program strictly in the sequence defined by the program. Later, in order to increase performance, computers were designed to execute instructions out of order when it could not be detected by a program.

When (shared memory) multiprocessors were developed, the same rules on out-of-order execution did not work. Now the second processor could see the first processor execute instructions out of order. The rules had to be revised to require once again that instructions be executed in order.

With the advent of caches came another change to the rules. Caches permitted multiple copies of an operand to exist within a system. This introduced the danger that one processor could change the value of a variable, but another processor might continue to make use of the unchanged value. The rules had to change to require write operations (to appear) to occur atomically.

Reasoning about the issues of distinguishability and indistinguishability requires the use of sets, factorials, and chromatic graphs (Chap. 3) and the formal definition of a model of a shared memory multiprocessor (Chap. 4).

The most important rule of all is the rule of computation, which describes how answers are calculated (Chap. 5). Often this rule is treated as being so obvious as not to merit description. In fact, however, an explicit statement of it is vital in reasoning about interactions between processes.

The many variations on the order rules are described in Chap. 6 and the atomicity rules in Chap. 7.

The synchronization rules in Chap. 8 are of the form: if a first statement performs some action before a second statement performs some action, then the first statement will perform some other action before the second statement performs some other action. These rules turn out to be quite important.

The intrastatement order rules in Chap. 9 are very similar in form to the synchronization rules, but turn out to have little value. They have the form: if a first statement performs some action before performing some other action, then a second statement will perform some action before performing some other action.

Chapter 10 states some general results about rules.

The major work of the book occurs in Chaps. 11 and 12. Frey's Theorem demonstrates a simple condition under which read operations can be performed out of order on a multiprocessor without the fact being detected (Chap. 11). The WSISWA Theorem shows that write operations will appear to occur instantaneously if all processors see all changes in the values of operands occur in the same order (Chap. 12). The performance improvement achievable through the use of the WSISWA Theorem is demonstrated in a ring-structured system (Chap. 13) and in a more detailed model of a multiprocessor (Chap. 14).

Finally, some conjectures on further relaxing the rules are offered (Chap. 15).

There was an early choice to be made in the structure of the book: to discuss first or to define first. I chose to discuss (1) testing machines for architecture errors and (2) the development of computer architecture first, rather than to delay addressing these topics until after the seven chapters which define the model and the rules, even though this meant that terms are used in the first two chapters that are not precisely defined until some chapters later.

There is a problem set at the end of most of the chapters. The more difficult or unsolved problems are starred.

William W. Collier

Acknowledgments

I am indebted to many people.

At Syracuse University Gideon Frieder, Ari M. Ghafoor, F. Lockwood Morris, Ernest Sibert, and Douglas R. Troeger encouraged this effort. Lockwood Morris in particular worked repeatedly to bring forth clarity and precision from muddled intuitions.

Sarita V. Adve, James K. Archibald, Mark D. Hill, Kevin P. McAuliffe, and Christoph Scheurich made valuable, detailed comments on early drafts of the manuscript. Charles Heimbach critiqued a late draft and wrote and ran the first programs to find (tentative) evidence of architecture failures.

For years Marie Wieck has been generous with good cheer and bedrock good sense. James A. Jackson was strong and supportive when it mattered most.

Jerry L. Amos, Gary S. Ditlow, Brian B. Moore, Kenneth E. Plambeck, James W. Rymarczyk, Ronald M. Smith, R. Timothy Tomaselli, Jason M. Warren, Charles F. Webb, and Luther J. Woodrum have been favorite partners in mostly amicable technical discussions over the years. For the opportunity to work with these and other talented and determined people on problems of lasting value, I am very grateful to the International Business Machines Corporation.

John Wait (formerly) at Prentice-Hall proposed that I write a book on computer architecture before I knew I wanted to. Thanks also to Greg Doench, Mike McDermott, Jean Lapidus and especially Joan Magrabi for conducting me through the mysteries of publishing.

To Joanne Voulellis Close, Werner M. Cohn, Inez M. Patrick, and Ronald and Gloria Robbins, there are debts that can never be repaid.

Special thanks to James Davis, Michael Dubois, Paul Easton, Dan Gross, Allan Gottlieb, Wally Kleinfelder, Evripidou Paraskevas, Harold Stone, Janice Stone, and Becky Wiesnewski.

I gratefully acknowledge the permission of Alfred A. Knopf, Inc. to quote from *The Trial* by Franz Kafka, (copyright 1937, 1956, and renewed 1965) and the permission of the International Business Machines Corp. to use material originally published in the following technical reports.

Principles of Architecture for Systems of Parallel Processes. TR 00.3100. IBM Corporation, Poughkeepsie, NY. March 25, 1981. 83 p.

Architectures for Systems of Parallel Processes. TR 00.3253. IBM Corporation, Poughkeepsie, NY. January 27, 1984. 72 p.

Write Atomicity in Distributed Systems. TR 00.3304. IBM Corporation, Poughkeepsie, NY. October 19, 1984. 9 p.

All errors remain solely my responsibility.

For each of these friends there is a story to tell:

Dennis Ackerman, Miriam Ayala, James Babb, George Bean, H. Carol Bernstein, David G. Bevier, Alice Bissell, Donna Boling, Hank and Rachel Bosch, James Broderick, Elaine Colandrea, Miles C. Dales, Bob Davis, Eric and Bonnie Davis, Mark DelCogliano, Sue Depew, Douglas Durant, Martin R. Eckstein, Anne Englehart, Carl and Margaret Englehart, Mathew and Jean Englehart, Fred and Kimiko Ek, A. Kenneth Fitzgerald, Jonathan Fram, Bradly G. Frey, Barbara Gayhart, Albert J. Gerney, Wally Gillman, Mike Graf, Joel Greenberg, Diana Hanson, Joseph T. Harth, Nany Hasan, Paul R. Heintz, Leo Hellerman, Richard Hemmes, Wolfgang and Kristin Hoppe, Hubert B. Ickes, Michael Ignatowski, Robert K. Jenner, Ruth Kava, Peter and Jo Kaestner, Henry T. Kieronski, David L. King, Pat King, Erik Kiviat, Eric and Gail Knutsen, Keith N. Langston, Edward and Leslie Lowry, Ted Lowry, Paul Lowy, Klim Maling, Alan F. Martens, Edward Matthews, Theo and Ronnie Maschas, Dennis D. Massanari, Gretchen McKenzie, William and Cecilia McWilliams, Robin Morris, Thomas R. Murphy, Yutaka Obayashi, Stewart Ogden, Rong-Yi Pan, Raymond P. Polivka, Marge Potenza, Robert Rabinowitz, George Rhoads, Steve Rosen, Thomas J. Ruane, Tim and Lisa Sanford, Howard and Ingrid Shipotofsky, John and Pat Simpson, Tito and Giulia Sorlini, Jim Stapleton, Henry and Janet Steck, David Stein, Lilo Stern, David Stickler, James and June Stickler, Joseph Stickler, Wendy Stuart, Nicholas Tindall, Marcelle Toor, Thomas B. Warnock, David B. Watts, John Western, Allen Wiener, Michael P. Witt, Mickey Wolf, and William A. Woods.

To my family: Charles and Ruth Collier, Ignatius and Eugenia Starzynski, Isabel DiGiusto, Robert and Sally Caiola, Roberta Collier, Jeffrey Collier, Jennifer Collier, Alessandra DiGiusto, and Patrick, Maria, and Madeleine ("Cookie") O'Neill, my thanks for your patience and understanding.

This book is dedicated to my wife, Yasuko Hatano-Collier, whose constant love and encouragement were expressed, even on the nights when even I could hardly stand myself, in a dinner that was attractive, adventurous, nourishing, and satisfying.

1

Seeing Architecture Failures

An architecture is the set of rules governing a machine's behavior which a programmer needs to know in order to determine what answers a program, running on the machine with a given set of input data, can generate.

The set of rules constituting an architecture for a machine specifies how the machine will (appear to) behave. Order and atomicity are the most visible rules. Order rules define the extent to which statements may be executed out of order. Atomicity specifies the degree to which certain operations appear to occur instantaneously, for example, whether or not a change in the value of an operand appears to all processes to occur at the same time.

There are other types of rules. As will be seen later, the most important, obvious, and yet least visible rule is the rule on how a machine performs computations.

Most programs are written with the expectation that they will be executed on a uniprocessor. The rules for uniprocessors are simple and are intuitively understood by both the engineers who build the machines and by the programmers who use them.

On systems, such as shared memory multiprocessors, where data is shared between independent processes, the interactions between processes can be subtle and complex. In such environments the rules must be thoroughly understood both by those building the systems and by those writing programs for them.

As Hofri [HOFR90] noted, most programmers first encounter the need to understand the rules when they take a course on operating systems and are assigned the task of writing a critical section routine [DEBR67, DIJK65, EISE72, KNUT66, LAMP74, RAYN86]. A critical section routine is a subroutine which may be executed simultaneously by any number of processes. The function of a critical section routine is to allow only one out of any number of calling processes at a time to execute a specific piece of code, the so-called critical section. The critical section routine is required to achieve this function using only the higher level language equivalents of Load, Store, Test, and Branch instructions. (Allowing the use of Test and Set or other atomic instructions makes the problem trivial to solve.)

Consider the following scenario. A programmer writes a critical section routine to run on a machine that obeys architecture A_1. The program is proven to be logically correct for such a machine. The program is then executed on a machine which obeys a subtly distinct architecture, architecture A_2. When the program is run, it performs differently from what is expected. It may never allow any process into the critical section of code. It may allow dozens at once. In either case, the machine, following the rules of architecture A_2, has performed a function (that is, calculated an answer) which could not be performed under architecture A_1.

It is not important what the source of the unexpected answer is. Perhaps the machine was intentionally built to obey the rules of architecture A_2, and the programmer mistakenly projected the rules of architecture A_1 onto the machine. Or the programmer may correctly have understood the architecture manual to specify architecture A_1, but the engineers failed to implement architecture A_1 and produced instead a machine which obeyed architecture A_2.

What is important is that execution of the program has had the effect of proving that the two architectures, A_1 and A_2, are distinct. The program produced a result under architecture A_2 which provably could not be produced under architecture A_1.

In this case, the erroneous result is more an existence proof than a constructive proof. It shows that the two architectures are distinct, but it does not identify the rules on which they differ. The natural question to ask then is whether or not programs can be written to perform simple calculations and then to identify what rules, if any, were not obeyed in the course of the calculations.

A PROGRAM TO TEST FOR A VIOLATION OF THE ARCHITECTURE CONSISTING OF THE RULES OF COMPUTATION, WRITE ORDER, AND READ ORDER

Consider Program 1, the parallel program in Fig. 1.1, running as two processes, P_1 and P_2.

If the two processes can be synchronized to start executing at exactly the same time, then k need be no larger than 2 in order to find a failure to obey the architecture. In practice such synchronization is impossible to achieve. An effective alternative is to choose k as large as possible and to trust the randomizing effect of operating system scheduling to cause at least part of the two processes to execute at the same time on different processors.

A Program to Test for a Violation of the Architecture

$$
\begin{array}{ll}
P_1 & P_2 \\
L_1: A:=1; & L_1: X[1]:=A; \\
L_2: A:=2; & L_2: X[2]:=A; \\
L_3: A:=3; & L_3: X[3]:=A; \\
\ldots & \ldots \\
L_k: A:=k; & L_k: X[k]:=A;
\end{array}
$$

Figure 1.1 Program 1.

If A has been initialized to zero, then what answers (preserved in the sequence of values X[1], X[2], . . . , X[k]) can Program 1 produce? The answers depend on the rules the machine obeys. If the value of the write operations in process P_1 are calculated in the way one intuitively expects and if the write operations occur in the order defined by the program, then operand A will take on the sequence of values 1, 2, . . . , k. If the values of the read operations from operand A in process P_2 are calculated in the way one intuitively expects and are performed in the order defined by the program, then the values of X[1], X[2], . . . , X[k] will end up obeying two conditions.

Condition 1. Every value is in the range from 0 through k.

Condition 2. The sequence of values is monotonically increasing, that is, each value is either the same as or greater than the preceding value.

Given any sequence of values meeting the two conditions, it is easy to construct an arrangement of statements to produce the sequence of values. For example, suppose $k = 5$ and the sequence of X values is 0, 3, 3, 3, 4. The arrangement of the statements of Program 1 shown in Fig. 1.2 produces the given sequence.

$$
\begin{array}{ll}
P_1 & P_2 \\
 & L_1: X[1]:=A; \\
L_1: A:=1; & \\
L_2: A:=2; & \\
L_3: A:=3; & \\
 & L_2: X[2]:=A; \\
 & L_3: X[3]:=A; \\
 & L_4: X[4]:=A; \\
L_4: A:=4; & \\
 & L_5: X[5]:=A; \\
L_5: A:=5; &
\end{array}
$$

Figure 1.2 Sequence to produce values of 0, 3, 3, 3, 4.

It is difficult to reason about the case in which the X sequence does not obey one or the other of the two conditions. For example, suppose X[2] ends up with the value 13. Clearly, the machine would have to malfunction for this to occur. Possibly one of the write operations in P_1 fetched a value between 1 and k, but stored a value of 13, which was subsequently copied into X[2]. Or perhaps the write operations in P_1 took place correctly, but a mishap occurred with one of the read operations in P_2; only values in the range of one through k were stored in A, but a read operation in P_2 incorrectly fetched the value 13 and then stored this result.

There is no general understanding of what it means for a machine to compute. The situation in which the value 13 is calculated is obviously an example of a failure to compute correctly, but at this stage it is as difficult to explain why 13 is wrong as it is to explain why answers in the range from 0 to k are right. The rule of computation is formally defined in Chap. 5. Until then, intuition must continue to suffice.

For sequences of X values which obey the two conditions, it is enough to work with whole statements to show how the sequences can be generated by the program. To analyze situations in which the two conditions do not both hold requires that a finer unit of granularity be adopted.

Each statement can be thought of as consisting of one read event and one write event, where each event is represented by a quadruple specifying the process, the statement in the process, the action (either "R" for a read operation or "W" for a write operation), and the operand. For the two statements in the following program there are four events.

$$P_1 \qquad\qquad P_2$$
$$L_1: A:=1; \qquad L_1: X:=A;$$

In statement L_1 in process P_1 there is a read event from the literal value 1 and a write event into operand A. These two events are represented by $(P_1,L_1,R,1)$ and (P_1,L_1,W,A). In statement L_1 in process P_2, there is a read event from operand A and a write event into operand X. These two events are represented by (P_2,L_1,R,A) and (P_2,L_1,W,X)

A rule expresses the idea that certain events happen in time before certain other events. Write $a < b$ (read "a happens before b") if a rule requires that event a happen before event b.

The rule of write order requires that for any pair of write events a, b, if a and b are in the same process and if a is in a statement which occurs before the statement containing event b, then $a < b$.

The rule of read order requires that for any pair of read events a, b, if a and b are in the same process and if a is in a statement which occurs before the statement containing event b, then $a < b$.

A sequence of events of the form $a < b < \ldots < a$ is called a circuit.

For a given program the rules of an architecture may require that there be several "happens before" relations between each pair of events for the program. If the rules, when applied to the program and its input and output data, imply that a circuit must exist among the events, then the program is said not to obey the architecture. Otherwise, the program does obey the architecture.

If the values $X[1], X[2], \ldots, X[k]$ are not monotonically increasing, then three facts are true.

1. There is an arrangement of the events in the program which calculates the values in the sequence and which obeys the rule of read order, but which does not obey the rule of write order.

2. There is an arrangement of the events in the program which calculates the values in the sequence and which obeys the rule of write order, but which does not obey the rule of read order.
3. There is no arrangement of the events in the program which calculates the values in the sequence and which obeys both write order and read order.

For example, in Program 1, how could the sequence 0, 0, 4, 3, 5 occur? If read order is obeyed, but write order is disobeyed, then the sequence of events in Fig. 1.3 calculates the sequence of X values.

P_1	P_2
	(P_2,L_1,R,A)
	$(P_2,L_1,W,X[1])$
	(P_2,L_2,R,A)
	$(P_2,L_2,W,X[2])$
$(P_1,L_1,R,1)$	
(P_1,L_1,W,A)	
$(P_1,L_2,R,2)$	
(P_1,L_2,W,A)	
$(P_1,L_3,R,3)$	
$(P_1,L_4,R,4)$	
(P_1,L_4,W,A)	
	(P_2,L_3,R,A)
	$(P_2,L_3,W,X[3])$
(P_1,L_3,W,A)	
	(P_2,L_4,R,A)
	$(P_2,L_4,W,X[4])$
$(P_1,L_5,R,5)$	
(P_1,L_5,W,A)	
	(P_2,L_5,R,A)
	$(P_2,L_5,W,X[5])$

Figure 1.3 Read order is obeyed, but not write order.

If write order is obeyed, but read order is disobeyed, then the arrangement of statements in Fig. 1.4 calculates the given sequence of X values.

Finally, the following argument shows that there is no arrangement of events which is both write ordered and read ordered and which calculates the given sequence of X values.

If the program obeys write order, then $(P_1,L_3,W,A) < (P_1,L_4,W,A)$.

For X[4] to have the value 3, it must be that (P_2,L_4,R,A) comes between (P_1,L_3,W,A) and (P_1,L_4,W,A), that is, $(P_1,L_3,W,A) < (P_2,L_4,R,A) < (P_1,L_4,W,A)$.

For X[3] to have the value 4, it must be that $(P_1,L_4,W,A) < (P_2,L_3,R,A)$.

If further, the program obeys read order, then $(P_2,L_3,R,A) < (P_2,L_4,R,A)$.

P_1	P_2
	(P_2, L_1, R, A)
	$(P_2, L_1, W, X[1])$
	(P_2, L_2, R, A)
	$(P_2, L_2, W, X[2])$
$(P_1, L_1, R, 1)$	
(P_1, L_1, W, A)	
$(P_1, L_2, R, 2)$	
(P_1, L_2, W, A)	
$(P_1, L_3, R, 3)$	
(P_1, L_3, W, A)	
	(P_2, L_4, R, A)
$(P_1, L_4, R, 4)$	
(P_1, L_4, W, A)	
	(P_2, L_3, R, A)
	$(P_2, L_3, W, X[3])$
	$(P_2, L_4, W, X[4])$
$(P_1, L_5, R, 5)$	
(P_1, L_5, W, A)	
	(P_2, L_5, R, A)
	$(P_2, L_5, W, X[5])$

Figure 1.4 Write order is obeyed, but not read order.

Combining these results shows that the following circuit exists among the events of the program under the architecture consisting of the rules of computation, write order, and read order.

$$(P_2, L_4, R, A) < (P_1, L_4, W, A)$$
$$< (P_2, L_3, R, A)$$
$$< (P_2, L_4, R, A)$$

Consequently, the program does not obey the architecture consisting of the rules of computation, write order, and read order.

The argument can easily be generalized to cover any nonmonotonic sequence of X values.

A PROGRAM TO TEST FOR A VIOLATION OF THE ARCHITECTURE CONSISTING OF THE RULES OF COMPUTATION, WRITE ORDER, READ ORDER, AND WRITE ATOMICITY

Other programs can be written to test machines for adherence to other architecture rules. For example, the rule of write atomicity requires that the effect of any given store operation appear to take place instantly throughout the system. Program 2 in

A Program to Test for a Violation of the Architecture

P_1	P_2	P_3	P_4
L_1: A:=1;	L_{A1}: U[1]:=A;	L_{B1}: X[1]:=B;	L_1: B:=1;
L_2: A:=2;	L_{B1}: V[1]:=B;	L_{A1}: Y[1]:=A;	L_2: B:=2;
. . .	L_{A2}: U[2]:=A;	L_{B2}: X[2]:=B;	. . .
L_k: A:=k;	L_{B2}: V[2]:=B;	L_{A2}: Y[2]:=A;	L_k: B:=k;
	. . .	. . .	
	L_{Ak}: U[k]:=A;	L_{Bk}: X[k]:=B;	
	L_{Bk}: V[k]:=B;	L_{Ak}: Y[k]:=A;	

Figure 1.5 Program 2.

Fig. 1.5 tests to see if a system fails to obey the rule of write atomicity, as well as the rules of computation, read order, and write order.

There are k statements in processes P_1 and in P_4. There are $2*k$ statements in processes P_2 and in P_3.

On a machine that is write atomic, a write operation appears to become visible to all processes at the same instant. If a machine is not write atomic, then it is possible to see a write operation become visible to different processes at different times.

To represent a failure to be write atomic, write events must have a finer granularity than before. Now, for each statement, there must be a separate write event associated with each process in the system. The event represents the moment at which the effect of the write operation becomes visible to the associated process. Equivalently, there is defined to be a separate store S_i for each process P_i, $i = 1, 2, \ldots , n$. A write event represents the moment at which the new value of the operand named in the event is recorded in store S_i. To represent this, a fifth component is added to each event to specify the store. Now

P_1	P_2
L_1: A:=1;	L_1: X:=A;

is represented by the events

P_1	P_2
$(P_1,L_1,R,1,S_1)$	
(P_1,L_1,W,A,S_1)	
(P_1,L_1,W,A,S_2)	
	(P_2,L_1,R,A,S_2)
	(P_2,L_1,W,X,S_1)
	(P_2,L_1,W,X,S_2)

Note that read events for process P_i always reference store S_i. This represents the fact that read operations are performed only from the store associated with the process performing the read.

As with Program 1, Condition 1 and Condition 2 can be tested for on the data resulting from running Program 2. If after running the program, the values of the sequence for U (or V, X, or Y) are not in the range from 0 through k, then the program has detected a failure of the machine to compute correctly.

If the values are all in the range from 0 through k, but in some sequence the values are not monotonically increasing, then the program, again as before, has detected a failure of the machine to obey the architecture consisting of the rules of computation, write order, and read order.

Suppose the values are all in the range from 0 through k and are monotonically increasing. Then there is another test that can be applied to see if the machine fails to obey the rule of write atomicity.

Condition 3. For all I, J, in the range from 1 to k, either $V[I] \geq X[J]$ or $Y[J] \geq U[I]$, or both.

Suppose Condition 3 does not hold. Then $V[I] < X[J]$ and $Y[J] < U[I]$. These inequalities have the following implications.

If the program obeys the rule of write order, then the value of B increases monotonically during execution of the program. Let n be the value of $X[J]$ at the completion of execution of the program.

If $V[I] < X[J]$, then the read operation on B in statement L_{BI} in process P_2 comes before the write operation (with value n) into B which in turn occurs before the read operation on B in statement L_{BJ} in process P_3. Expressed in terms of events this is

$$(P_2, L_{BI}, R, B, S_2) < (P_4, L_n, W, B, S_2)$$

and

$$(P_4, L_n, W, B, S_3) < (P_3, L_{BJ}, R, B, S_3)$$

The rule of write atomicity requires that the write events for one statement all appear to happen at the same time. Therefore, if $(P_2, L_{BI}, R, B, S_2) < (P_4, L_n, W, B, S_2)$, then $(P_2, L_{BI}, R, B, S_2) < (P_4, L_n, W, B, S_3)$. Consequently,

$$(P_2, L_{BI}, R, B, S_2) < (P_4, L_n, W, B, S_3) < (P_3, L_{BJ}, R, B, S_3)$$

Similarly, if the terminal value of $U[I]$ is m, then $Y[J] < U[I]$ implies that

$$(P_3, L_{AJ}, R, A, S_3) < (P_1, L_m, W, A, S_2) < (P_2, L_{AI}, R, A, S_2)$$

If the program obeys the rule of read order, then

$$(P_2, L_{AI}, R, A, S_2) < (P_2, L_{BI}, R, B, S_2)$$

and

$$(P_3, L_{BJ}, R, B, S_3) < (P_3, L_{AJ}, R, A, S_3)$$

Combining the four results yields the following circuit:

$$\begin{aligned}
(P_1, L_m, W, A, S_2) &< (P_2, L_{AI}, R, A, S_2) \\
&< (P_2, L_{BI}, R, B, S_2) \\
&< (P_4, L_n, W, B, S_3) \\
&< (P_3, L_{BJ}, R, B, S_3) \\
&< (P_3, L_{AJ}, R, A, S_3) \\
&< (P_1, L_m, W, A, S_2)
\end{aligned}$$

Thus, if for any I, J in the range from 1 through k, it is the case that $V[I] < X[J]$ and $Y[J] < U[I]$, then the machine on which the program occurred could not have obeyed the rules of computation, read order, and write atomicity.

CONCLUSION

In order to write programs consisting of processes that interact correctly on shared data, it is vital to understand the architecture of the machine executing the program. Failure to do so can lead to software bugs which are virtually impossible to reproduce, much less identify and repair.

Conventional hardware verification programs seek to ensure the correct operation of individual hardware components. The program is expected to identify both the nature of the failure and the potential culprit components. The more a program is tailored to stress a specific component, the less likely the program is to detect an error from any other source. Programs such as Programs 1 and 2 are needed to test the system as a whole. It is possible that two components may each appear to work correctly when considered in isolation, but may together interact erroneously. Programs such as Programs 1 and 2 can help to detect such cases.

Program 1 and Program 2 are based on Theorem A7 and Theorem A38, respectively, in App. A. Other theorems in App. A can also be used to form test programs. Examples are worked out in Appendix D. Running such programs on a machine can provide assurance that the programmer understands the machine and that the machine conforms to its architecture.

The mechanisms employed in this chapter in reasoning about Program 1 and Program 2 are primitive. The rules and objects are described in a way that is more intuitive than exact. In order to reason effectively about parallel architectures, the intuitive perceptions about how processes interact on shared data must be translated into precisely defined concepts within the framework of a formal model. Chap. 2 reviews prior work and previews the major results obtained. Chap. 3 presents the elements of set theory, factorials, and chromatic graph theory. Chap. 4 then defines the model used throughout the text.

PROBLEMS

1.1. Consider each sequence of X values below (for $k = 5$) as the result of executing Program 1.
  a. If the sequence obeys both Condition 1 and Condition 2, then show an arrangement of events (statements will do) that computes the X sequence.
  b. If the sequence violates Condition 1, say how.
  c. If the sequence obeys Condition 1, but violates Condition 2, then show an arrangement of statements that computes the X sequence, but violates the rule of write order. Do the same for read order.
  a. 1, 2, 2, 3, 5.
  b. 1, 2, 147, 3, 5.
  c. 1, 2, 4, 3, 5.

1.2. Assume four runs were made using Program 2 (with $k = 5$) to see if a machine obeyed the architecture consisting of the rules of computation, write order, read order, and write atomicity. For each set of output data shown, say what rule, if any, the data shows the machine not to obey.

a.

U	V	X	Y
1	0	0	4
2	1	3	4
2	1	4	5
4	1	7	5
5	1	7	5

b.

U	V	X	Y
0	1	1	4
2	1	2	5
4	1	4	5
3	2	4	5
4	2	4	5

c.

U	V	X	Y
2	0	1	2
5	1	1	3
5	4	3	4
5	5	3	5
5	5	4	5

d.

U	V	X	Y
0	2	0	1
3	2	0	1
3	2	0	3
4	2	5	4
4	3	5	5

1.3. A failure to be write atomic means that two write events in the same statement can be shown not to have happened at the same time. Use the "happens before" relations in the section on atomicity to show that $(P_4, L_n, W, B, S_3) < \ldots < (P_4, L_n, W, B, S_2)$ in Program 2.

1.4. A straightforward search for a violation of Condition 3 involves $2 * k ** 2$ tests: test for $V[I] < X[J]$ and test for $Y[J] < U[I]$ at each point (I, J) on the grid that follows.

```
k  •  •  •  •  •  ···  •
   .  .  .  .  .
   .  .  .  .  .
   .  .  .  .  .
5  •  •  •  •  •  ···  •
4  •  •  •  •  •  ···  •
3  •  •  •  •  •  ···  •
2  •  •  •  •  •  ···  •
1  •  •  •  •  •  ···  •
   1  2  3  4  5       k
```

Assume that the values in the U, V, X, and Y sequences are monotonically increasing and find a search that requires only $2 * k$ tests. (Hint. If $V[I] \geq X[J]$, then what is known about $V[I + D]$ and $X[J]$, for $D > 0$?)

1.5. Consider the following variation on Program 1 in Fig. 1.6. If the program is executed on a machine that obeys the rules of computation, read order, and write order, then what will the value of the A sequence be? Of the X sequence? What can be determined from a suitable pattern of X values?

$$
\begin{array}{ll}
P_1 & P_2 \\
L_1: A[1]:=1; & L_1: X[1]:=A[1]; \\
L_2: A[2]:=2; & L_2: X[2]:=A[2]; \\
L_3: A[3]:=3; & L_3: X[3]:=A[3]; \\
\quad \cdots & \quad \cdots \\
L_k: A[k]:=k; & L_k: X[k]:=A[k];
\end{array}
$$

Figure 1.6 Program 3.

1.6. The execution in Fig. 1.7 occurs on a machine that is reputed to obey the rules of computation, read order, and write atomicity. Identify the circuit which shows this not to be the case.

Initially, $A = B = C = R = S = U = V = X = Y = 0$.

$$
\begin{array}{llllll}
P_1 & P_2 & P_3 & P_4 & P_5 & P_6 \\
L_1: A:=1; & L_1: R:=A; & L_1: B:=1; & L_1: U:=B; & L_1: C:=1; & L_1: X:=C; \\
 & L_2: S:=B; & & L_2: V:=C & & L_2: Y:=A;
\end{array}
$$

Terminally, $A = B = C = R = U = X = 1, S = V = Y = 0$.

Figure 1.7 Program 4.

REFERENCES

DEBR67 N. G. DEBRUIJN. Additional comments on a problem in concurrent programming control. *Comm. ACM* 10:3 (1967), 137–138.

DIJK65 E. W. DIJKSTRA. Solution of a problem in concurrent programming control. *Comm. ACM* 8:9 (1965), 569.

EISE72 M. A. EISENBERG AND M. R. MCGUIRE. Further comments on Dijkstra's concurrent programming control problem, *Comm. ACM* 15:11 (1972), 999.

HOFR90 M. HOFRI. Proof of a mutual exclusion algorithm—A 'class'ic example. *Operating Systems Review*, 24:1 (1990), 18–22.

KNUT66 D. E. KNUTH. Additional comments on a problem in concurrent programming control. *Comm. ACM* 9:5 (1966), 321–322.

LAMP74 L. LAMPORT. A new solution to Dijkstra's concurrent programming problem. *Comm. ACM*, 17:8 (1974), 453–455.

RAYN86 M. RAYNAL. *Algorithms for Mutual Exclusion*. MIT Press, Cambridge, MA. 1986.

2

History

Suppose that there are two machines M_1 and M_2 and that for every program and every set of inputs, any output that can be generated by machine M_1 can also be generated by machine M_2. Then the set of outputs generated by machine M_1 is contained in the set of outputs generated by machine M_2 and so write $M_1 \Rightarrow M_2$ (read "M_1 implies M_2").

If $M_1 \Rightarrow M_2$ and $M_2 \Rightarrow M_1$, then write $M_1 \Leftrightarrow M_2$ (read "M_1 and M_2 are indistinguishable"). If either $M_1 \Rightarrow M_2$ is false or $M_2 \Rightarrow M_1$ is false, then say that M_1 and M_2 are distinguishable. (These ideas will be restated more formally in Chap. 4 in terms of architectures, rather than machines.)

Let M_1 be a machine with a simple user interface. Let M_2 be a machine that is faster and more complex than M_1, but that is indistinguishable from M_1. Then machine M_2 can be presented to the customer as machine M_1. The result is a machine that appears to be as simple as machine M_1 but as fast as machine M_2. In the rest of this chapter, the history of computer architecture is presented in terms of the development of successively more sophisticated indistinguishable machines.

ORDER RULES

The computers of the 1950s and early 1960s had only a single processor. Programs and data resided in main storage. A processor fetched an instruction and interpreted its operands. The operands were fetched from main storage to the processor. The processor manipulated the operands and returned results to storage. Then the processor performed the same actions all over again beginning with the next instruction. A machine which operates in this fashion is said to obey the rule of program order. Let U_2 be such a machine. (U_1 will be defined in a moment.)

If it were efficient for machines always to execute instructions strictly in program order, then only this one order rule would be necessary. This is not the case. There are situations in which it is faster to execute statements out of order than it is to execute them in order. Suppose that on a uniprocessor system, operand B is available to the processor and operand A is deep down in the storage hierarchy when the machine is about to execute

$$P_1$$
$$L_1: X:=A;$$
$$L_2: Y:=B;$$

Instead of waiting for operand A to arrive from main storage before executing statement L_2, it is faster to initiate the fetch of operand A, then to copy B into Y, and then to finish the first statement when operand A arrives at the processor. Furthermore, it is safe to do so since the program cannot detect that the reversal in the order of fetches has happened.

Let U_1 be a uniprocessor that is identical to U_2 except that U_1 executes statements out of order when, as described previously, it cannot be detected. Then U_2 and U_1 are indistinguishable, $U_1 \Leftrightarrow U_2$.

The fact that some operations could occur out of order without being detected was well understood during the era of uniprocessors [ANDE67] and [TOMA67].

The rules defining what behaviors were and were not allowed on uniprocessors were first laid out explicitly by Kuck et al. [KUCK80]. (See the UWR, URW, and UWW rules in Chap. 6.) The rules for a U_1 machine were simple (by today's standards), because on a uniprocessor the only observers of a program's behavior were the program itself during the run and the programmer at the end of the run.

Later, when multiprocessing systems were developed, it was found that what worked on uniprocessor systems did not necessarily work on multiprocessor systems. On multiprocessing systems it was found that there was a third, new observer of a process' behavior, namely, the process running on the other processor.

Smith [SMIT72], reasoning from the example in Fig. 2.1 (Theorem A4 in App. A), was the first to observe that two programs executing at the same time could reveal a failure of the implementation of a machine to obey an architectural requirement that instructions be executed in order. The argument goes as follows: if statements are executed in order, then statement L_1 in process P_1 occurs before statement L_2. Similarly with statements L_1 and L_2 in process P_2. Since Y ends up with a value of 1, the write of 1 into A in statement L_2 of process P_1 occurs before the read of A in statement L_1 in process P_2. Similarly, L_2 in P_2 occurs before L_1 in P_1. Consequently, there is a circuit in time among the statements of the execution. This is impossible.

$$\text{Initially, } A = B = X = Y = 0.$$

```
       P₁                P₂
L₁:  X:=B;         L₁:  Y:=A;
L₂:  A:=1;         L₂:  B:=1;
```

$$\text{Terminally, } A = B = X = Y = 1.$$

Figure 2.1 Visible out-of-order execution.

As a result of this execution and others (see Theorems A5 and A6 in App. A), for a long time out-of-order execution was avoided in the design of multiprocessing systems.

Let M_2 be a multiprocessor which executes statements in order. Let M_1 be identical to M_2 except that statements are allowed to execute out of order in the same way as on U_1. Then it is easy to reorder statements in Smith's execution to show that it can occur on machine M_1. The preceding argument showed that the execution could not occur on machine M_2. Consequently, M_1 and M_2 are distinguishable, $M_1 \neg \Rightarrow M_2$.

In 1986 Bradly Frey [FREY86] found a case in which read operations can be done out of order without the fact being detected. In Fig. 2.2, processor P_1 can fetch operand B before fetching operand A providing the value of B is not changed by another process after P_1 fetches the value of B and before P_1 fetches the value of A. Let M_3 be a machine which obeys Frey's rule. The proof that M_2 and M_3 are indistinguishable, $M_2 \Leftrightarrow M_3$, is given in Chap. 11.

```
       P₁                P₂
L₁:  X:=A;         L₁:  B:=Z;
L₂:  Y:=B;
```

Figure 2.2 Seeing out-of-order reads.

ATOMICITY RULES

Most programs exhibit some regularity in the pattern in which operands are accessed in main storage. Once an operand has been referenced, it is often referenced again a short time later. This is known as locality of temporal reference. Further, once an operand has been referenced, other operands nearby in main storage are often referenced a short time later. This is known as locality of spatial reference.

In the early 1970s a way was found to make use of locality of reference to increase system performance greatly at a relatively small increase in system cost. A small, expensive, high-speed memory was built close to the processor. This memory was called a cache. Operands were copied into the cache whenever they were referenced in main storage. On a subsequent reference to the same operand a short time later, the processor would often find the operand already in the cache and so fetch it from the cache instead of from main storage, at a considerable savings in time. This exploited locality of temporal reference.

It was efficient to load into the cache not just individual operands, but a fixed-size section of storage, called a line. Thus, when a processor referenced a sequence of operands in storage, the first reference would cause a line to be loaded into the cache, and subsequent references to operands in the sequence would find the operands already loaded into the cache. This exploited locality of spatial reference.

Virtually all programs exhibit a large measure of locality of reference. In scientific calculations typically upwards of 95 percent of all operand references are satisfied via the cache. Even with programs with more random patterns of storage access, such as database programs and operating systems, the percentage of operand references satisfied via the cache is often 80 percent or more. Thus, a cache can have an enormous impact on system performance since it enables more than 80 to 95 percent of all storage accesses to be satisfied at the speed of the cache, instead of at the speed of main storage.

At first it was not evident what a large conceptual step caches represented. On early systems there was only one place for a processor to look for an operand: always in main storage. Now there could be two copies of an operand, one in main storage and one in the cache. Of course, programs could create multiple copies of an operand on secondary storage and in main storage. What was new was that the processor alone, not any program, now had responsibility for creating and controlling a second copy of the operand.

The rules for such a system were simple: (1) to find the most recent copy of an operand, always look first in the cache, and if not found, then look in main storage, and (2) whenever the cache becomes full, erase one or more unchanged operands (actually lines) and possibly write back to main storage one or more lines which had been changed while in the cache.

When two processors with caches were first combined into one multiprocessing system, there was the potential for each operand to exist in three copies, one in main storage and one in each of the caches associated with the two processors. If the two processors each independently followed the rules for uniprocessor systems, then the two processors could each set the value of their copy of an operand (in each of their own caches) to different values, repeatedly use the value in their own cache, and not be aware of the conflict. Just as with the case of the order rules, it became apparent that more sophisticated rules were required for a multiprocessing system than for a uniprocessor system. The solution adopted for this problem on the IBM System/370 system was to require that the system appear to have a single level store [IBMC88], that is, the system was required to be indistinguishable from a system which had no caches and on which all storage accesses were made from main storage.

INTUITIONS ABOUT INSTANTANEOUS WRITE OPERATIONS

There are many intuitions about what it means to say that write operations occur instantaneously in a system. The most common meaning of the term is that of single copy atomicity. A system exhibits single copy atomicity if the following two conditions are met:

Intuitions about Instantaneous Write Operations

1. After every two write operations to a shared operand, either the value of the first write operation or the value of the second write operation remains in the operand. Thus, it is impossible for part of the value of the first write operation and part of the value of the second write operation to remain in the operand.
2. When a read operation and a write operation occur to the same operand, the value obtained by the read operation is either the value of the operand before the write operation or the value of the operand after the write operation. It is never the case that the value of the read operation is partly the value of the operand before the write operation and partly the value of the operation after the write operation.

In contrast to the idea of single copy atomicity is the idea of multiple copy atomicity. A system which permits different processors to see an operand change value at different times is equivalent to a system in which each processor has its own separate copy of all of storage. Multicopy atomicity requires that all copies of an operand change value at the same instant.

Throughout the text single copy atomicity is assumed. Henceforth, "atomicity" always refers to multiple copy atomicity.

Each intuition about multiple copy atomicity can be represented by a separate machine. While it is not possible to prove rigorously that machines based on intuitions are equivalent, it can still be possible to gain insight into the different concepts.

Consider four multiprocessing machines, A_1, A_2, A_3, and A_4. In the A_1 machine there is only one store. A change to any operand in the store is necessarily visible to all processors in the system at the same time.

In the A_2 machine there is a separate store for each processor; each write operation is represented by one write event for each store in the system. Each write event for a given operation changes an operand's value at exactly the same instant as the other write events for the given operation. A change in the value of operand A followed by a change in the value of operand B in a system with four stores can be represented by the diagram in Fig. 2.3. First operand A changes instantly everywhere and then operand B changes instantly everywhere.

Clearly, $A_1 \Leftrightarrow A_2$.

B	B	B	B
A	A	A	A
S_1	S_2	S_3	S_4

Figure 2.3 A2: A write atomic machine.

In the A_3 machine the write events for a given write operation can occur at different times, but no other event can intervene between any two of the write events for the same operation. This idea underlies the definition of atomic operation given in Chap. 7. In an A_3 system events for the store into operand A and the store into operand B might be represented as in Fig. 2.4.

```
                B
                              B
                                    B
                      B
                                    A
              A
                      A
      A
      S₁      S₂      S₃      S₄
```

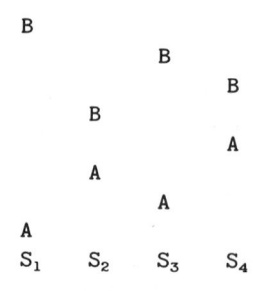

Figure 2.4 A3: A machine indistinguishable from a write atomic machine.

The execution of any program on the A_3 machine can be translated into an execution of the program on the A_2 machine by combining the write events for a write operation into a single event, and vice versa. Thus, $A_2 \Leftrightarrow A_3$.

Censier and Feautrier [CENS78] defined a system to be cache coherent if every load instruction for a given operand sees the most recent value stored into the operand. Call this machine CF. CF is more relaxed than A_2 since it allows distinct copies of an operand to change value at distinct times. Hence, $A_2 \Rightarrow CF$. (Possibly the original intent was that $A_2 \Leftrightarrow CF$.)

In the A_4 machine the write events for each individual statement may occur at different times and other events may intervene. However, for every pair of statements the following rule, called the rule of write synchronization, holds.

Let A and B be any pair of operands which change value during some time interval. If one process sees operand A change before seeing operand B change, then all processes see operand A change before seeing operand B change. This can be restated in terms of stores as: if a first statement writes into a store before a second statement writes into the same store, then the first statement writes into each other store before the second statement writes into each other store. (Also, there is no restriction on the intermingling of events from other statements.) Figure 2.5 represents an interval of time in which A and B change values in the same order, first A and then B, in all stores.

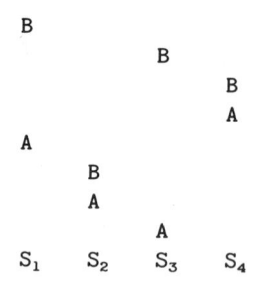

```
      B
                      B
                                    B
                                    A
      A
              B
              A
                              A
      S₁      S₂      S₃      S₄
```

Figure 2.5 A4: A write synchronized machine.

Write synchronization is so much weaker than write atomicity that it might seem an easy matter to find an execution which obeys write synchronization, but does not obey write atomicity, thereby demonstrating that machines A_3 and A_4 are distinguishable. It turns out that write synchronization is distinguishable from write atomicity only in the presence of the rule of read synchronization. (Fortunately, read synchronization is not a rule that a multiprocessing system would be expected to obey. See Chap. 8.) In the absence of the rule of read synchronization, the two rules, write synchronization and write atomicity, are indistinguishable. Every execution which obeys one, obeys the other. This is Theorem 12.1, called the WSISWA theorem, in Chap. 12. Thus effectively, $A_2 \Leftrightarrow A_4$. (An early version of the proof of the WSISWA theorem appeared in [COLL84].)

The connection between write synchronization and write atomicity has been glimpsed before. Figures 2 and 3 in [LAMP78] strongly suggest that a write synchronized execution is indistinguishable from a write atomic execution (though the text does not explicitly state the idea). Gelenbe and Sevcik [GELE79] wrote that "Among conflicting updates originating nearly simultaneously from different nodes only one can be allowed, and among the updates allowed, they must be applied in the same order at each node." Nicholas [NICH89] quotes Archibald [ARCH87] as defining a system to be totally write ordered "if all caches observe all writes in the same order."

The preceding discussion established that machines A_1, A_2, A_3, and A_4 are indistinguishable, that is, $A_1 \Leftrightarrow A_2 \Leftrightarrow A_3 \Leftrightarrow A_4$. Since also $A_2 \Rightarrow CF$, it is the case that $A_4 \Rightarrow A_3 \Rightarrow A_2 \Rightarrow CF$, that is, write synchronization is a solution to the problem of cache coherence.

A machine which obeys the rule of write synchronization almost certainly contains some central mechanism which controls the sending out of write events to the processors on which the processes run. On the other hand, programs for parallel processes are typically written with the image of N coequal processes in mind. Given that write synchronization, and hence the central control mechanism, must exist for the system to operate correctly, it is reasonable to ask whether or not the central control mechanism ought to become a visible part of the architecture of the machine, and if so, then what other functions it might be assigned to perform.

APPLICATIONS

There are four areas in which the ideas in this text may be applied.

1. Below the machine interface, that is, to the internal implementation of machines.
2. At the machine (assembly language) interface.
3. In the definition of higher level languages.
4. In software systems, such as operating systems, networks, and distributed data bases.

Below the Machine Interface

Lamport [LAMP79] defined a multiprocessor to be sequentially consistent if the result of any execution could also be obtained by executing the operations of all the processors in some sequential order in which the operations of each processor appear in the order defined by the program executed by the processor.

Implicit in the idea of sequential consistency is the concept of indistinguishable architectures. A machine is not required to be sequentially consistent in fact; it only has to appear to be, in the sense that any answer it calculates could also be calculated by a sequentially consistent machine.

Also implicit in sequential consistency is the idea of correctness, that there is only one logical standard by which to determine whether or not a machine performs correctly.

Dubois et al., [DUBO86] introduced the concepts of strong ordering and weak ordering. Strong ordering requires that a machine obey (1) the rule of program order and (2) a form of write atomicity which disallows the occurrence of the execution in Fig. 2.6 (Theorem A29 in App. A).

```
Initially, A = B = X = Y = 0.

   P₁              P₂              P₃
L₁: A:=1;      L₁: B:=A;       L₁: X:=B;
                               L₂: Y:=A;

Terminally, A = B = X = 1, Y = 0.
```

Figure 2.6 Dubois, Scheurich, and Briggs's execution.

Strong order was originally proposed to be indistinguishable from sequential consistency. Later it was shown by Adve and Hill [ADVE90a] to be distinguishable.

The concept of sequential consistency has stimulated a great deal of research. Scheurich and Dubois [SCHE87] and Adve and Hill [ADVE90b] defined conditions sufficient to ensure sequential consistency in a multiprocessor.

Other examples of indistinguishable architectures to be applied below the interface are Frey's Theorem and the WSISWA theorem previously described. The focus of this book is specifically and solely on learning to reason about distinguishable and indistinguishable architectures, applied below the interface.

At the Machine Interface

The intent of weakly ordered architectures is to give the programmer higher performance in exchange for assuming more responsibility for the correctness of calculations by exercising greater control over a more complex machine.

Weak ordering, as defined by Dubois et al. [DUBO86], allows a processor to ignore certain architectural rules about the order of operations in between synchronization points. However, at synchronization points all variables must be restored to the state they would have had had the rules been obeyed all along. One effect of weak ordering is to structure the data accessed by the processors since the data used to achieve synchronization is subjected to more rigorous rules than other data.

Adve and Hill [ADVE90a, ADVE90b] argue that correct execution is achieved if the status of a machine at each synchronization point is reset to a state consistent with a sequentially consistent architecture.

An earlier and more limited version of weak order is found on the IBM System/370 machines. The architecture for these machines guarantees that read operations will occur in order and write operations will occur in order, but full program order is not guaranteed. Thus, it is possible for read operations to appear to occur early (or, equivalently, for write operations to appear to occur late) as in Theorem A5 in App. A. If the programmer wants to ensure that full program order occurs between two given instructions, then the programmer can execute the BCR 15,0 instruction between the given instructions. This instruction forces all prior instructions to complete before any subsequent instructions commence. The widespread use of such machines shows that complete program order is not always necessary, and therefore the standard of correctness required by sequential consistency is slightly too high.

In other areas it is efficient to ask the machine to assume a greater share of the burden. Although critical section routines can be written using only Load and Store instructions on shared data, it is more efficient to let the machine assist with this function, as with the Compare and Swap instruction [IBMC88] or the Fetch and Op instruction [EDLE85].

Higher Level Languages

It is hard to make the semantics of operations on shared variables in a higher level language explicit in the language definition without increasing the visibility of the underlying assembly language interface, thereby undermining one purpose for which the higher level language was created. Consequently, some higher level languages conceal shared data by preventing access to it by any program other than the one which has exclusive ownership of it. Some languages define shared data out of existence by requiring that all program calls be serial. Other languages simply note that unexpected answers can result from simultaneous operations on shared data. Judging from Wegner [WEGN89] there is little appreciation in the area of higher level languages of the importance of understanding the degree to which interactions on shared data obey rules of order and atomicity. Nicholas [NICH89] discussed what sequential consistency might mean in a higher level language.

Software Systems

The issues of distinguishable and indistinguishable architectures occur also in software system design. In software systems it is important for users to know the rules a sytem is intended to obey. For example, an operating system, after receiving, in a short period of time, several requests to access the data on a disk, may ignore the order in which the requests are received and may instead perform the operations in the order in which the requested data is stored on the disk. This reduces the time required to access the data, and therefore to perform the operations. However, if two programs communicate via shared disk storage, and if the two programs assume the equivalent of program order in their interactions, the reordering of accesses can produce incorrect results. Here the issue is one of discovering unexpectedly that two architectures are distinguishable.

A fundamental goal in the design of data-base systems is achieving serialization of data base updates [PAPA79]. (In Chap. 4 the discussion of representing events in time suggests that serialization is too strong a concept and that transaction atomicity is more appropriate.) The execution in Theorem A25 (App. A) shows that a machine can obey all of the architectural rules defined in subsequent chapters, other than statement atomicity, and the failure to be statement atomic can still be visible. Since statement atomicity is a weaker rule than transaction atomicity, there appears to be no covert way of achieving transaction atomicity the way write synchronization makes it possible to achieve write atomicity. Here the issue is to invent an architecture which is indistinguishable from a transaction atomic architecture.

PREVIEW

Topics in subsequent chapters are as follows.

Define some basic mathematical constructs, namely, sets, factorials, chromatic graphs, sets of chromatic graphs, and the product of sets of chromatic graphs. Derive several lemmas on the existence of circuits in sets of chromatic graphs (Chap. 3).

Define a simple model of a multiprocessing system. An execution represents the act of executing a program. Decompose executions into events. Represent an architectural rule as a set of graphs on the events of an execution. Define an architecture to be a set of rules, represented by the product of the graph sets for the rules. Explain the utility of representing events in time, not as points on the real line, but as nodes in a (partly) circuit-free set of graphs (Chap. 4).

Identify rules that can be attributed to the behavior of a multiprocessor. The rules fall into five groups: the computation rule (Chap. 5), order rules (Chap. 6), atomicity rules (Chap. 7), interstatement rules (Chap. 8), and intrastatement rules (Chap. 9). Show how a failure to obey each of the rules can be made visible by a program. In doing so, show how to prove that architectures can be distinguished. Show which rules imply which other rules (Chap. 10).

Show how to prove theorems that architectures are indistinguishable. These theorems are of the form:

Let architecture A be any subset of some large set of rules. Let architecture A_1 be A plus the rule R_1 and A_2 be A plus the rule R_2, where R_1 and R_2 are rules not in A. Then A_1 and A_2 are indistinguishable.

Since A_1 and A_2 are allowed to consist of (almost) any combination of rules, it is necessary to define all the rules before addressing the topic of indistinguishable architectures. Prove Frey's Theorem (Chap. 11). Prove the WSISWA Theorem (Chap. 12). Apply WSISWA to the architecture of a ring-structured system (Chap. 13). Apply WSISWA to the architecture of a shared memory, directory-based multiprocessor (Chap. 14). Conjecture on possible extensions (Chap. 15).

PROBLEM

2.1. In Chap. 1, the analysis of Program 2 showed that when a program failed to obey the architecture rules of computation, read order, write order, and write atomicity, then a circuit existed among the events. Problem 1.3 required that a part of this circuit could be construed as a path which demonstrates a failure to be write atomic. Now select a part of this path to show that Program 2 did not obey CF.

REFERENCES

ADVE90a S. V. ADVE AND M. D. HILL. Weak Ordering—A New Definition and Some Implications. Proceedings of the Seventeenth Annual International Symposium on Computer Architecture 18:2 (1990), pp. 2–14.

ADVE90b S. V. ADVE AND M. D. HILL. Implementing Sequential Consistency in Cache-Based Systems. Proceedings of the Nineteenth International Symposium on Parallel Processing, St. Charles, IL., August 1990. pp. I:47–50.

ANDE67 D. W. ANDERSON, F. J. SPARACIO, AND R. M. TOMASULO. The IBM System/360 Model 91: Machine philosophy and instruction handling. *IBM J. Res. and Dev.*, 11:1 (1967), 8–24.

ARCH87 J. K. ARCHIBALD. The Cache Coherence Problem in Shared-Memory Multiprocessors. Ph.D. Thesis, University of Washington, Seattle, WA. March, 1987.

CENS78 L. M. CENSIER AND P. FEAUTRIER. A new solution to coherence problems in multicache systems. *IEEE Transactions on Computers*, 27:12 (1978). 1112–1118.

COLL84 W. W. COLLIER. Architectures for Systems of Parallel Processes, Technical Report TR 00.3253, IBM Corporation, Poughkeepsie, NY, Jan. 27, 1984.

DUBO86 M. Dubois, C. Scheurich, and F. A. Briggs. Memory Access Buffering in Multiprocessors, Proceedings of the Thirteenth Annual International Symposium on Computer Architecture 14:2 (1986), 434–442.

EDLE85 J. Edler, A. Gottlieb, C. P. Kruskal, K. P. McAuliffe, L. Rudolph, M. Snir, P. J. Teller, and J. Wilson. Issues Related to MIMD Shared-memory Computers: the NYU Ultracomputer Approach. Twelfth Annual Symposium on Computer Architecture, 13:3 (1985), Boston, MA. pp. 126–135.

FREY86 B. G. Frey, private communication. 1986.

GELE79 E. Gelenbe and K. Sevcik. Analysis of update synchronization for multiple copy data bases, *IEEE Transactions on Computers*, C28:10 (1979), 737–747.

IBMC88 System Architecture/370 Principles of Operation. IBM Corporation, Publication Number SA22-7200-0, 1988.

KUCK80 D. J. Kuck, R. H. Kuhn, B. Leasure, and M. Wolfe. The Structure of an Advanced Vectorizer for Pipelined Processors. Proceedings of the IEEE Computer Software and Applications Conference (4th), COMPSAC 80, Chicago, IL. 1980. pp. 709–715.

LAMP78 L. Lamport. Time, clocks, and the ordering of events in a distributed system. *Comm. ACM* 21:7 (1978), 558–565.

LAMP79 L. Lamport. How to make a multiprocessor computer that correctly executes multiprocess programs. *IEEE Trans. on Computers*, vol. C28:9 (1979), 690–691.

NICH89 K. E. Nicholas. Levels of Ordering and Consistency in Shared-Memory Multiprocessors. Masters thesis, Dept. of Electrical and Computer Engineering, Brigham Young University. Provo, UT. April, 1989.

PAPA79 C. H. Papadimitriou. The serializability of concurrent database updates. *Journal of the ACM*, 26:4 (1979), 631–653.

SCHE87 C. Scheurich, and M. Dubois. Correct Memory Operation of Cache-based Multiprocessors. Fourteenth Annual Symposium on Computer Architecture, 15:2 (1987), Pittsburgh, PA. pp. 234–243.

SMIT72 R. M. Smith, private communication, 1972.

TOMA67 R. M. Tomasulo. An efficient algorithm for exploiting multiple arithmetic units. *IBM J. Res. and Dev.*, 11:1 (1967), 25–33.

WEGN89 P. Wegner, (ed.) Special Issue on Programming Language Paradigms. *ACM Computing Surveys*, 21:3 (1989).

3

Basics

SETS

A set S is a collection of zero or more objects. The objects are called elements or members of S. Elements are said to be in S. Sets can be finite or infinite. Write S = {a,b,c} to show that S is a finite set consisting of the objects a, b, and c. Write S = {a,b,c, . . . } to show that S is an infinite set of which the initial members are a, b, and c.

The set of symbols in a natural language alphabet is a finite set. The set of statements in a program is a finite set. The set of positive integers {1, 2, 3, . . . } is an infinite set. The set of all programs is an infinite set.

The empty set, denoted $\emptyset$, is the set which contains no elements.

If set S_3 consists of exactly those elements which are in set S_1, or are in set S_2, or are in both S_1 and S_2, then S_3 is called the union of S_1 and S_2, written $S_3 = S_1 + S_2$.

If set S_3 consists of exactly those elements which are both in set S_1 and in set S_2, then S_3 is called the intersection of S_1 and S_2.

If every element of a set S_1 is also in set S_2, then S_1 is called a subset of S_2 and is said to be contained in S_2. If, in addition, S_2 contains elements not in S_1, then S_1 is said to be properly contained in S_2.

FACTORIALS

The factorial of an integer $n \geq 0$, fact(n), is defined as follows:

1. Fact(0) = 1.
2. Fact(n) = n * fact(n − 1).

Lemma 3.1. There are fact(n) distinct ways to arrange the n elements of a finite set in a linear order.

Proof. For a set of only one element there is only one way to arrange the element in a linear order. Assume the lemma is true for a set of $n-1$ elements. For a set of n elements, the first element can occupy any of n positions in the linear order. By assumption the remaining $n-1$ elements can be arranged in fact($n-1$) linear orders in the remaining $n-1$ positions. Consequently, the total number of linear orders of the n elements is n * fact($n-1$) = fact(n) orderings. ∎

GRAPHS

A graph G = (S,R) is a finite set S and a set R of triplets (a, b, c) where a and b are distinct elements of S and c is a label (alternatively, a color) associated with a and b. The elements of S are called points or nodes of G.

The set R is called a rule.

The triplet (a, b, c) is called an arc from a to b with label c. Think of an arrow, colored with color c, extending from node a to node b. The triplet may also be represented by writing $a <_c b$, or, if the label is immaterial, by writing either $a < b$ or (a, b).

If $a < b$, the arc is said to be incident into b and incident out of a.

A graph is simple if all the triplets have the same color. Otherwise it is compound.

A path is a sequence of arcs of the form (a_1, a_2, c_1), (a_2, a_3, c_2), . . . , (a_k, a_{k+1}, c_k). (The colors c_1, c_2, . . . , c_k may be the same or different.) A path is a circuit if $a_{k+1} = a_1$.

Two paths are adjacent if they have no nodes in common except their beginning and ending nodes.

If X = (S,R_1) and Y = (S,R_2) are graphs, then the sum of X and Y, denoted X + Y is (S, $R_1 + R_2$).

A graph set (GS) is a set of graphs such that all of the graphs in the set have the same set of nodes.

A graph set is simple if all the triplets in all the graphs have the same color. Otherwise it is compound.

A graph set is circuit-full if every graph in the graph set contains a circuit.

A graph set is partly circuit-free if it is not circuit-full, that is, if at least one graph in the graph set contains no circuit.

The graph set product of two graph sets is a graph set which exists only if the graphs in both graph sets have the same set of nodes. If GS_1 and GS_2 are graph sets with the same set of nodes, then the graph set product $GS_1 * GS_2$ is a graph set

Graphs

consisting of exactly those graph sums $G_1 + G_2$ such that G_1 is in GS_1 and G_2 is in GS_2. More explicitly, if $GS_1 = \{G_{11}, G_{12}, \ldots, G_{1m}\}$ and $GS_2 = \{G_{21}, G_{22}, \ldots, G_{2n}\}$, then $GS_1 * GS_2 =$

$$\{ G_{11} + G_{21}, G_{11} + G_{22}, \ldots, G_{11} + G_{2n},$$
$$G_{12} + G_{21}, G_{12} + G_{22}, \ldots, G_{12} + G_{2n},$$
$$\ldots$$
$$G_{1m} + G_{21}, G_{1m} + G_{22}, \ldots, G_{1m} + G_{2n} \}$$

Lemma 3.2 shows that the product of graph sets is commutative.

Lemma 3.2. If $GS_1 * GS_2$ is defined, then $GS_1 * GS_2 = GS_2 * GS_1$.

Proof. From the definitions of graph set product, the sum of graphs, and the union of sets. ■

Lemmas 3.3 and 3.4 show that removing one or more arcs from one or more graphs in a graph set which is partly circuit-free creates a new graph set which is also partly circuit-free.

Lemma 3.3. Let GS_1 be any graph set which is partly circuit-free. Let GS_2 be identical to GS_1, except that one arc in one graph of GS_1 is deleted. Then GS_2 is partly circuit-free.

Proof. Deleting an arc in a graph does not create a new circuit, so if GS_1 is partly circuit-free, then so is GS_2. ■

Lemma 3.4. If $GS_3 = GS_1 * GS_2$ is partly circuit-free, then so is GS_1.

Proof. Let G_3 be a circuit-free graph in GS_3. $G_3 = G_1 * G_2$, where G_1 is some graph in GS_1, and G_2 is some graph in GS_2. To obtain G_1 from G_3, delete the arcs in G_3 which are not in G_1. Deleting arcs creates no circuits. Hence G_1 is circuit-free also. ■

Here is an important case in which the product of two partly circuit-free graphs is also partly circuit-free.

Lemma 3.5. Let GS_1 be any graph set. Let $GS_2 = \{(S,\{a < b\}), (S,\{b < a\})\}$ where a and b are arbitrary distinct nodes in the set S of nodes for the graphs in GS_1. Then GS_1 is partly circuit-free if and only if $GS_1 * GS_2$ is partly circuit-free.

Proof. If $GS_1 * GS_2$ is partly circuit-free, then by Lemma 3.4 so is GS_1. So assume that GS_1 is partly circuit-free but that $GS_1 * GS_2$ is circuit-full. Choose any circuit-free graph G in GS_1. Consider $G * GS_2$. By the assumption both $G_1 = G * \{(S,\{a < b\})\}$ and $G_2 = G * \{(S,\{b < a\})\}$ contain circuits. In G_1 the circuit must have the form $a < b < x_1 < \ldots < x_n < a$. In G_2 the circuit must have the form $b < a < y_1 < \ldots < y_m < b$. Then, contrary to the assumption, G must contain the circuit $b < x_1 < \ldots < x_n < a < y_1 < \ldots < y_m < b$. ■

A graph is complete if there is exactly one triplet (a, b, c) in R for every unordered pair (a, b) of points in S, that is, if there is exactly one arc between every two points in S.

A path of a graph G is complete if each node of G appears exactly once in the path.

Complete graphs are encountered frequently later on. It is useful to know that if they are circuit-free, they contain a unique complete path.

Lemma 3.6. Let G be a complete graph of two or more nodes. Then G contains a complete path. If G is circuit-free, then the path is unique.

Proof of existence (by induction). The lemma is obviously true for a graph of two nodes. Assume it is true for any graph of $n - 1$ nodes. Let G_2 be a complete graph of n nodes. Choose some point c in G_2, and let G_1 be the graph formed from the other $n - 1$ nodes. G_1 is complete and so by the induction hypothesis contains a complete path $a < \ldots < b$. Consider the arc between c and a and the arc between c and b. There are four cases.

1. $c < a$ and $b < c$.
2. $c < a$ and $c < b$.
3. $a < c$ and $b < c$.
4. $a < c$ and $c < b$.

For each of the four cases there is a path in G_2 containing each node of G_2 exactly once.

1. $c < a \ldots < b$.
2. $c < a \ldots < b$.
3. $a < \ldots < b < c$.
4. Let x and y be successive nodes in the path $a < \ldots < b$ such that x is the last node to have an arc directed to c. (There exists at least one such node, namely, a.) Then $c < y$ since the graph is complete and it is impossible for $y < c$ since x is the last node in the path from which an arc is directed to c. Thus, $a < \ldots < x < c < y < \ldots < b$ is the desired complete path. (If $x = b$, then the path is $a < \ldots < b < c$.)

Proof of circuit-free uniqueness. Assume not, that is, assume there are two distinct complete paths. Let a_1 and a_2 be their respective first nodes. If $a_1 = a_2$, then let a_x be the last node at which the two complete paths are the same. The next nodes, a_y and a_z, are distinct. The nodes a_y and a_z cannot occur earlier in the complete paths, because that would show a circuit exists. Therefore, they occur later. Since the first path is complete, it contains a path from a_y to a_z. Since the second path is complete, it contains a path from a_z to a_y. Therefore, a circuit exists, contrary to assumption. If $a_1 < a_2$, then that fact plus the fact that $a_2 < \ldots < a_1$

occurs in the second path shows that there is a circuit in the graph, which is also a contradiction. Similarly, if $a_2 < a_1$. ∎

PROBLEMS

3.1. What is the union of {2, 7, 8} and {1, 2, 6}? What is the intersection?

3.2. What is the union of the set of even integers and the set of odd integers? What is the intersection?

3.3. What is the smallest value of k for which fact(k) > 10 ** k? (Hint: Use a calculator.)

3.4. The product of two simple graphs can be a compound graph. Explain.

3.5. A graph set is a set of graphs, but a set of graphs may fail to be a graph set. Explain.

3.6. Even though $G * G = G$, it is not generally true that for a graph set GS_1, $GS_1 * GS_1 = GS_1$. Explain.

3.7. Let GS_1 and GS_2 be simple graph sets with distinct colors. Let GS_1 have n_1 elements and GS_2 have n_2 elements. How many elements are there in $GS_1 * GS_2$?

3.8. Let GS_1 and GS_2 be simple graph sets, both with the same color and let $S = \{a, b, c\}$. Let $GS_1 = \{(S,\{a < b, b < c\}), (S,\{a < b\})\}$ and $GS_2 = \{(S,\{b < c\})\}$. Find the product of GS_1 and GS_2 and so conclude that no general result holds as with the preceding problem.

3.9. Show that the product of two partly circuit-free graph sets may result in circuit-full graph set.

3.10. Let S be a set of k points. Let $G = \{G_1, G_2, \ldots, G_n\}$ be the largest possible simple graph set on S. How many elements are there in G, that is, what is the value of n in terms of k? Calculate n for $k = 5$.

3.11. Let S be a set of n elements. Let GS_1 be the graph set consisting of all of the complete simple graphs of S.
   a. How many elements does GS_1 have?
   (Hint. Construct a simple graph set $\{G_1, G_2, \ldots, G_m\}$ as follows. For each pair of points a,b in S, construct the graph set $\{(S,\{a < b\}),(S,\{b < a\})\}$. How many such graph sets are there? Take the product of all these graph sets. How many graphs are there in the graph set product? What does this procedure construct?)
   b. How many elements of GS_1 are circuit-free?
   c. How many elements of GS_1 contain a circuit?
   d. Compute the answers to a., b., and c., for $n = 4$.

REFERENCE

While the preceding discussion of sets and factorials is elementary by any measure, the treatment of graphs skips over beginning topics such as

Undirected graphs. There is at most one, undirected arc, between each pair of nodes.

Directed graphs. There are at most two, directed arcs (one in each direction) between each pair of nodes.

See [BERG62] for a more typical introduction.

BERG62. C. BERGE. *The Theory of Graphs and Its Applications*. John Wiley and Sons. New York, NY. 1962.

4

The Model

BUILDING MODELS

The process of building a model has four steps. Step one is to decide what answers are sought. Step two is to reduce the complexity of the real world to its essence, eliminating the irrelevant and approximating the unmanageable. Step three is to translate the essence into a formally defined system within which one can make deductions. The final step is to test the deductions in the real world, to see if what the model teaches either illuminates or can be applied.

The value of each step of the process can be disputed. Different people have different goals. One person's irrelevancy is another's obsession. The translation from intuitive perception to mathematical model can be accomplished in many ways. A highway map is not a road system, and the applicability of any model to reality can always be challenged.

Any perception of value of a model is ultimately based on consensus. Reality is not mathematically tractable, and models are not reality. There can be no proof that a model is correct, right, or true.

GOALS FOR A MODEL OF ARCHITECTURES

The architecture for a computer is the list of rules which determine what outputs a set of programs running on the computer can generate from a given set of inputs. (The possibility of multiple outputs arises from the nondeterminism present in a multiprocessing system.)

The first goal for a model of architectures is to express all the rules that are commonly or might reasonably be attributed to a multiprocessing system.

The second goal is to show how to demonstrate that two architectures are distinguishable, that is, to show how an answer can be calculated under one architecture which cannot be calculated under the other architecture. The intent is to increase appreciation for the power of programs to detect, in almost all cases, the subtlest differences between architectures.

The third goal is to show how to demonstrate that two architectures are indistinguishable, that is, to show how to prove that every answer which can be calculated under one architecture can also be calculated under the other architecture. The intent is to find cases of indistinguishable architectures A_1 and A_2 such that A_1 presents a simple interface to programmers while A_2 is faster, though typically more complex, than A_1.

THE ESSENCE OF A MULTIPROCESSING SYSTEM

A multiprocessing system consists of a set of processes. The processes read input data, calculate results, and record the results as output data.

There is a single store shared by all the processes.

Each process consists solely of a finite sequence of assignment statements.

Data may be read and written by more than one process. Such data are called global data.

Other data, which are read and/or written by only one process, are called local data.

When a new value is written into a global operand, distinct processes may see the operand assume the new value at distinct times.

Much is omitted from this definition of the essence. In a real multiprocessing system processors operate simultaneously. Each processor may be indefinitely delayed. A processor can be interrupted away from one process and reassigned to another process in a seemingly arbitrary fashion. Execution of instructions may be pipelined, so each processor may overlap the execution of several instructions at once There may be multiple operands in each instruction. Copies of the same operand may be in use in several processors simultaneously. Programs have complex loop within loop structures. Instructions can move data between any combination of local and global operands. Input and output operations proceed in parallel with the operation of the processors. The contents of storage are moved around automatically, by both hardware and software, with no control over the process by any user program.

To keep the model simple, processes consist solely of assignment statements. Statements which govern the flow of control are not essential. Within a process, the only rules that apply are computation and order rules. These rules can be modeled adequately with assignment statements. Between processes there are many rules that govern the interaction between processes. The only way processors can affect each other's behavior is by fetching and storing data into global operands. At the

A Model of a Multiprocessing System

interface between processor and storage every process, no matter how complex, appears to be solely a sequence of fetch and store operations.

The operation of addition between source operands apparently allows all the essential complexity of a real system to be expressed. It is an open question whether or not other operations would significantly affect the model.

A MODEL OF A MULTIPROCESSING SYSTEM

Executions

An execution consists of the following:

1. a finite set of one or more processes, P_1, P_2, ... , each consisting of a finite sequence of assignment statements,
2. for each process P_i a store S_i, consisting of a copy of all the operands named anywhere in the execution,
3. for each process P_i a list defining initial values of operands in S_i,
4. for each process P_i a list defining terminal values of operands in S_i,

Each assignment statement consists of a line number, one sink operand, and one or more, possibly literal, source operands connected by the addition operator.

When the initial (terminal) value of an operand is the same for every store, the value is specified only once in the list of initial (terminal) values.

Operands can be either local, that is, accessed by only one process, or global, that is, accessed by more than one process. Global operands are named A, B, C, ... Local operands are named Z, Y, X, ...

An execution, as in Fig. 4.1, represents an instance of a set of programs executing on a computer. For each operand there is an initial value of the operand. The initial values of the operands may be viewed as representing input data. The processes represent programs each of which runs on a separate processor. The terminal values of the operands represent output data, computed by the processes from the input data.

```
              Initially, A = B = X = Y = 0.

                    P₁              P₂
                    L₁: X:= B;      L₁: Y:= A;
                    L₂: A:= 1;      L₂: B:= 1;

              Terminally, A = 1, B = 1, X = 0, Y = 0.
```

Figure 4.1 An execution in which the initial value and the terminal value of each operand is the same in all stores.

In the description of the essence of a multiprocessing system there was a statement that there was only one store, but that different processes saw operands change value at different times. In the model this is represented (1) by having each process have a separate copy of each of the operands in the system, (2) by having each process read only from its own store, and (3) by having each statement write a new value for an operand into the individual copy of the operand in each store in the system.

The intent is to model a system in which each process reads values from the copies of operands in its own store and writes values into storage in such a way that it is possible for new values to arrive at different times at different stores.

Events

Events are the elemental units from which all other objects are constructed. In other models additional details could be incorporated. For example, read and write events might be broken down into still smaller operations, or a statement might decompose into both events on storage and events in the execution unit, or, as in Chap. 14, an event might read and write both data and status flags.

For each statement in an execution there is one read event per source operand and one write event per process. Each event has five components. Each component can be determined by inspection of the execution from which the event is derived. The five components are:

1. the name of the process in which the statement occurs,
2. the label of the statement,
3. the character "R" for a read event or "W" for a write event,
4. for a read event, a source operand, or for a write event, the sink operand,
5. for a read event, the name of the store for the process in which the statement occurs, or, for a write event, the name of any one of the stores in the execution:

For the execution in Fig. 4.1 the events are

$$(P_1, L_1, R, B, S_1) \quad (P_2, L_1, R, A, S_2)$$
$$(P_1, L_1, W, X, S_1) \quad (P_2, L_1, W, Y, S_1)$$
$$(P_1, L_1, W, X, S_2) \quad (P_2, L_1, W, Y, S_2)$$
$$(P_1, L_2, R, 1, S_1) \quad (P_2, L_2, R, 1, S_2)$$
$$(P_1, L_2, W, A, S_1) \quad (P_2, L_2, W, B, S_1)$$
$$(P_1, L_2, W, A, S_2) \quad (P_2, L_2, W, B, S_2)$$

The Value of an Event

The computation rule, defined in Chap. 5, generates a graph set for each execution and assigns, via the value function, an integer value to each event. The value of an event depends on the structure of the graph containing the event. The value function may assign one value to an event in one graph in a graph set and

A Model of a Multiprocessing System

another value to the same event in a different graph in the graph set. Thus, the value of an event is an entity separate from the event and is not part of the event. However, it is convenient to treat the value of an event as if it were just another component of the event itself, and so the convention is adopted of recording the value of an event as the fourth component of the event itself. (The operand and store components then become the fifth and sixth components.) When the value of an event has not yet been determined, the value component is filled in with a dash "−." Then, for the execution in Fig. 4.1 the events are

$$(P_1, L_1, R, -, B, S_1) \quad (P_2, L_1, R, -, A, S_2)$$
$$(P_1, L_1, W, -, X, S_1) \quad (P_2, L_1, W, -, Y, S_1)$$
$$(P_1, L_1, W, -, X, S_2) \quad (P_2, L_1, W, -, Y, S_2)$$
$$(P_1, L_2, R, 1, 1, S_1) \quad (P_2, L_2, R, 1, 1, S_2)$$
$$(P_1, L_2, W, 1, A, S_1) \quad (P_2, L_2, W, 1, B, S_1)$$
$$(P_1, L_2, W, 1, A, S_2) \quad (P_2, L_2, W, 1, B, S_2)$$

To represent the possibility that each process can see an operand change value at a different time, there is, for each statement, a separate write event for each process. Thus, for the statement $A := 1$; in Figure 4.1 preceding, there is a write event to S_1, the store for P_1, and another write event to S_2, the store for P_2. The two events represent the (possibly) different times at which P_1 and P_2 see operand A change value.

Most of the time the write events for a single statement will all be shown as occurring together, that is, with no other events intervening. In such a case it will be a convenient abbreviation to represent this situation with what looks like a single event for store "S." The preceding events would then be represented by

$$(P_1, L_1, R, -, B, S_1) \quad (P_2, L_1, R, -, A, S_2)$$
$$(P_1, L_1, W, -, X, S) \quad (P_2, L_1, W, -, Y, S)$$
$$(P_1, L_2, R, 1, 1, S_1) \quad (P_2, L_2, R, 1, 1, S_2)$$
$$(P_1, L_2, W, 1, A, S) \quad (P_2, L_2, W, 1, B, S)$$

The use of this notation is only a convenience and is not to be construed as representing an act of writing instantaneously into all stores at once.

Architectures

Even though the rules have yet to be defined, it is possible to describe how the rules fit together to form architectures.

Denote by $A(R_1, R_2, \ldots, R_n)$ the architecture consisting of rules $R_1, R_2, \ldots, R_n$.

An architecture consisting of a single rule maps the events of an execution into a graph set. The mapping is different for each different rule. The exact mappings are defined in Chaps. 5 through 9. For a given execution the graphs in the graph set have as nodes the events of the execution. Some rules define only a single graph for the events of an execution. Other rules define a graph set consisting of a factorially large number of graphs. Within each graph an arc from event E_1 to event E_2 represents E_1 occurring earlier in time than E_2. The intent of having an architecture rule define a graph set is to represent concretely and explicitly via the graph set all of the possible orderings of events permitted by the architecture rule.

Suppose $A(R_1)$ maps the events of execution E into GS_1 and $A(R_2)$ maps the events of execution E into GS_2. Then $A(R_1, R_2)$, the architecture consisting of rules R_1 and R_2, is defined to map the events of execution E into GS_3, where $GS_3 = GS_1 * GS_2$. Instead of referring to the underlying graph sets, it will be convenient simply to write $A(R_1, R_2) = A(R_1) * A(R_2)$.

An execution E is said to obey an architecture if the graph set induced by the architecture on the events of E is partly circuit-free. If the graph set is partly circuit-free, then the events in some element of the graph set that is circuit-free can be linearized, and the linear ordering of the events can be viewed as being the order in time in which the events occurred on a machine obeying the architecture.

An architecture divides the set of all executions into two subsets: those which obey the architecture and those which do not.

Architecture A_1 implies architecture A_2, written $A_1 \Rightarrow A_2$, if whenever an execution obeys A_1, it also obeys A_2.

It will sometimes be convenient to write $R_1 \Rightarrow R_2$, instead of the more accurate $A(R_1) \Rightarrow A(R_2)$, or to write that an execution obeys R_1, rather than $A(R_1)$.

Two architectures are indistinguishable, written $A_1 \Leftrightarrow A_2$, if every execution which obeys one architecture also obeys the other. In terms of graph sets, two architectures are indistinguishable if and only if for every execution the graph set for the execution under one architecture is partly circuit-free whenever the graph set for the execution under the other architecture is partly circuit-free.

Two architectures are distinguishable if there is an execution which obeys one of the architectures, but does not obey the other. Such an execution is said to distinguish the two architectures. In practice, one of the architectures, say A_1, will have fewer and/or weaker rules than the other architecture, say A_2, and so the set of executions obeying A_2 will be a proper subset of the executions obeying A_1. In such a case it will be convenient to write $A_1 \neg \Rightarrow A_2$ to indicate, not only that A_1 and A_2 are distinguishable, but, more explicitly, that the set of executions obeying A_1 is not contained in the set of executions obeying A_2.

Transition Templates

For each rule R defined in Chaps. 5 through 9 there are one or more transition templates also defined. Transition templates identify the information which is preserved when moving from one event to another event along an arc in a graph.

Transition templates have the form

$$(P,L,A,V,O,S) \quad <_R \quad (-,-,-,-,-,-)$$

where R is a rule.

For example, the transition template for program order has the form

$$(P,L,A,V,O,S) \quad <_{PO} \quad (=,-,-,-,-,-)$$

The process, statement, action, value, operand, and store components of the events on the left-hand end of the arc are represented as having the values P, L, A, V, O, S, respectively. The action component A represents either a read event or a write event. If the left-hand event were restricted to being only a read event (write event), then the action component would be R (W). The arc is labeled with the rule that generates it, in this case, the rule of program order.

The right-hand event shows which components of the left-hand event appear also in the right-hand event. In the case of program order, only the process component is guaranteed to be the same. The other components, since they cannot be determined from the left-hand event, are filled in with a dash (–).

Transition templates are used in Chaps. 11, 12, and 14 in proving theorems about architectures being indistinguishable.

Not all information about the rule appears in the transition template. In the case of program order the statement component of the right-hand event is always greater than the statement component of the left-hand event. Since this information is not needed in the proofs of indistinguishable architectures, it is not represented in the transition template.

THE VALUE OF THE GRAPH SET STRUCTURE AS A MODEL OF TIME

The usual model of time is the real line. Each event is assigned a distinct point on the line (though in some models events are allowed to coincide [LAMP74], cited in Chap. 1). The distance between points is irrelevant.

The graph set structure makes it possible

1. to add rules, without obscuring arcs due to other rules, since the arcs for each rule are labeled distinctively,
2. to delete rules, without erasing arcs due to other rules,
3. to represent all the ordering information and only the ordering information implied by the rules.

    In the graph set model arcs exist only as required by the architectural rules.

Under the real line model of time for every pair of events x,y either $x < y$ or $y < x$. This introduces extraneous arcs which interfere with efforts to reason about arcs due solely to architectural rules.

4. to represent all the essentially distinct ways an execution can obey the rules.

The mechanism for generating the graph set for each rule will be seen to generate all possible patterns of arcs between the events of an execution that are allowed by the rule.

For an architecture consisting of multiple rules, the product of the graph sets for each rule ensures that all possible combinations of arcs are generated.

For an execution of n events under the real time model there are fact(n) linearizations of the events, many of which differ only irrelevantly.

5. to treat as equally legitimate those graph sets being circuit-full and those being partially circuit-free.

To analyze the executions in Chap. 1 in terms of events on the real line would lead to the uncomfortable conclusion that, for certain terminal values of the operands, there is a circuit among the points of the real line. The value of the graph set construct is that it translates the discussion of events in time into a discussion of whether or not a set of graphs all have, or do not all have, circuits. If a graph set is partly circuit-free, then each circuit-free element of the graph set may, when linearized, be taken as representing a possible ordering of the events in time. The process may be viewed as being akin to that of taking a problem stated in the real numbers, translating it to and solving it in the domain of complex numbers, and then interpreting the results back in the realm of real numbers.

PROBLEMS

4.1. Write down the events for the following execution.

Initially, A = B = 0.

P_1 P_2
L_1: A:= 1; L_1: B:= 1;
L_2: B:= 2; L_2: A:= 2;

Terminally, A = B = 1.

4.2. For some execution E with set of events $S = \{a, b, c\}$, rule R_1 defines the graph set $\{(S,\{a < b, c < a\}),(S,\{c < b\})\}$ and rule R_2 defines the graph set $\{(S,\{b < c\})\}$. Does E obey $A(R_1)$? $A(R_2)$? $A(R_1, R_2)$?

4.3. Rule R_1 defines the graph set $\{(S,\{(a < b)\})\}$ for execution E and $\emptyset$ for all other executions. Rule R_2 defines the graph set $\{(S,\{(b < a)\})\}$ for execution E and for all other executions. Then $A(R_1) \Leftrightarrow A(R_2)$. Explain.

5
The Rule of Computation

When an assignment statement is executed on a computer, the source operands for the statement are fetched, a value is computed, and the computed value is written into the sink operand. The value recorded in a sink operand by one statement may serve as a source operand to other statements. The history by which any given operand comes to have a particular value can be described by a tree structure of events extending back into the past: each present value of an operand is based on the values of one or more other operands, which in turn are based on the values of yet other operands, and so on.

COMPUTATION SUBRULES

There are four subrules of the rule of computation. Collectively, the four subrules are known as the CMP rule, and an execution which obeys CMP is said to compute. CMP is the most complex of any of the rules. Ideally, it would be presented last, but since it is essential to proving anything at all about an execution (see Theorem 10.4), it must come first.

The following examples show how the several computation subrules arise. A later section shows the mechanism for generating the graph sets for an execution which obeys A(CMP).

The Statement-Read-Write Subrule (SRW)

An arc, labeled $<_{SRW}$, leads from each read event in a statement to each write event in the same statement. The intent of the SRW subrule is to represent the fact that source operands in a statement are fetched before the computed value is stored into the sink operand in the statement. Fig. 5.1 shows an execution used in explaining the rule of SRW.

Initially, A = B = C = X = Y = 0.

P_1 P_2
L_1:X:=A; L_1:B := Y + C;

Terminally, A = B = C = X = Y = 0.   **Figure 5.1**   Example of SRW.

Under A(CMP) the GS for the execution of Fig. 5.1. contains six arcs labeled $<_{SRW}$. There are three read events. From each read event there is one arc to each of the two write events in the same statement as the read event. Specifically, the arcs are

$(P_1, L_1, R, -, A, S_1)$ $<_{SRW}$ $(P_1, L_1, W, -, X, S_1)$
$(P_1, L_1, R, -, A, S_1)$ $<_{SRW}$ $(P_1, L_1, W, -, X, S_2)$
$(P_2, L_1, R, -, Y, S_2)$ $<_{SRW}$ $(P_2, L_1, W, -, B, S_1)$
$(P_2, L_1, R, -, Y, S_2)$ $<_{SRW}$ $(P_2, L_1, W, -, B, S_2)$
$(P_2, L_1, R, -, C, S_2)$ $<_{SRW}$ $(P_2, L_1, W, -, B, S_1)$
$(P_2, L_1, R, -, C, S_2)$ $<_{SRW}$ $(P_2, L_1, W, -, B, S_2)$

The transition template for SRW is

(P, L, R, V, O, S) $<_{SRW}$ $(=, =, W, -, -, -)$

The transition template for SRW records the fact that both of the events occur in the same statement (the process and statement components of the events are equal). The left-hand statement is a read event; the right a write event. The other entries are immaterial.

The Compute-Write-Read Subrule (CWR)

An arc with a $<_{CWR}$ label leads from a write event to a read event, where the two events have the same operand and store components. The two events and the arc connecting them represent the case in which a write operation stores a value into an operand in a store and a subsequent read operation fetches the value from the same operand in the same store. Fig. 5.2 shows an example of the rule of CWR.

Computation Subrules

Initially, $A = X = 0$.

$P_1 \qquad P_2$
$L_1: A := 1; \qquad L_1: X := A;$

Figure 5.2 Example of CWR.

Terminally, $A = 1, X = 1$.

If the execution in Fig. 5.2 obeys A(CMP), then every element of the graph set for the execution contains the following path.

$$(P_1, L_1, W, 1, A, S_2) \quad <_{CWR} \quad (P_2, L_1, R, 1, A, S_2)$$

Transition template for CWR.

$$(P, L, W, V, O, S) \quad <_{CWR} \quad (-, -, R, =, =, =)$$

If $W <_{CWR} R$, then the value V written into operand O in store S by event W is the same as the value read by event R from operand O in store S.

The Compute-Read-Write Subrule (CRW)

An arc with a $<_{CRW}$ label leads from a read event to a write event, where the two events have the same operand and store components. The two events and the arc connecting them represent the case in which a read operation fetches the value of an operand in a store prior to the time a subsequent write operation stores a (possibly different) value in the same operand and same store. Fig. 5.3 shows an example of the rule of CRW.

Initially, $A = X = 0$.

$P_1 \qquad P_2$
$L_1: A := 1; \qquad L_1: X := A;$

Figure 5.3 Example of CRW.

Terminally, $A = 1, X = 0$.

If the execution in Fig. 5.3 obeys A(CMP), then every element of the graph set for the execution contains the following path.

$$(P_1, L_2, R, 0, A, S_2) \quad <_{CRW} \quad (P_1, L_1, W, 1, A, S_2)$$

Transition template for CRW.

$$(P, L, R, V, O, S) \quad <_{CRW} \quad (-, -, W, -, =, =)$$

If $R <_{CRW} W$, then the two events reference the same operand O in the same store S.

The Compute-Write-Write Subrule (CWW)

An arc with a $<_{CWW}$ label leads from one write event to another write event, where the two events have the same operand and store components. The two events and the arc connecting them represent the case in which the first write operation writes the value of an operand in a store prior to the time a second write operation writes a (possibly different) value in the same operand and same store. Fig. 5.4 shows an example of the rule of CWW.

```
Initially, A = 0.

   P₁              P₂
L₁: A:= 1;    L₁: A:= 2;

Terminally, A = 2.
```

Figure 5.4 Example of CWW.

If the execution in Fig. 5.4 obeys A(CMP), then every element of the graph set for the execution contains the following two paths. (Recall that saying that $A = 2$ terminally is shorthand for saying that terminally $A = 2$ in S_1 and $A = 2$ in S_2.)

$$(P_1, L_1, W, 1, A, S_1) <_{CWW} (P_2, L_1, W, 2, A, S_1)$$
$$(P_1, L_1, W, 1, A, S_2) <_{CWW} (P_2, L_1, W, 2, A, S_2)$$

The transition template for CWW is

$$(P, L, W, V, O, S) <_{CWW} (-, -, W, -, =, =)$$

If $W1 <_{CWW} W2$, then the two write events reference the same operand O in the same store S.

CREATING THE GRAPH SET FOR CMP

The first step in creating the graph set for the rule CMP is to enumerate all possible combinations of orderings of events containing the same operand and store components. Succeeding steps successively winnow the possibilites.

Step 1. Create graph set GS_1 to represent all the possible orderings of events with the same operand and the same store components. Partition the events of execution E into sets, where each set contains the events which have the same operand and store components. (Each event with a literal source operand goes into a separate set.) Call such sets SOSS sets, for same-operand-same-store sets. Let

Creating the Graph Set for CMP

$<_{SOS}$ define a linear ordering on a SOSS set. If there are n elements in a SOSS set, there are fact(n) $<_{SOS}$ orderings of the SOSS set.

Enumerate all combinations of $<_{SOS}$ orderings of all SOSS sets. For each element of the enumeration, define one element of GS_1.

The number of SOSS sets for an execution can be calculated as follows. There is one SOSS set for each literal source operand. For each distinct sink operand there is one SOSS set for each store in the system. For each distinct source operand not included in either of the above groups there is one SOSS set for each process in which the source operand is referenced.

The number of elements of GS_1 is equal to the product of the factorials of the number of elements of the SOSS sets.

Figure 5.5 shows an example of an execution and its SOSS sets.

```
        Execution 1.
        Initially, A = B = X = Y = 0.

              P₁              P₂
        L₁: X:= B;       L₁: Y:= A;
        L₂: A:= 1;       L₂: B:= 1;

        Terminally, A = 1, B = 1, X = 1, Y = 0.
```

There are two SOSS sets for events with literal operands.

$$\{(P_1, L_2, R, -, 1, S_1)\}$$
$$\{(P_2, L_2, R, -, 1, S_2)\}$$

The other SOSS sets are

$$\{(P_1, L_1, W, -, X, S_1)\}$$
$$\{(P_1, L_1, W, -, X, S_2)\}$$
$$\{(P_1, L_2, W, -, A, S_2), (P_2, L_1, R, -, A, S_2)\}$$
$$\{(P_1, L_2, W, -, A, S_1)\}$$
$$\{(P_2, L_1, W, -, Y, S_1)\}$$
$$\{(P_2, L_1, W, -, Y, S_2)\}$$
$$\{(P_2, L_2, W, -, B, S_1), (P_1, L_1, R, -, B, S_1)\}$$
$$\{(P_2, L_2, W, -, B, S_2)\}$$

Figure 5.5 Example of SOSS sets.

Therefore, the number of graphs in GS_1 for the execution is fact(1) * fact(1) * fact(1) * fact(1) * fact(2) * fact(1) * fact(1) * fact(1) * fact(2) * fact(1) = 4

Step 2. For each element of GS_1 draw additional arcs, labeled $<_{CWW}$, $<_{CWR}$, or $<_{CRW}$, according to the following rules. Let W1 and W2 be write events; let R1 and R2 be read events.

If W1 $<_{SOS}$ R1 $<_{SOS}$ R2 $<_{SOS}$ ..., then draw arcs labeled $<_{CWR}$ from W1 to R1, from W1 to R2, ...

If . . . $<_{SOS}$ R2 $<_{SOS}$ R1 $<_{SOS}$ W1, then draw arcs labeled $<_{CRW}$ from . . . , from R2 to W1, from R1 to W1.

If W1 $<_{SOS}$ . . . $<_{SOS}$ W2, then draw an arc labeled $<_{CWW}$ from W1 to W2.

Step 3. Create graph set GS_2 to represent the distinct orderings due to CWR, CRW, and CWW. Take each element of GS_1, delete the arcs labeled $<_{SOS}$, and then add the element to GS_2. (Distinct elements of GS_1 may translate to the same element of GS_2. See Prob. 5.13.)

Step 4. Create graph set GS_3 to represent the additional arcs due to SRW. Choose each element of GS_2 in turn. For each element select the events for each statement. Draw arcs labeled $<_{SRW}$ from each read event in the statement to each write event in the statement. Test each new element to see whether or not the element remains circuit-free. If so, add the element to GS_3. (See Prob. 5.14.)

Step 5. For each element of GS_3 apply the value function in order to assign a value to each event in the element.

Choose any read event R in the graph in GS_3. (Write events are handled similarly.) Create sets $S_1, S_2, \ldots, S_n$ as follows. Event R is the only element of S_1. In S_2 place all the write events W such that W $<_{CWR}$ R. In S_3 place all the read events R_* such that $R_* <_{SRW}$ W, for some write event W in S_2. Repeat the two steps until a set is generated which is empty. Such a set must eventually be generated since the graph is circuit-free and contains only a finite number of events. Let S_n be the last nonempty set. The elements of S_n are all read events since only read events have no arcs incident into them. (Each write event has at least one arc labeled $<_{SRW}$ incident into it.)

Assign to each event in S_n the initial value of the operand defined in the execution. (If there is a literal value rather than an operand, assign the event the literal value.) Record the value in the fourth component of the event.

After values have been assigned to the elements of S_n, consider the write events in the set S_{n-1}. Assign to each write event W in S_{n-1} the sum of the values of the read events R_* in S_n such that $R_* <_{SRW}$ W. (From the construction of the sequence all such read events are in S_n.)

Now assign to each read event R in S_{n-2} the value of the write event W in S_{n-1} such that W $<_{CWR}$ R.

Repeat the last two steps until a value has been assigned to the read event in S_1.

Step 6. Create graph set GS_4 from GS_3. Since all read events have arcs labeled $<_{SRW}$ incident out from them, the only events having no arcs emanating from them are write events. If the value of each such write event matches the terminal value specified in the execution, then add the graph to GS_4.

If GS_4 is not empty, then the execution is said to compute, or to obey rule CMP.

Figure 5.6 continues the example of Execution 1 in Figure 5.5.

Creating the Graph Set for CMP

Initially, $A = B = X = Y = 0$.

P_1 P_2
L_1: $X := B$; L_1: $Y := A$;
L_2: $A := 1$; L_2: $B := 1$;

Terminally, $A = 1$, $B = 1$, $X = 1$, $Y = 0$.

There are only two SOSS sets of interest

$\{(P_1, L_2, W, -, A, S_2), (P_2, L_1, R, -, A, S_2)\}$
$\{(P_2, L_2, W, -, B, S_1), (P_1, L_1, R, -, B, S_1)\}$

Figure 5.6 SOSS sets of interest in Fig. 5.5.

GS_2 for Fig. 5.5 contains four graphs. Each graph contains one of these four pairs of paths, where each pair is derived in Step 2 from the two SOSS sets.

$(P_1, L_2, W, -, A, S_2)$ $<_{CWR}$ $(P_2, L_1, R, -, A, S_2)$
$(P_2, L_2, W, -, B, S_1)$ $<_{CWR}$ $(P_1, L_1, R, -, B, S_1)$

$(P_1, L_2, W, -, A, S_2)$ $<_{CWR}$ $(P_2, L_1, R, -, A, S_2)$
$(P_1, L_1, R, -, B, S_1)$ $<_{CRW}$ $(P_2, L_2, W, -, B, S_1)$

$(P_2, L_1, R, -, A, S_2)$ $<_{CRW}$ $(P_1, L_2, W, -, A, S_2)$
$(P_2, L_2, W, -, B, S_1)$ $<_{CWR}$ $(P_1, L_1, R, -, B, S_1)$

$(P_2, L_1, R, -, A, S_2)$ $<_{CRW}$ $(P_1, L_2, W, -, A, S_2)$
$(P_1, L_1, R, -, B, S_1)$ $<_{CRW}$ $(P_2, L_2, W, -, B, S_1)$

If values are assigned to events according to Step 5, then the resulting values of the four operands are as shown

			Resulting values			
			A	B	X	Y
$(P_1, L_2, W, 1, A, S_2)$	$<_{CWR}$	$(P_2, L_1, R, 1, A, S_2)$	1	1	1	1
$(P_2, L_2, W, 1, B, S_1)$	$<_{CWR}$	$(P_1, L_1, R, 1, B, S_1)$				
$(P_1, L_2, W, 1, A, S_2)$	$<_{CWR}$	$(P_2, L_1, R, 1, A, S_2)$	1	1	0	1
$(P_1, L_1, R, 0, B, S_1)$	$<_{CRW}$	$(P_2, L_2, W, 1, B, S_1)$				
$(P_2, L_1, R, 0, A, S_2)$	$<_{CRW}$	$(P_1, L_2, W, 1, A, S_2)$	1	1	1	0
$(P_2, L_2, W, 1, B, S_1)$	$<_{CWR}$	$(P_1, L_1, R, 1, B, S_1)$				
$(P_2, L_1, R, 0, A, S_2)$	$<_{CRW}$	$(P_1, L_2, W, 1, A, S_2)$	1	1	0	0
$(P_1, L_1, R, 0, B, S_1)$	$<_{CRW}$	$(P_2, L_2, W, 1, B, S_1)$				

In the third graph the resulting values are the same as the terminal values in the execution. Therefore, GS_4 is nonempty and so the execution in Fig. 5.5 obeys the CMP rule.

Now consider the execution of Fig. 5.5 under A(CMP, PO). (Under the rule of program order (PO) there is an arc, labeled $<_{PO}$, from each event in one statement to every event in another statement further down in the program. See Chap. 6.) The GS for the execution under A(CMP) has one graph, as shown. The graph set for any execution under A(PO) has only one graph. The graph set for an execution E under A(CMP, PO) is the product of the graph set for E under A(CMP) with the graph set for E under A(PO). Therefore, the graph set product for the execution under A(CMP, PO) has just one graph. Is this one graph circuit-free? If so, the execution obeys A(CMP, PO). Otherwise, it doesn't.

A graph is circuit-free if and only if it is extendable to a linear ordering. Therefore, the following linear ordering of the events of Execution 5.5, which obeys CMP and PO, shows that the GS for the execution in A(CMP, PO) is circuit-free. Hence, the execution obeys A(CMP, PO).

P_1 P_2
          $(P_2,L_1,R,0,A,S_2)$
          $(P_2,L_1,W,0,Y,S_1)$
          $(P_2,L_1,W,0,Y,S_2)$
          $(P_2,L_2,R,1,1,S_2)$
          $(P_2,L_2,W,1,B,S_1)$
          $(P_2,L_2,W,1,B,S_2)$
$(P_1,L_1,R,1,B,S_1)$
$(P_1,L_1,W,1,X,S_1)$
$(P_1,L_1,W,1,X,S_2)$
$(P_1,L_2,R,1,1,S_1)$
$(P_1,L_2,W,1,A,S_1)$
$(P_1,L_2,W,1,A,S_2)$

Figure 5.7 shows an execution which differs from the execution in Figure 5.5 only in the terminal value of Y, but whose GS under A(CMP, PO) is quite distinct.

Execution 2.
Initially, A = B = X = Y = 0.

P_1 P_2
L_1: X:= B; L_1: Y:= A;
L_2: A:= 1; L_2: B:= 1;

Terminally, A = 1, B = 1, X = 1, Y = 1.   **Figure 5.7** A Variation on Fig. 5.5.

GS_3 for Execution 2 under A(CMP) is the same as for Execution 1. Now the sole member of GS_4 is

Creating the Graph Set for CMP

			Resulting values			
			A	B	X	Y
$(P_1, L_2, W, 1, A, S_2)$	$<_{CWR}$	$(P_2, L_1, R, 1, A, S_2)$	1	1	1	1
$(P_2, L_2, W, 1, B, S_1)$	$<_{CWR}$	$(P_1, L_1, R, 1, B, S_1)$				

The GS for Execution 2 under A(PO) is the same as for Execution 1. In particular, there are the following arcs between events in the single member of the GS.

$$(P_1, L_1, R, 1, B, S_1) <_{PO} (P_1, L_2, W, 1, A, S_2)$$
$$(P_2, L_1, R, 1, A, S_2) <_{PO} (P_2, L_2, W, 1, B, S_1)$$

Does the execution obey A(CMP, PO)? The graph set for the execution under A(CMP, PO) is formed by taking the product of the graph set for the execution under A(CMP) and the graph set for the execution under A(PO). Since every element of the first graph set contains the arcs

$$(P_1, L_1, R, 1, B, S_1) <_{PO} (P_1, L_2, W, 1, A, S_2)$$
$$(P_2, L_1, R, 1, A, S_2) <_{PO} (P_2, L_2, W, 1, B, S_1)$$

and every member of the second graph set contains the arcs

$$(P_1, L_2, W, 1, A, S_2) <_{CWR} (P_2, L_1, R, 1, A, S_2)$$
$$(P_2, L_2, W, 1, B, S_1) <_{CWR} (P_1, L_1, R, 1, B, S_1)$$

it must be that every element of the product graph set contains the following circuit:

$$
\begin{aligned}
(P_1, L_1, R, 1, B, S_1) &<_{PO} (P_1, L_2, W, 1, A, S_2) \\
&<_{CWR} (P_2, L_1, R, 1, A, S_2) \\
&<_{PO} (P_2, L_2, W, 1, B, S_1) \\
&<_{CWR} (P_1, L_1, R, 1, B, S_1)
\end{aligned}
$$

Consequently, the execution in Fig. 5.7 does not obey architecture A(CMP, PO).

The same analysis as for Execution 1 shows that Execution 2 can also compute the terminal value A = B = X = Y = 1 under A(CMP). Then the analysis of Execution 2 showed that it does not obey A(CMP, PO). This proves Theorem A4 in App. A that the architecture A(CMP) is distinguishable from the architecture A(CMP, PO).

PROBLEMS

5.1. If the following execution obeys A(CMP), what label appears on the arc from $(P_1,L_1,W,1,A,S_1)$ to $(P_1,L_2,R,1,A,S_1)$?

$$\text{Initially, } A = B = 0.$$

$$P_1$$
$$L_1: A := 1;$$
$$L_2: B := A;$$

$$\text{Terminally, } A = B = 1.$$

5.2. If the following execution obeys A(CMP), what label appears on the arc from $(P_1,L_1,R,0,A,S_1)$ to $(P_1,L_2,W,1,A,S_1)$?

$$\text{Initially, } A = B = 0.$$

$$P_1$$
$$L_1: B := A;$$
$$L_2: A := 1;$$

$$\text{Terminally, } A = 1, B = 0.$$

5.3. If the following execution obeys A(CMP), what label appears on the arc from $(P_1,L_1,W,1,A,S_1)$ to $(P_1,L_2,W,2,A,S_1)$?

$$\text{Initially, } A = 0.$$

$$P_1$$
$$L_1: A := 1;$$
$$L_2: A := 2;$$

$$\text{Terminally, } A = 2.$$

5.4. If the following execution obeys A(CMP), what labels appear on the arc from $(P_1,L_2,W,1,A,S_2)$ to $(P_2,L_1,R,1,A,S_2)$ and from $(P_2,L_2,W,1,B,S_1)$ to $(P_1,L_1,R,1,B,S_1)$?

$$\text{Initially, } A = B = X = Y = 0.$$

$$\begin{array}{ll} P_1 & P_2 \\ L_1: Y := B; & L_1: X := A; \\ L_2: A := 1; & L_2: B := 1; \end{array}$$

$$\text{Terminally, } A = B = X = Y = 1.$$

5.5. If the following execution obeys A(CMP), what labels appear on the arcs from $(P_2,L_2,R,0,A,S_2)$ to $(P_1,L_1,W,1,A,S_2)$ and from $(P_1,L_1,W,1,A,S_2)$ to $(P_2,L_1,R,1,A,S_2)$?

Initially, A = X = Y = 0.

P_1 P_2
L_1: A:= 1; L_1: X:= A;
                   L_2: Y:= A;

Terminally, A = X = 1, Y = 0.

5.6. If the following execution obeys A(CMP), what labels appear on the arc from $(P_1,L_2,W,2,B,S_1)$ to $(P_2,L_1,W,1,B,S_1)$ and from $(P_2,L_2,W,2,A,S_1)$ to $(P_1,L_1,W,1,A,S_1)$?

Initially, A = B = 0.

P_1 P_2
L_1: A:= 1; L_1: B:= 1;
L_2: B:= 2; L_2: A:= 2;

Terminally, A = B = 1.

5.7. If the following execution obeys A(CMP), what labels appear on the arc from $(P_1,L_2,R,0,B,S_1)$ to $(P_2,L_1,W,1,B,S_1)$ and from $(P_2,L_2,W,2,A,S_1)$ to $(P_1,L_1,W,1,A,S_1)$?

Initially, A = B = X = 0.

P_1 P_2
L_1: A:= 1; L_1: B:= 1;
L_2: X:= B; L_2: A:= 2;

Terminally, A = B = 1, X = 0.

5.8. Under A(CMP) the following execution can compute a terminal value of either 3 or 7 for X. Explain.

Initially, X = 0.

P_1
L_1: X:= 3;
L_2: X:= 7;

Terminally, X = ?.

5.9. What terminal values can C have if the following execution obeys A(CMP)? A(CMP, PO)?

$$\text{Initially, A = B = C = 0.}$$

$$\begin{array}{ll} P_1 & P_2 \\ L_1: A:= 1; & L_1: C:= A + B; \\ L_2: B:= 2; & \end{array}$$

$$\text{Terminally, A = 1, B = 2, C = ?.}$$

5.10. Answer the following questions for this execution.

$$\text{Initially, A = 0.}$$

$$\begin{array}{l} P_1 \\ L_1: A:= 1; \end{array}$$

$$\text{Terminally, A = 7.}$$

(a) What are the SOSS sets?
(b) Display the computation tree for A in S_1.
(c) At which of the five steps in forming the graph set for CMP does the execution fail to compute?

5.11. How many elements are there in GS_1 for the following execution?

$$\text{Initially, A = B = X = 0.}$$

$$\begin{array}{lll} P_1 & P_2 & P_3 \\ L_1: A:= 3; & L_1: B:= 4; & L_1: X:= A + B: \end{array}$$

$$\text{Terminally, A = 3, B = 4, X = 7.}$$

5.12. Assume the execution in Prob. 5.11 obeys A(CMP). Label the arcs and fill in the values of the events in the graph which shows how X obtains the value 7.

$$\begin{array}{cc} (P_1,L_1,R,\_\_,3,S_1) & (P_2,L_1,R,\_\_,4,S_2) \\ | & | \\ (P_1,L_1,W,\_\_,A,S_3) & (P_2,L_1,W,\_\_,B,S_3) \\ | & | \\ (P_3,L_1,R,\_\_,A,S_3) & (P_3,L_1,R,\_\_,B,S_3) \\ \searrow & \swarrow \\ & (P_3,L_1,W,\_\_,X,S_3) \end{array}$$

5.13. What is the source of the duplicates which are eliminated in Step 3?

5.14. Show the elements of GS_1, GS_2, and GS_3 for the following execution. In particular show how there are fewer elements of GS_3 than of GS_2 due to circuits being created when $<_{SRW}$ arcs are added to the elements of GS_2.

$$\text{Initially, } A = 1, B = 2.$$

$$\begin{array}{ll} P_1 & P_2 \\ L_1: A := B; & L_1: B := A; \end{array}$$

$$\text{Terminally, } A = 2, B = 1.$$

5.15. The elements of GS_2 are circuit-free. Prove.

6

The Rules of Program Order

The order rules are the simplest rules of all. Each order rule defines only a single graph. The intent of the order rules is to express the idea that statements which occur earlier in a program are executed before those which occur later. Because the ideas are so simple to express, it is easy to propose a great many variations on the basic rule of program order.

There are two categories of order rules: uniprocessor order rules and multiprocessor order rules. The rules of uniprocessor order are rules that must be obeyed on a uniprocessor and within each separate process on a multiprocessor. Both categories of rules apply both to local and to global operands. (However, it may be that the multiprocessor rules need to be defined to apply only to global operands. See Chap. 15.)

The rules of uniprocessor order at first sight appear to be similar to the CWR, CRW, and CWW subrules. They are quite distinct. The CMP rules derive from the need for a mechanism to exist whereby inital values of operands are transformed into the terminal values of the operands. The uniprocessor rules are based solely on the order of events in a process.

For the sake of simplifying the definitions which follow, define the following rule. For every pair of events E_1 and E_2 in the same process there is an arc, labeled $<_O$, from event E_1 to event E_2 if event E_1 is in a statement which occurs earlier in the process than the statement in which E_2 occurs. Just as the $<$sos rule was used solely to define the computation rules, the $<_O$ rule is used solely for the purpose of defining the order rules.

THE RULE OF UNIPROCESSOR-WRITE-READ ORDER (UWR)

The intent of the rule of uniprocessor write-read order is to express the idea that in the process

$$P_1$$
$$L_1: \ X := 1;$$
$$L_2: \ Y := X;$$

the write event in statement L_1 occurs before the read event in statement L_2.

To form the single graph in the graph set for an execution E under A(UWR) draw an arc, labeled $<_{UWR}$, from write event W_1 to read event R_1 if

1. $W_1 <_O R_1$,
2. W_1 and R_1 are in the same process and have the same operand and store components.

The transition template for UWR is

$$(P, L, W, V, O, S) \quad <_{UWR} \quad (=, -, R, -, =, =)$$

An arc labeled $<_{UWR}$ occurs only from a write event to a read event. Both the write event and the read event are in the same process. Both reference the same operand and the same store. The store is not arbitrary; it is precisely the store associated with process P.

Not all relevant information about UWR is recorded in the transition template. The statement number for the read event must be higher than the statement number for the write event.

In Fig. 6.1 an execution shows a failure to be Uniprocessor-Write-Read Ordered (Theorem A1).

Initially, X = Y = 0.

$$P_1$$
$$L_1: \ X := 1;$$
$$L_2: \ Y := X;$$

Figure 6.1 A failure to obey UWR.

Terminally, X = 1, Y = 0.

The following linear ordering of the events of the execution shows that the execution obeys A(CMP).

P_1
$(L_1, R, 1, 1, S_1)$
$(L_2, R, 0, X, S_1)$
$(L_1, W, 1, X, S_1)$
$(L_2, W, 0, Y, S_1)$

Under architecture A(CMP) every member of the graph set for the execution includes the following path:

$(P_1, L_2, R, 0, X, S_1) <_{CRW} (P_1, L_1, W, 1, X, S_1)$

The path shows that the read event in statement L_2 for operand X occurs before the write event in statement L_1 for operand X. Therefore, the execution does not obey A(CMP, UWR). Equivalently, if the execution occurs on a machine known to obey A(CMP), then the execution reveals a failure of the machine to obey UWR.

THE RULE OF UNIPROCESSOR-READ-WRITE ORDER (URW)

The intent of the rule of uniprocessor-read-write order is to express the idea that in the following process:

P_1
L_1: Y := X;
L_2: X := 1;

the read event in statement L_1 for operand X in store S_2 occurs before the write event in statement L_2 for operand X in store S_2.

To form the single graph in the graph set for an execution E under A(URW) draw an arc, labeled $<_{URW}$, from read event R_1 to write event W_1 if

1. $R_1 <_O W_1$,
2. R_1 and W_1 are in the same process and have the same operand and store components.

The transition template for URW is

$(P, L, R, V, 0, S) <_{URW} (=, -, W, -, =, =)$

An arc labeled $<_{URW}$ occurs only from a read event to a write event. Both the read event and the write event are in the same process. Both reference the same operand and the same store. The store is not arbitrary; it is explicitly the store associated with process P.

The Rule of Uniprocessor-Write-Write Order (UWW)

Not all relevant information about URW is recorded in the transition template. The statement number for the read event must be higher than the statement number for the write event.

In Fig. 6.2 an execution shows a failure to be Uniprocessor-Read-Write Ordered (Theorem A2).

Initially, X = Y = 0.

P_1
L_1: Y:= X;
L_2: X:= 1;

Figure 6.2 A failure to obey URW.

Terminally, X = Y = 1.

The following linear ordering of the events of the execution shows that the execution obeys A(CMP).

P_1
$(L_2, R, 1, 1, S_1)$
$(L_2, W, 1, X, S_1)$
$(L_1, R, 1, X, S_1)$
$(L_1, W, 1, Y, S_1)$

Under architecture A(CMP) every member of the graph set for the execution includes the following path.

$(P_1, L_2, W, 1, X, S_1) <_{CWR} (P_1, L_1, R, 1, X, S_1)$

The path shows that the write event in statement L_2 for operand X occurs before the read event in statement L_1 for operand X. Therefore, the execution does not obey A(CMP, URW). Equivalently, if the execution occurs on a machine known to obey A(CMP), then the execution reveals a failure of the machine to obey URW.

THE RULE OF UNIPROCESSOR-WRITE-WRITE ORDER (UWW)

The intent of the rule of uniprocessor-write-read order is to express the idea that in the following process:

P_1
L_1: X:= 1;
L_2: X:= 2;

the write event in statement L_1 occurs before the write event in statement L_2.

To form the single graph in the graph set for an execution E under A(UWW) draw an arc, labeled $<_{UWW}$, from write event W_1 to write event W_2 if

1. $W_1 <_O W_2$,
2. W_1 and W_2 are in the same process and have the same operand and store components.

The transition template for UWW is

$$(P,L,W,V,O,S) \quad <_{UWW} \quad (=,-,W,-,=,=)$$

An arc labeled $<_{UWW}$ occurs only from a write event to another write event. Both write events are in the same process. Both reference the same operand and the same store. The store is not arbitrary; it is explicitly the store associated with process P.

Not all relevant information about UWW is recorded in the transition template. The statement number for the read event must be higher than the statement number for the write event.

In Fig. 6.3 an execution shows a failure to be Uniprocessor-Write-Write Ordered (Theorem A3).

```
Initially, X = 0.

    P₁
L₁: X:= 2;
L₂: X:= 1;

Terminally, X = 2.
```

Figure 6.3 A failure to obey UWW.

The following linear ordering of the events of the execution shows that the execution obeys A(CMP).

$$P_1$$
$$(L_1,R,2,2,S_1)$$
$$(L_2,R,1,1,S_1)$$
$$(L_2,W,1,X,S_1)$$
$$(L_1,W,2,X,S_1)$$

Under architecture A(CMP) every member of the graph set for the execution includes the following path.

$$(P_1,L_2,W,1,X,S_1) \quad <_{CWW} \quad (P_1,L_1,W,2,X,S_1)$$

The path shows that the write event in statement L_2 for operand X occurs before the write event in statement L_1 for operand X. Therefore, the execution does not obey

The Rule of Program Order (PO)   **57**

A(CMP, UWW). Equivalently, if the execution occurs on a machine known to obey A(CMP), then the execution reveals a failure of the machine to obey UWW.

THE RULE OF UNIPROCESSOR ORDER (UPO)

The intent of the rule of uniprocessor order is to express the idea that the three rules, UWR, URW, and UWW, are all obeyed.

To form the single graph in the graph set for an execution E under A(UPO), form the graph sets for the execution under UWR, URW, and UWW. Take the product of the three graphs. Relabel all arcs $<_{UPO}$.

The transition template for UPO is

$$(P,L,A,V,O,S) \quad <_{UPO} \quad (=,-,-,-,=,=)$$

which is just the transition template for UWR, URW, and UWW, without any indication that the events are either read events or write events.

The obvious relationships hold among the four rules.

Theorem 6.1.   UPO $\Rightarrow$ UWR.

Proof. The graph for any execution under A(UPO) is the product of the graphs for A(UWR), A(URW), and A(UWW). By Lemma 3.3 if the graph for an execution under A(UPO) is circuit-free, then its graph under A(UWR) is also circuit-free. Hence A(UPO) $\Rightarrow$ A(UWR). ∎

Theorem 6.2.   UPO $\Rightarrow$ URW.

Theorem 6.3.   UPO $\Rightarrow$ UWW.

The proofs are similar to that for Theorem 6.1. (See Prob. 6.1.)

THE RULE OF PROGRAM ORDER (PO)

The intent of the rule of program order is to express the idea that if statement L_i precedes statement L_j in a program, then when the program is executed, the events in statement L_i will occur in time before the events in statement L_j.

To form the single graph in the graph set for an execution E under A(PO), draw an arc, labeled $<_{PO}$, from E_1 to E_2 if $E_1 <_O E_2$.

The transition template for PO is

$$(P,L,A,V,O,S) \quad <_{PO} \quad (P,-,-,-,-,-)$$

An arc labeled $<_{PO}$ occurs only between events in the same process.

In addition, the statement number for the left-hand event is lower than the statement number for the right-hand event.

In Fig. 6.4 an execution shows a failure to be Program Ordered (Theorem A4).

```
Initially, A = B = X = Y = 0.

   P₁              P₂
L₁: Y:= B;      L₁: X:= A;
L₂: A:= 1;      L₂: B:= 1;

Terminally, A = B = X = Y = 1.
```

Figure 6.4 A failure to obey PO.

There are two events in the SOSS set for operand A in store S_2.

$$(P_1, L_2, W, -, A, S_2)$$
$$(P_2, L_1, R, -, A, S_2)$$

The two events can be arranged in one of two orders.

$$(P_1, L_2, W, -, A, S_2) <_{CWR} (P_2, L_1, R, -, A, S_2)$$
$$(P_2, L_1, R, -, A, S_2) <_{CRW} (P_1, L_2, W, -, A, S_2)$$

Once values are assigned, the events are

$$(P_1, L_2, W, 1, A, S_2) <_{CWR} (P_2, L_1, R, 1, A, S_2)$$
$$(P_2, L_1, R, 0, A, S_2) <_{CRW} (P_1, L_2, W, 1, A, S_2)$$

The latter possibility requires that the value of the read event be 0 which requires that the terminal value of X be 0. Consequently, the only possible SOSS sequence for A in S_2 is

$$(P_1, L_2, W, 1, A, S_2) <_{CWR} (P_2, L_1, R, 1, A, S_2)$$

Similarly, the only possible SOSS sequence for B in S_2 is

$$(P_2, L_1, W, 1, B, S_2) <_{CWR} (P_1, L_2, R, 1, B, S_1)$$

The Rule of Program Order (PO)

Thus, under architecture A(CMP) every member of the graph set for the execution includes the following two paths:

$$(P_1,L_2,W,1,A,S_2) <_{CWR} (P_2,L_1,R,1,A,S_2)$$
$$(P_2,L_2,W,1,B,S_1) <_{CWR} (P_1,L_1,R,1,B,S_1)$$

The following linear ordering of the events of the execution shows that the execution obeys A(CMP).

P_1	P_2
	$(L_2,R,1,1,S_2)$
	$(L_2,W,1,B,S)$
$(L_1,R,1,B,S_1)$	
$(L_1,W,1,Y,S)$	
$(L_2,R,1,1,S_1)$	
$(L_2,W,1,A,S)$	
	$(L_1,R,1,A,S_2)$
	$(L_1,W,1,X,S)$

Under architecture A(PO) every member of the graph set for the execution contains the following paths.

$$(P_1,L_1,R,-,B,S_1) <_{PO} (P_1,L_2,R,1,A,S_1)$$
$$(P_1,L_1,R,-,B,S_1) <_{PO} (P_1,L_2,W,1,A,S_1)$$
$$(P_1,L_1,R,-,B,S_1) <_{PO} (P_1,L_2,W,1,A,S_2)$$

$$(P_1,L_1,W,-,Y,S_1) <_{PO} (P_1,L_2,R,1,A,S_1)$$
$$(P_1,L_1,W,-,Y,S_1) <_{PO} (P_1,L_2,W,1,A,S_1)$$
$$(P_1,L_1,W,-,Y,S_1) <_{PO} (P_1,L_2,W,1,A,S_2)$$

$$(P_1,L_1,W,-,Y,S_2) <_{PO} (P_1,L_2,R,1,A,S_1)$$
$$(P_1,L_1,W,-,Y,S_2) <_{PO} (P_1,L_2,W,1,A,S_1)$$
$$(P_1,L_1,W,-,Y,S_2) <_{PO} (P_1,L_2,W,1,A,S_2)$$

$$(P_2,L_1,R,-,A,S_2) <_{PO} (P_2,L_2,R,1,B,S_2)$$
$$(P_2,L_1,R,-,A,S_2) <_{PO} (P_2,L_2,W,1,B,S_1)$$
$$(P_2,L_1,R,-,A,S_2) <_{PO} (P_2,L_2,W,1,B,S_2)$$

$$(P_2,L_1,W,-,X,S_1) <_{PO} (P_2,L_2,R,1,B,S_2)$$
$$(P_2,L_1,W,-,X,S_1) <_{PO} (P_2,L_2,W,1,B,S_1)$$
$$(P_2,L_1,W,-,X,S_1) <_{PO} (P_2,L_2,W,1,B,S_2)$$

$$(P_2,L_1,W,-,X,S_2) <_{PO} (P_2,L_2,R,1,B,S_2)$$
$$(P_2,L_1,W,-,X,S_2) <_{PO} (P_2,L_2,W,1,B,S_1)$$
$$(P_2,L_1,W,-,X,S_2) <_{PO} (P_2,L_2,W,1,B,S_2)$$

The following linear ordering of the events of the execution shows that the execution obeys A(PO).

$$P_1$$
$(L_1,R,1,B,S_1)$
$(L_1,W,1,Y,S)$
$(L_2,R,1,1,S_1)$
$(L_2,W,1,A,S)$

$$P_2$$
$(L_1,R,1,A,S_2)$
$(L_1,W,1,X,S)$
$(L_2,R,1,1,S_2)$
$(L_2,W,1,B,S)$

Computing the product of the graph set for the execution under A(CMP) and the graph set for the execution under A(PO) yields the graph set for the execution under A(CMP,PO). Under architecture A(CMP,PO) every member of the graph set for the execution contains the following circuit.

$(P_1,L_1,R,1,B,S_1)$ $<_{PO}$ $(P_1,L_2,W,1,A,S_2)$
$<_{CWR}$ $(P_2,L_1,R,1,A,S_2)$
$<_{PO}$ $(P_2,L_2,W,1,B,S_1)$
$<_{CWR}$ $(P_1,L_1,R,1,B,S_1)$

Therefore, the execution does not obey A(CMP,PO). Equivalently, if the execution occurs on a machine known to obey A(CMP), then the execution reveals a failure of the machine to obey PO.

THE RULE OF WRITE ORDER (WO)

The intent of the rule of write order is to express the idea that if statement L_i precedes statement L_j in a program, then when the program is executed, the sink operands in statement L_i will be stored before the sink operands in statement L_j.

To form the single graph in the graph set for an execution E under A(WO), draw an arc, labeled $<_{WO}$, from E_1 to E_2 if

1. $E_1 <_O E_2$,
2. E_1 and E_2 are both write events.

The transition template for WO is

(P,L,W,V,O,S) $<_{WO}$ $(=,-,W,-,-,-)$

An arc labeled $<_{WO}$ occurs only between write events in the same process. If $E_1 <_{WO} E_2$, then $E_1 <_{WO} E_*$ for all write events E_* in the same statement as E_2.

In addition, the statement number for the left-hand event must be lower than the statement number for the right-hand event.

The Rule of Write Order (WO)

Theorem 6.4. PO $\Rightarrow$ WO.

Proof. If an execution E obeys an architecture A_1 which includes the rule PO, then there is a circuit-free graph G_1 of the graph set for E under A_1. From G_1 construct a second graph G_2 via the following steps. Erase the arcs labeled $<_{PO}$ which are incident into or out of read events. Relabel the remaining arcs from $<_{PO}$ to $<_{WO}$. By Lemma 3.3, G_2 is also circuit-free, and G_2 occurs in the graph set for the execution under an architecture which is identical to A_1 except that WO is substituted for PO. ∎

In Fig. 6.5 an execution shows a failure to be Write Ordered (Theorem A6).

```
                Initially, A = B = 0.

            P₁                  P₂
        L₁: A:= 1;          L₁: B:= 1;
        L₂: B:= 2;          L₂: A:= 2;

                Terminally, A = B = 1.
```

Figure 6.5 A failure to obey WO.

The two events in the SOSS set for operand A in store S_1 can be arranged in one of two orders.

$$(P_2, L_2, W, 2, A, S_1) <_{CWW} (P_1, L_1, W, 1, A, S_1)$$
$$(P_1, L_1, W, 1, A, S_1) <_{CWW} (P_2, L_2, W, 2, A, S_1)$$

Only the former accords with the terminal value of A.

A similar restriction applies in the case of the SOSSs for each of A in S_2, B in S_1, and B in S_2. Thus, under architecture A(CMP) every member of the graph set for the execution includes the following paths:

$$(P_2, L_2, W, 2, A, S_1) <_{CWW} (P_1, L_1, W, 1, A, S_1)$$
$$(P_2, L_2, W, 2, A, S_2) <_{CWW} (P_1, L_1, W, 1, A, S_2)$$
$$(P_1, L_2, W, 2, B, S_1) <_{CWW} (P_2, L_1, W, 1, B, S_1)$$
$$(P_1, L_2, W, 2, B, S_2) <_{CWW} (P_2, L_1, W, 1, B, S_2)$$

The following linear ordering of the events of the execution shows that the execution obeys A(CMP).

```
            P₁                      P₂
      (L₁, R, 1, 1, S₁)
                                (L₁, R, 1, 1, S₂)
                                (L₂, R, 2, 2, S₂)
                                (L₂, W, 2, A, S)
      (L₁, W, 1, A, S)
      (L₂, R, 2, 2, S₁)
      (L₂, W, 2, B, S)
                                (L₁, W, 1, B, S)
```

Under architecture A(WO) every member of the graph set for the execution contains the following path:

$$(P_1, L_1, W, 1, A, S_1) <_{WO} (P_1, L_2, W, 2, B, S_1)$$
$$(P_1, L_1, W, 1, A, S_1) <_{WO} (P_1, L_2, W, 2, B, S_2)$$
$$(P_1, L_1, W, 1, A, S_2) <_{WO} (P_1, L_2, W, 2, B, S_1)$$
$$(P_1, L_1, W, 1, A, S_2) <_{WO} (P_1, L_2, W, 2, B, S_2)$$

$$(P_2, L_1, W, 1, B, S_1) <_{WO} (P_2, L_2, W, 2, A, S_1)$$
$$(P_2, L_1, W, 1, B, S_1) <_{WO} (P_2, L_2, W, 2, A, S_2)$$
$$(P_2, L_1, W, 1, B, S_2) <_{WO} (P_2, L_2, W, 2, A, S_1)$$
$$(P_2, L_1, W, 1, B, S_2) <_{WO} (P_2, L_2, W, 2, A, S_2)$$

Under architecture A(CMP, WO) every member of the graph set for the execution contains the two circuits, for $S_x = S_1$ or S_2.

$$(P_1, L_1, W, 1, A, S_x) <_{WO} (P_1, L_2, W, 2, B, S_x)$$
$$<_{CWW} (P_2, L_1, W, 1, B, S_x)$$
$$<_{WO} (P_2, L_2, W, 2, A, S_x)$$
$$<_{CWW} (P_1, L_1, W, 1, A, S_x)$$

Therefore, the execution does not obey A(CMP, WO). Equivalently, if the execution occurs on a machine known to obey A(CMP), then the execution reveals a failure of the machine to obey A(WO).

THE RULE OF READ ORDER (RO)

The intent of the rule of read order is to express the idea that if statement L_i precedes statement L_j in a program, then when the program is executed, the source operands in statement L_i will be fetched before the source operands in statement L_j are fetched.

To form the single graph in the graph set for an execution E under A(RO), draw an arc, labeled $<_{RO}$, from E_1 to E_2 if

1. $E_1 <_O E_2$,
2. E_1 and E_2 are both read events.

The transition template for RO is

$$(P, L, R, V, 0, S) <_{RO} (=, -, R, -, -, =)$$

An arc labeled $<_{RO}$ occurs only between read events in the same process.

The Rule of Read Order (RO)

In addition, the statement number for the left-hand event must be lower than the statement number for the right-hand event. If $E_1 <_{RO} E_2$, then $E_1 <_{RO} E_*$ for all read events E_* in the same statement as E_2.

In Figure 6.6 an execution shows a failure to be Read Ordered (Theorem A13).

Initially, $A = X = C = 0$.

$$
\begin{array}{ll}
P_1 & P_2 \\
L_1: A := 1; & L_1: X := A; \\
& L_2: Y := A;
\end{array}
$$

Figure 6.6 A failure to obey RO.

Terminally, $A = X = 1, Y = 0$.

The SOSS set for operand A in store S_2 contains three events. The only way the three events can be ordered so as to calculate the terminal values of X and Y is

$$(P_2, L_2, R, 0, A, S_2) <_{CRW} (P_1, L_1, W, 1, A, S_2)$$
$$<_{CWR} (P_2, L_1, R, 1, A, S_2)$$

Under architecture A(CMP) every member of the graph set for the execution contains this path.

The following linear ordering of the events of this execution shows that the execution obeys A(CMP).

$$
\begin{array}{ll}
P_1 & P_2 \\
 & (L_2, R, 0, A, S_2) \\
(L_1, R, 1, 1, S_1) & \\
(L_1, W, 1, A, S) & \\
 & (L_1, R, 1, A, S_2) \\
 & (L_1, W, 1, X, S) \\
 & (L_2, W, 0, Y, S)
\end{array}
$$

The path

$$(P_2, L_2, R, 0, A, S_2) <_{CRW} (P_1, L_1, W, 1, A, S_2)$$
$$<_{CWR} (P_2, L_1, R, 1, A, S_2)$$

shows that in process P_2 the read event in statement L_2 occurs before the read event in statement L_1. Therefore, the execution does not obey A(CMP, RO). Equivalently, if the above execution occurs on a machine known to obey A(CMP), then the execution reveals a failure of the machine to obey RO.

THE RULE OF PROGRAM ORDER BY STORE (POS)

The intent of the rule of program order by store is to express a specialization of the idea of program order, namely, that events in a process which reference the store associated with the process occur in program order.

To form the single graph in the graph set for an execution E under A(POS) draw an arc, labeled $<_{POS}$, from E_1 to E_2 if

1. $E_1 <_O E_2$.
2. The store components of E_1 and E_2 are both for the store associated with the process containing E_1 and E_2.

The transition template for POS is

$$(P, L, A, V, O, S) \quad <_{POS} \quad (=, -, -, -, -, =)$$

An arc labeled $<_{POS}$ occurs only between events in the same process. The store component of both events is specifically for the store associated with the process containing the events.

In addition, the statement number for the left-hand event must be lower than the statement number for the right-hand event.

Theorem 6.5. POS $\Rightarrow$ RO.

Theorem 6.6. PO $\Rightarrow$ POS.

Proofs. See Prob. 6.1.

In Fig. 6.7 an execution shows a failure to be Program Ordered by Store (Theorem A21).

```
Initially, A = B = X = 0.

     P₁                P₂
L₁: A:= 1;        L₁: B:= 1;
L₂: X:= B;        L₂: A:= 2;

Terminally, A = B = 1, X = 0.
```
Figure 6.7 A failure to obey POS.

Under A(CMP) every element of the graph set for the execution contains the following paths:

$$(P_1, L_2, R, 0, B, S_1) \quad <_{CRW} \quad (P_2, L_1, W, 1, B, S_1)$$
$$(P_2, L_2, W, 2, A, S_1) \quad <_{CWW} \quad (P_1, L_1, W, 1, A, S_1)$$
$$(P_2, L_2, W, 2, A, S_2) \quad <_{CWW} \quad (P_1, L_1, W, 1, A, S_2)$$

The Rule of Program Order by Store (POS)

Under A(WO) every element of the graph set for the execution contains the following paths:

$$(P_1, L_1, W, 1, A, S_1) <_{WO} (P_1, L_2, W, -, X, S_1)$$
$$(P_1, L_1, W, 1, A, S_1) <_{WO} (P_1, L_2, W, -, X, S_2)$$
$$(P_1, L_1, W, 1, A, S_2) <_{WO} (P_1, L_2, W, -, X, S_1)$$
$$(P_1, L_1, W, 1, A, S_2) <_{WO} (P_1, L_2, W, -, X, S_2)$$

$$(P_2, L_1, W, 1, B, S_1) <_{WO} (P_2, L_2, W, 2, A, S_1)$$
$$(P_2, L_1, W, 1, B, S_1) <_{WO} (P_2, L_2, W, 2, A, S_2)$$
$$(P_2, L_1, W, 1, B, S_2) <_{WO} (P_2, L_2, W, 2, A, S_1)$$
$$(P_2, L_1, W, 1, B, S_2) <_{WO} (P_2, L_2, W, 2, A, S_2)$$

Under A(POS) every element of the graph set for the execution contains the following paths:

$$(P_1, L_1, R, 1, 1, S_1) <_{POS} (P_1, L_2, R, -, B, S_1)$$
$$(P_1, L_1, R, 1, 1, S_1) <_{POS} (P_1, L_2, W, -, X, S_1)$$

$$(P_1, L_1, W, 1, A, S_1) <_{POS} (P_1, L_2, R, -, B, S_1)$$
$$(P_1, L_1, W, 1, A, S_1) <_{POS} (P_1, L_2, W, -, X, S_1)$$

$$(P_2, L_1, R, 1, 1, S_2) <_{POS} (P_2, L_2, R, 2, 2, S_2)$$
$$(P_2, L_1, R, 1, 1, S_2) <_{POS} (P_2, L_2, W, 2, A, S_2)$$

$$(P_2, L_1, W, 1, B, S_2) <_{POS} (P_2, L_2, R, 2, 2, S_2)$$
$$(P_2, L_1, W, 1, B, S_2) <_{POS} (P_2, L_2, W, 2, A, S_2)$$

The following linear ordering of the events of the execution shows that the execution obeys A(CMP, WO).

P_1	P_2
$(L_1, R, 1, 1, S_1)$	
$(L_2, R, 0, B, S_1)$	
	$(L_1, R, 1, 1, S_2)$
	$(L_1, W, 1, B, S)$
	$(L_2, R, 2, 2, S_2)$
	$(L_2, W, 2, A, S)$
$(L_1, W, 1, A, S)$	
$(L_2, W, 0, X, S)$	

Under architecture A(CMP, WO, POS) every member of the graph set for the execution contains the following circuit:

$$(P_1, L_2, R, 0, B, S_1) <_{CRW} (P_2, L_1, W, 1, B, S_1)$$
$$<_{WO} (P_2, L_2, W, 2, A, S_1)$$
$$<_{CWW} (P_1, L_1, W, 1, A, S_1)$$
$$<_{POS} (P_1, L_2, R, 0, B, S_1)$$

Therefore, the execution does not obey A(CMP, WO, POS). Equivalently, if the execution occurs on a machine which is known to obey A(CMP, WO), then the execution reveals a failure of the machine to obey POS.

THE RULE OF WRITE ORDER BY STORE (WOS)

The intent of the rule of write order by store is to express a specialization of the idea of write order, namely, that write events to the store for the process containing the events occur in program order.

To form the single graph in the graph set for an execution E under A(WOS), draw an arc, labeled $<_{WOS}$, from E_1 to E_2 if

1. $E_1 <_O E_2$.
2. E_1 and E_2 are write events.
3. The store components of E_1 and E_2 are both for the store associated with the process containing E_1 and E_2.

The transition template for WOS is

$$(P,L,W,V,O,S) \quad <_{WOS} \quad (=,-,W,-,-,=)$$

An arc labeled $<_{WOS}$ occurs only between write events in the same process. The store component of both events is for the store associated with the process containing the events.

In addition, the statement number for the left-hand event must be lower than the statement number for the right-hand event.

Theorem 6.7. POS $\Rightarrow$ WOS.

Proof. See Prob. 6.1.

UWW orders write events in the same process which have the same operand component. WOS orders write events in the same process which have the same store component. The execution in Fig. 6.3, which shows a failure to obey UWW, can also be used to show a failure to obey WOS. (See Prob. 6.10.)

PROBLEMS

6.1. Prove
    (a) UPO $\Rightarrow$ URW.
    (b) UPO $\Rightarrow$ UWW.
    (c) PO $\Rightarrow$ WO.
    (d) PO $\Rightarrow$ RO.

(e) PO ⇒ POS
(f) WO ⇒ WOS.
(g) POS ⇒ RO.
(h) POS ⇒ WOS.

6.2. Argue for or against the position that a datum which is only read from, never written into, should be considered a local datum, not a global datum, even though it may be referenced by many different processes.

In the next several problems the phrase "rule set" refers to a set consisting of the following rules.

CWR	CRW	CWW	SRW	
UWR	URW	UWW		
PO	WO	RO	POS	WOS

6.3. In the graph set for the execution

$$\text{Initially, } X = 0.$$

$$P_1$$
$L_1: X := 3;$
$L_2: X := 7;$

$$\text{Terminally, } X = 7.$$

which rules in the rule set require that an arc occur from $(P_1, L_1, W, 3, X, S_1)$ to $(P_1, L_2, W, 7, X, S_1)$?

6.4. In the graph set for the execution

$$\text{Initially, } X = Y = 0.$$

$$P_1$$
$L_1: X := 1;$
$L_2: Y := X;$

$$\text{Terminally, } X = Y = 1.$$

which rules in the rule set require that an arc occur from $(P_1, L_1, W, 1, X, S_1)$ to $(P_1, L_2, R, 1, X, S_1)$?

6.5. In the graph set for the execution

$$\text{Initially, } X = Y = 0.$$

$$P_1$$
$L_1: Y := X;$
$L_2: X := 1;$

$$\text{Terminally, } X = 1, Y = 0.$$

which rules in the rule set require that an arc occur from $(P_1, L_1, R, 0, X, S_1)$ to $(P_1, L_2, W, 1, X, S_1)$?

6.6. In the graph set for the execution

$$\text{Initially, } X = Y = Z = 0.$$

$$\begin{array}{l} P_1 \\ L_1: Y := X; \\ L_2: Z := X; \end{array}$$

$$\text{Terminally, } X = Y = Z = 0.$$

which rules in the rule set require that an arc occur from $(P_1,L_1,R,0,X,S_1)$ to $(P_1,L_2,R,0,X,S_1)$?

6.7. While POS $\Rightarrow$ UPO, it is not true that UPO $\Rightarrow$ POS. Explain why not.

6.8. In the discussion of the execution exhibiting a failure to be program ordered, the statement was made that the only possible SOSS sequence for B in S_2 is

$$(P_2,L_1,W,1,B,S_1) <_{CWR} (P_1,L_2,R,1,B,S_1)$$

Explain why.

6.9. For rule PO there is rule POS. For WO there is WOS. There is a rule named RO, but none named ROS. Why not?

6.10. Use the execution in Fig. 6.3 that was used to show a failure to obey the rule of UWW to show a failure to obey the rule of WOS.

* 6.11. The theorem underlying the design of uniprocessors is that A(CMP, UPO) $\Leftrightarrow$ A(CMP, PO). Or, more generally, let A be any set of rules that contains neither UPO or PO. Let $A_1 = A * A(UPO)$ and $A_2 = A * A(PO)$. Then on a uniprocessor $A_1 \Leftrightarrow A_2$.

Even though the methods for proving architectures to be indistinguishable are not demonstrated until Chap. 11, try now to prove that A(CMP, UPO) $\Leftrightarrow$ A(CMP, PO) on a system consisting of only a single process.

(Hint. Proof of $\Leftarrow$. PO $\Rightarrow$ UPO. Proof of $\Rightarrow$. Assume the contrary. Then there is an execution E which obeys A(CMP, UPO), but does not obey A(CMP, PO). Let GS_1 be the graph set for E under A(CMP, UPO). Let GS_2 be the graph set for E under A(CMP, PO). Let GS_3 be the graph set for E under A(CMP, UPO, PO).

Choose some circuit-free graph G_1 in the graph set GS_1 for E under A(CMP, UPO).

Consider the element G_3 of GS_3 formed from the product of G_1 and the graph set of E under A(PO).

G_3 contains a circuit C_3 since all members of GS_2 contain a circuit, and G_3 is obtained from some member of GS_2 by adding arcs labeled $<_{UPO}$. Further C_3 contains an arc labeled $<_{PO}$, since G_1 is circuit-free.

Complete the proof of the theorem by inventing another circuit C_4 which does not have an arc labeled $<_{PO}$ and which must occur also in G_1, contrary to assumption.)

* 6.12. The rule of PO applies to all events in a process. The rule of POS applies only to the events in a process whose store component is the store specifically associated with the process. Thus, POS is a specialization of PO. Another way to specialize PO is to define a rule, POO, which applies only to those events in a process which have the same operand component. The rules of RO and WO can be similarly specialized to obtain rules ROO and WOO. The transition templates of the new rules are

$$(P,L,A,V,O,S) \quad <_{POO} \quad (=,-,-,-,=,-)$$

$$(P,L,R,V,O,S) \quad <_{ROO} \quad (=,-,R,-,=,-)$$

$$(P,L,W,V,O,S) \quad <_{WOO} \quad (=,-,W,-,=,-)$$

Are the new rules essentially different from the rule of UPO? ROO forces read events to be ordered in a way that UPO does not, but there appears to be no way to take advantage of that. Prove or disprove: A(CMP, UPO) ⇔ A(CMP, POO).

7

The Rules of Atomicity

**SEEING THE FAILURE OF A SET OF EVENTS
TO OCCUR INSTANTANEOUSLY**

When a programmer writes the statement $X := A + B$;, the intent may be that the two global operands, A and B, be fetched at the same instant of time. On most systems this will not happen. An assembly language instruction will fetch one of the operands from storage. Then a second instruction will fetch the other operand. Between the two instructions an interrupt could occur, causing the two fetches to be separated by an arbitrarily long interval of time.

When a programmer writes $A := 1$; (where A is a shared variable whose previous value was not 1) the intent usually is that the new value of A be visible instantly to programs running on all processors in the system. This will not happen because signals take a finite amount of time to propagate. It may appear to happen, though, if the machine has been properly constructed.

When a programmer writes the statement $X := B$; the intent may be that there be an instant when X and B have the same value. Normally, such a statement will be compiled into a fetch instruction and a store instruction. Again, due to an interrupt an arbitrarily long interval can occur between the two.

The sole logical requirement of an implementation of an architecture is that it not be possible to execute a program which demonstrates that the implementation violates the architecture. Suppose one wants to build a machine whose architecture includes some principle of instantaneity. The first step is to understand how it is possible to see a failure of an action to be instantaneous. The second step is to understand how to avoid building a machine in which failures of actions to be instantaneous are visible.

The General Rule of Atomicity

Suppose E is an execution which obeys architecture A, and suppose S is a set $\{X_1, X_2, \ldots, X_n\}$ of events within E which are all required to appear to occur at the same instant. To prove that this is not the case, it suffices to prove that there is another event or path Y which occurs between two events, say X_1 and X_2, of S. This can only happen if the rules of architecture A make it possible to deduce that there is an arc from X_1 to Y and an arc from Y to X_2:

$$X_1 < Y \text{ and } Y < X_2$$

In order for it to be impossible to show that the events in S did not all occur at the same instant means that either $X_1 < Y$ or $Y < X_2$ must be false, that is, that either

$$Y < X_1 \text{ and } Y < X_2$$

or

$$X_1 < Y \text{ and } X_2 < Y$$

must be true. In other words, for a set of events S to appear to be atomic, it suffices that for any other event Y, either $Y < X_*$ for all X_* in S or $X_* < Y$ for all X_* in S. This observation leads to the following procedure for constructing the graph set to represent a general rule of atomicity.

THE GENERAL RULE OF ATOMICITY

Let $S = \{s_1, s_2, \ldots, s_k\}$ be a set of disjoint subsets of the events of an execution E. Choose any element s in S and any event E_1 not in s. Create a graph set consisting of two graphs. In the first graph draw arcs, labeled $<_a$, from E_1 to each event of s. In the second element draw arcs, labeled $<_a$, from each event in s to E_1. Continue, over all elements s of S and over all events E_1 not in s, the operation of forming graph sets consisting of pairs of graphs. Let GS_1 be the product of all of the graph sets. Let GS_2 be the set of graphs in GS_1 which are circuit-free. Then, GS_2 is the graph set for execution E under the rule of atomicity.

Three different sets are used to formulate architectural rules about atomicity: the set of all events within a statement (statement atomicity), the set of all write events within a statement (write atomicity), and the set of all read events within a statement (read atomicity).

The Rule of Statement Atomicity (SA)

The atomic sets are the sets of events for each statement.

The rule of statement atomicity expresses the idea that each statement is executed instantaneously.

The transition template for SA is

$$(P,L,A,V,O,S) \quad <_{SA} \quad (-,-,-,-,-,-)$$

If $ev_1 <_{SA} ev_2$, then nothing is known from ev_1 about ev_2.

The Rule of Write Atomicity (WA)

The atomic sets are the sets of write events for each statement.

The rule of write atomicity expresses the idea that the set of write events for each statement is executed instantaneously.

The transition template for WA is

$$(P,L,A,V,O,S) \quad <_{WA} \quad (-,-,-,-,-,-)$$

The Rule of Read Atomicity (RA)

The atomic sets are the sets of read events for each statement.

The rule of read atomicity expresses the idea that the set of read events for each statement is executed instantaneously.

The transition template for RA is

$$(P,L,A,V,O,S) \quad <_{RA} \quad (-,-,-,-,-,-)$$

A CONVENIENT NOTATION

Consider an execution that obeys an architecture which is write atomic. Let W_1 and W_2 be write events in a given statement and let E_1 be any event not in the given statement. It will often be convenient to deduce that, since $E_1 < W_1$, it must also be that $E_1 <_{WA} W_1$ and so $E_1 <_{WA} W_2$. As a matter of notational convenience, this will be abbreviated as $E_1 < W_1 =_{WA} W_2$. Similarly, $=_{RA}$ ($=_{SA}$) will be used to connect two members of a read atomic set (statement atomic set).

The transition templates for $=_{SA}$, $=_{WA}$, and $=_{RA}$ are

$$(P,L,A,V,O,S) \quad =_{SA} \quad (=,=,A,-,-,-)$$
$$(P,L,W,V,O,S) \quad =_{WA} \quad (=,=,W,=,=,-)$$
$$(P,L,R,V,O,S) \quad =_{RA} \quad (=,=,R,-,-,=)$$

It will be convenient to use XA to denote any of the rules SA, WA, or RA. Also, $<_{XA}$ ($=_{XA}$) will be used to denote $<_{SA}$, $<_{WA}$, or $<_{RA}$ ($=_{SA}$, $=_{WA}$, or $=_{RA}$).

If $E_1 =_{XA} E_2$, then $E_1 =_{XA} E_*$ for all other events E_* in the same atomic set as E_1 and E_2.

There is a reason not to define arcs labeled $=_{XA}$ to be part of the graph sets for an execution under A(XA). Suppose they were. Then every atomic set would be a complete graph with arcs labeled $=_{XA}$, that is, every graph for an execution under A(XA) would contain a circuit. Thus, it would be necessary to modify the definition of an execution obeying an architecture as being "circuit-free outside of atomic sets." The choice of considering $=_{XA}$ to be a notational convenience is just simpler. (See also the discussion of conditional relationships in Chap. 15.)

RELATIONSHIPS BETWEEN SA, WA, AND RA

Theorem 7.1. SA $\Rightarrow$ WA.

Proof. Let E be any execution which obeys SA. Let G_1 be a circuit-free element of the graph set for E under A(SA). Create a new graph G_2 from G_1 by the following steps. Delete the arcs labeled $<_{SA}$ from a read event or to a read event. Relabel the rest of the arcs $<_{WA}$. Then by Lemma 3.3, the new graph is circuit-free. By the construction of the graph set for E under A(SA) and under A(WA), it is also an element of the latter. Thus E obeys WA. ∎

Theorem 7.2. SA $\Rightarrow$ RA.

Proof. See Prob. 7.1.

An Execution Showing a Failure to Be Statement Atomic (Theorem A25)

Consider the execution in Fig. 7.1.

Initially, A = 0, B = 1.

P_1 $\qquad$ P_2
L_1: A:= B; $\quad$ L_1: B:= A;

Figure 7.1 Not statement atomic. $\qquad$ Terminally, A = 1 and B = 0.

There are two events in the SOSS set for operand A in store S_2.

$$(P_2, L_1, R, -, A, S_2)$$
$$(P_1, L_1, W, -, A, S_2)$$

The two events can be arranged in one of two orders

$$(P_2, L_1, R, -, A, S_2) \quad <_{CRW} \quad (P_1, L_1, W, -, A, S_2)$$
$$(P_1, L_1, W, -, A, S_2) \quad <_{CWR} \quad (P_2, L_1, R, -, A, S_2)$$

Once values are assigned, the events are

$$(P_2, L_1, R, 0, A, S_2) <_{CRW} (P_1, L_1, W, 1, A, S_2)$$
$$(P_1, L_1, W, 1, A, S_2) <_{CWR} (P_2, L_1, R, 1, A, S_2)$$

The latter possibility requires that the value of the read event be one, which requires that the terminal value of B be one. Consequently, the only possible SOSS sequence for A in S_2 is

$$(P_2, L_1, R, 0, A, S_2) <_{CRW} (P_1, L_1, W, 1, A, S_2)$$

Similarly, the only possible SOSS sequence for B in S_1 is

$$(P_1, L_1, R, 1, B, S_1) <_{CRW} (P_2, L_1, W, 0, B, S_1)$$

The following linear ordering of the events of the execution shows that the graph set for the execution under A(CMP) is not circuit-full. Therefore, the execution obeys A(CMP).

```
        P₁                      P₂
 (L₁, R, 1, B, S₁)
                        (L₁, R, 0, A, S₂)
 (L₁, W, 1, A, S)
                        (L₁, W, 0, B, S)
```

Since $(P_1, L_1, W, 1, A, S_2)$ and $(P_2, L_1, R, 0, A, S_2)$ are in different statements, in each graph in the graph set for the execution under A(SA) one of the following is true:

$$(P_2, L_1, R, 0, A, S_2) <_{SA} (P_1, L_1, W, 1, A, S_2)$$
$$(P_1, L_1, W, 1, A, S_2) <_{SA} (P_2, L_1, R, 0, A, S_2)$$

If the execution is assumed to obey A(CMP, SA), then there is no circuit among the events and so both of the following are true.

$$(P_2, L_1, R, 0, A, S_2) <_{CRW} (P_1, L_1, W, 1, A, S_2)$$
$$(P_2, L_1, R, 0, A, S_2) <_{SA} (P_1, L_1, W, 1, A, S_2)$$

But by virtue of statement atomicity it must also then be true that

$$(P_2, L_1, R, 0, A, S_2) <_{SA} (P_1, L_1, R, 1, B, S_1)$$

This can be more simply stated using the abbreviation $=_{SA}$

$$(P_2, L_1, R, 0, A, S_2) <_{CRW} (P_1, L_1, W, 1, A, S_2)$$
$$=_{SA} (P_1, L_1, R, 1, B, S_1)$$

Relationships Between SA, WA, and RA

Similarly, one obtains for B that

$$
\begin{aligned}
(P_1,L_1,R,1,B,S_1) \quad &<_{CRW} \quad (P_2,L_1,W,0,B,S_1) \\
&=_{SA} \quad (P_2,L_1,R,0,A,S_2)
\end{aligned}
$$

Combining the preceding two results shows that every member of the graph set for the execution contains the following circuit:

$$
\begin{aligned}
(P_1,L_1,R,1,B,S_1) \quad &<_{CRW} \quad (P_2,L_1,W,0,B,S_1) \\
&=_{SA} \quad (P_2,L_1,R,0,A,S_2) \\
&<_{CRW} \quad (P_1,L_1,W,1,A,S_2) \\
&=_{SA} \quad (P_1,L_1,R,1,B,S_1)
\end{aligned}
$$

Therefore, the execution does not obey A(CMP, SA), contrary to the assumption. Equivalently, if the machine is known to obey A(CMP), and if the execution occurs on the machine, then the execution reveals a failure of the machine to be statement atomic.

An Execution Showing a Failure to Be Write Atomic (Adapted from Theorem A38)

Consider the execution in Fig. 7.2.

Initially, $A = B = U = V = X = Y = 0$.

P_1	P_2	P_3	P_4
L_1: $A := 1$;	L_1: $U := A$;	L_1: $X := B$;	L_1: $B := 1$;
	L_2: $V := B$;	L_2: $Y := A$;	

Terminally, $A = B = 1$,
$U = X = 1$,
$V = Y = 0$.

Figure 7.2 Not write atomic.

There are four SOSS sets for A: A and S_1, A and S_2, A and S_3, and A and S_4. The first and last consist only of a single event and are of no interest. The second and third each consist of two events; in order to compute the terminal values of U and Y the SOSS sequences must be

$$
\begin{aligned}
(P_3,L_2,R,0,A,S_3) \quad &<_{CRW} \quad (P_1,L_1,W,1,A,S_3) \\
(P_1,L_1,W,1,A,S_2) \quad &<_{CWR} \quad (P_2,L_1,R,1,A,S_2)
\end{aligned}
$$

Similarly, the significant SOSS sequences for B are

$$(P_2, L_2, R, 0, B, S_2) <_{CRW} (P_4, L_1, W, 1, B, S_2)$$
$$(P_4, L_1, W, 1, B, S_3) <_{CWR} (P_3, L_1, R, 1, B, S_3)$$

These paths occur in every element of the graph set for the execution under A(CMP).

Under A(CMP, WA) the arcs above labeled $<_{CRW}$ imply that the following arcs also exist:

$$(P_3, L_2, R, 0, A, S_3) <_{WA} (P_1, L_1, W, 1, A, S_2)$$

$$(P_2, L_2, R, 0, B, S_2) <_{WA} (P_4, L_1, W, 1, B, S_3)$$

This can more succinctly be expressed as

$$
\begin{array}{rl}
(P_3, L_2, R, 0, A, S_3) & <_{CRW} \; (P_1, L_1, W, 1, A, S_3) \\
& =_{WA} \; (P_1, L_1, W, 1, A, S_2) \\
& <_{CWR} \; (P_2, L_1, R, 1, A, S_2) \\
(P_2, L_2, R, 0, B, S_2) & <_{CRW} \; (P_4, L_1, W, 1, B, S_2) \\
& =_{WA} \; (P_4, L_1, W, 1, B, S_3) \\
& <_{CWR} \; (P_3, L_1, R, 1, B, S_3)
\end{array}
$$

Under A(RO) the single element of the graph set for the execution contains the following paths:

$$(P_2, L_1, R, -, A, S_2) <_{RO} (P_2, L_2, R, -, B, S_2)$$
$$(P_3, L_1, R, -, B, S_3) <_{RO} (P_3, L_2, R, -, A, S_3)$$

Consequently, under A(CMP, RO, WA) every element of the graph set for the execution contains the following circuit:

$$
\begin{array}{rl}
(P_3, L_2, R, 0, A, S_3) & <_{CRW} \; (P_1, L_1, W, 1, A, S_3) \\
& =_{WA} \; (P_1, L_1, W, 1, A, S_2) \\
& <_{CWR} \; (P_2, L_1, R, 1, A, S_2) \\
& <_{RO} \; (P_2, L_2, R, 0, B, S_2) \\
& <_{CRW} \; (P_4, L_1, W, 1, B, S_2) \\
& =_{WA} \; (P_4, L_1, W, 1, B, S_3) \\
& <_{CWR} \; (P_3, L_1, R, 1, B, S_3) \\
& <_{RO} \; (P_3, L_2, R, 0, A, S_3)
\end{array}
$$

Relationships Between SA, WA, and RA

Therefore, the execution does not obey A(CMP, RO, WA). Equivalently, if the execution occurs on a machine known to obey A(CMP,RO) (see the following), then the execution reveals a failure of the machine to be write atomic.

That the execution can occur on a machine which obeys A(CMP, RO) is shown by the following linear ordering of the events of the execution.

P_1	P_2	P_3	P_4
$(L_1, R, 1, 1, S_1)$			
$(L_1, W, 1, A, S_1)$			
$(L_1, W, 1, A, S_2)$			
	$(L_1, R, 1, A, S_2)$		
	$(L_1, W, 1, U, S)$		
	$(L_2, R, 0, B, S_2)$		
	$(L_2, W, 0, V, S)$		
			$(L_1, R, 1, 1, S_4)$
			$(L_1, W, 1, B, S)$
		$(L_1, R, 1, B, S_3)$	
		$(L_1, W, 1, X, S)$	
		$(L_2, R, 0, A, S_3)$	
		$(L_2, W, 0, Y, S)$	
$(L_1, W, 1, A, S_3)$			
$(L_1, W, 1, A, S_4)$			

An Execution Showing a Failure to Be Read Atomic (Theorem A32)

Consider the execution in Fig. 7.3.

Initially, $A = B = X = 0$.

P_1 P_2
L_1: $X := A + B$; L_1: $A := 1$;
     L_2: $B := 2$;

Figure 7.3 Not read atomic.   Terminally, $A = 1$, $B = 2$, $X = 2$.

There are two SOSS sets of interest, for B and S_1 and for A and S_1. Given the terminal value of X, the only possible ordering of the SOSS sequences is

$(P_2, L_2, W, 2, B, S_1)$ $<_{CWR}$ $(P_1, L_1, R, 2, B, S_1)$
$(P_1, L_1, R, 0, A, S_1)$ $<_{CRW}$ $(P_2, L_1, W, 1, A, S_1)$

These paths occur in every element of the graph set for the execution under A(CMP).

The following linear ordering of the events of the execution shows that the execution obeys A(CMP, WO).

```
        P₁                      P₂
                          (L₁,R,1,1,S₂)
   (L₁,R,0,A,S₁)
                          (L₁,W,1,A,S)
                          (L₂,R,2,2,S₂)
                          (L₂,W,2,B,S)
   (L₁,R,2,B,S₁)
   (L₁,W,2,X,S)
```

Under A(CMP, WO, RA) every element of the graph set for the execution contains the following circuit:

$$
\begin{aligned}
(P_2,L_2,W,2,B,S_1) \quad &<_{CWR} \quad (P_1,L_1,R,2,B,S_1) \\
&=_{RA} \quad (P_1,L_1,R,0,A,S_1) \\
&<_{CRW} \quad (P_2,L_1,W,1,A,S_1) \\
&<_{WO} \quad (P_2,L_2,W,2,B,S_1)
\end{aligned}
$$

Therefore, the execution does not obey A(CMP, WO, RA). Equivalently, if the machine is known to obey A(CMP, WO), and if the execution occurs on the machine, then the execution reveals a failure of the machine to be read atomic.

ARCS LABELED $<_{RA}$, $<_{WA}$, AND $<_{SA}$

If $x <_{WA} y$, then the transition template for WA shows that nothing can be deduced about the components of y from the components of x. This makes it very difficult to reason about circuits containing arcs labeled $<_{WA}$. On the other hand, if $x =_{WA} y$, then quite a bit can be deduced about the components of y from the components of x. What is needed is a justification for ignoring arcs labeled $<_{WA}$ and for focusing instead on arcs labeled $=_{WA}$. Lemma 7.2 provides such justification. (Obviously, the same remarks apply to $<_{RA}$ and $<_{SA}$.)

Let $a_1, a_2, \ldots, a_k$ be members of an atomic set in an execution under architecture A(XA), where XA represents either RA, WA, or SA. Let x and y be any events in the execution which are not in the atomic set. The arguments which follow begin with an arc labeled $<_{XA}$ from x to a_i, but are trivially adaptable to begin with the case of an arc from a_i to x. If there is a path from x to a_i, where the path does not contain an arc labeled $<_{XA}$, then arcs labeled $<_{XA}$ from x to $a_1, a_2, \ldots, a_k$ are called determined, and the path is called the determining path. Otherwise, such arcs are called nondetermined.

Let G_1 be any graph. A circuit in G_1 is maximal if there is no other circuit containing the same nodes in the same order. Clearly, any graph containing a circuit contains at least one maximal circuit.

Arcs Labeled $<_{RA}$, $<_{WA}$, and $<_{SA}$

Let A_1 be any architecture not containing XA. Let $A_2 = A_1 * A(XA)$.

Lemma 7.1. Let G_1 be a graph in the graph set, GS_1, for an execution under architecture A_2. If G_1 contains a maximal circuit containing a nondetermined arc labeled $<_{XA}$ (from x to some member of an atomic set), then there is a graph G_2 in GS_1 such that (1) G_2 is identical to GS_1 except that the direction of the nondetermined arcs labeled $<_{XA}$ are reversed (they run from members of the atomic set to x), and (2) G_2 contains no circuits not also found in G_1.

Proof. Let C_1 be a maximal circuit in G_1, containing a nondetermined arc labeled $<_{XA}$, say from x to a_i. By the definition of the graph set for XA there are arcs labeled $<_{XA}$ from x to $a_1, a_2, \ldots, a_k$. Further, there is another graph G_2 in graph set GS_1 which is identical to G_1 except that the direction of the arcs between x and members of the atomic set are reversed.

G_2 contains no circuits not also found in G_1. To see this, assume the contrary. Then there is an arc labeled $<_{XA}$ from some member of the atomic set, say, a_j, to x and a path from x back to a_j. The path must exist also in G_1 since G_1 and G_2 are identical except for the single set of arcs labeled $<_{XA}$. The length of the path must be either one or more than one. If the length of the path is one, then the label on the path (arc) cannot also be $<_{XA}$, and so the arc labeled $<_{XA}$ from x to a_i is determined, contrary to the original conditions. If the length of the path is more than one, then circuit C_1 was not maximal, also contrary to the original conditions. ∎

Lemma 7.2. Let G_1 be a graph in the graph set, GS_1, for an execution E which does not obey architecture A_2. Then G_1 contains a circuit which does not contain any arcs labeled $<_{XA}$, but may contain arcs labeled $=_{XA}$.

Proof. Choose any maximal circuit C_1 in G_1. If C_1 contains any nondetermined arcs labeled $<_{XA}$, then by Lemma 7.1 there exists graph G_2 in GS_1, containing at least one less circuit. Repeat the process until graph G_x is obtained containing circuit C_x which contains no nondetermined arcs. (The process cannot end in a circuit-free graph since E does not obey A_2. The process must terminate since the number of circuits is reduced at each step.)

If C_x contains no arcs labeled $<_{XA}$, then the lemma is proved. So let C_x contain a determined arc, labeled $<_{XA}$. If the determining path is adjacent to the determined arc, then create circuit C_{x+1} in which the determined arc is replaced by the determining path. Repeat wherever possible to obtain circuit C_y. (The repetition must end since the number of determined arcs is finite and is reduced by one at each repetition.)

If there are no determined arcs in C_y, then the lemma is proved, so let C_y contain one or more determined arcs. For these arcs the determining path is not adjacent to the determined arc. The determined arc goes from x to a_i, say, but the determining path goes from x to a_j. Then create circuit C_{y+1} in which the determined arc is replaced by the determining path plus the arc $a_j =_{XA} a_i$. Repeat once for each of the finite number of remaining determined arcs to obtain circuit C_z. Then C_z is the sought for circuit. ∎

PROBLEMS

7.1. Prove: if there are n statements in an execution which obeys A(SA), then there are fact(n) circuit-free elements of the graph set for the execution under A(SA).

7.2. Prove SA $\Rightarrow$ RA (Theorem 7.2).

7.3. If an execution fails to be statement atomic, then for some events e_1 and e_2 in the same statement there is another event e_3 (or path), not in the statement, such that $e_1 < e_3 < e_2$. In the example showing a failure to be statement atomic, what event can be shown to occur between $(P_1,L_1,R,1,B,S_1)$ and $(P_1,L_1,W,1,A,S_2)$? (Fill in the blanks.)

$$(P_1,L_1,R,1,B,S_1) \quad <_{CRW} \quad (P\_\_,L\_\_,\_\_,\_\_,\_\_,S\_\_)$$
$$=_{SA} \quad (P\_\_,L\_\_,\_\_,\_\_,\_\_,S\_\_)$$
$$<_{CRW} \quad (P_1,L_1,W,1,A,S_2)$$

7.4. Same question for the write atomic example.

$$(P_1,L_1,W,1,A,S_2) \quad <_{CWR} \quad (P\_\_,L\_\_,\_\_,\_\_,\_\_,S\_\_)$$
$$<_{RO} \quad (P\_\_,L\_\_,\_\_,\_\_,\_\_,S\_\_)$$
$$<_{CRW} \quad (P\_\_,L\_\_,\_\_,\_\_,\_\_,S\_\_)$$
$$=_{WA} \quad (P\_\_,L\_\_,\_\_,\_\_,\_\_,S\_\_)$$
$$<_{CWR} \quad (P\_\_,L\_\_,\_\_,\_\_,\_\_,S\_\_)$$
$$<_{RO} \quad (P\_\_,L\_\_,\_\_,\_\_,\_\_,S\_\_)$$
$$<_{CRW} \quad (P_1,L_1,W,1,A,S_3)$$

7.5. Same question for the read atomic example.

$$(P_1,L_1,R,0,A,S_1) \quad < \_\_\_ \quad (P\_\_,L\_\_,\_\_,\_\_,\_\_,S\_\_)$$
$$< \_\_\_ \quad (P\_\_,L\_\_,\_\_,\_\_,\_\_,S\_\_)$$
$$< \_\_\_ \quad (P_1,L_1,R,2,B,S_1)$$

7.6. Consider the following execution under A(SA).

$$\begin{array}{ll} P_1 & P_2 \\ L_1: A:=B; & L_1: X:=Y; \\ L_2: C:=B; & \end{array}$$

It contains nine events. How many nodes does each element of the graph set contain? How many statement atomic sets are there? How many elements of the graph set are there before the elements with circuits are thrown away? After the elements with circuits are thrown away? How many arcs are there in each element of the graph set?

Chap. 7 Problems

7.7. Consider the following execution and its events.

$$\text{Initially, } A = 0, B = 1.$$

$$\begin{array}{ll} P_1 & P_2 \\ L_1: A := B; & L_1: B := A; \end{array}$$

$$\text{Terminally, } A = 1 \text{ and } B = 0.$$

Consider the graph of these events with the following arcs:

$$(P_1, L_1, R, -, B, S_1) <_{WA} (P_2, L_1, W, -, B, S_1)$$
$$(P_1, L_1, R, -, B, S_1) <_{WA} (P_2, L_1, W, -, B, S_2)$$
$$(P_1, L_1, W, -, A, S_1) <_{WA} (P_2, L_1, W, -, B, S_1)$$
$$(P_1, L_1, W, -, A, S_1) <_{WA} (P_2, L_1, W, -, B, S_2)$$
$$(P_1, L_1, W, -, A, S_2) <_{WA} (P_2, L_1, W, -, B, S_1)$$
$$(P_1, L_1, W, -, A, S_2) <_{WA} (P_2, L_1, W, -, B, S_2)$$
$$(P_2, L_1, R, -, A, S_2) <_{WA} (P_2, L_1, W, -, B, S_1)$$
$$(P_2, L_1, R, -, A, S_2) <_{WA} (P_2, L_1, W, -, B, S_2)$$

$$(P_2, L_1, R, -, A, S_2) <_{WA} (P_1, L_1, W, -, A, S_1)$$
$$(P_2, L_1, R, -, A, S_2) <_{WA} (P_1, L_1, W, -, A, S_2)$$
$$(P_2, L_1, W, -, B, S_1) <_{WA} (P_1, L_1, W, -, A, S_1)$$
$$(P_2, L_1, W, -, B, S_1) <_{WA} (P_1, L_1, W, -, A, S_2)$$
$$(P_2, L_1, W, -, B, S_2) <_{WA} (P_1, L_1, W, -, A, S_1)$$
$$(P_2, L_1, W, -, B, S_2) <_{WA} (P_1, L_1, W, -, A, S_2)$$
$$(P_1, L_1, R, -, B, S_1) <_{WA} (P_1, L_1, W, -, A, S_1)$$
$$(P_1, L_1, R, -, B, S_1) <_{WA} (P_1, L_1, W, -, A, S_2)$$

Does this graph occur in the graph set for the execution under A(WA) before the graphs with circuits have been thrown away?

7.8. The events for the SOSS set for A and S_2 in the execution that follows are $(P_1, L_1, W, 1, A, S_2)$, $(P_2, L_1, R, 0, A, S_2)$, and $(P_2, L_1, W, 0, A, S_2)$. Show the order in which the events occur in the SOSS sequence to compute the terminal value of 0 for A.

$$\text{Initially, } A = 0.$$

$$\begin{array}{ll} P_1 & P_2 \\ L_1: A := 1; & L_1: A := A; \end{array}$$

$$\text{Terminally, } A = 0.$$

From this conclude that the execution does not obey A(CMP, SA).

7.9. Under the example of a failure to be statement atomic it was stated that the only possible SOSS sequence for B in S_1 is

$$(P_1, L_1, R, 1, B, S_1) <_{CRW} (P_2, L_1, W, 0, B, S_1)$$

Derive this statement in the same way as was done for A in S_2.

8

The Rules of Synchronization

The rules of synchronization and the rules of intrastatement order (Chap. 9) are similar in form. The definition of each type of rule involves four events, two in one statement and two in another statement. Both express an idea that if a first event occurs before a second, then a third event occurs before a fourth. The difference between the two types of rule is that the synchronization rules define arcs to occur between events in different statements, whereas the intrastatement rules, as the name implies, define arcs to occur between events within the same statement.

There are three synchronization rules. In a write synchronized execution, changes to the values of operands become visible to each store in the same order. In a consistent execution, each store sees each operand assume the same sequence of values. Consistency is a special case of write synchronization. Thus, in a write synchronized execution if one store saw operand B get the value 2, then operand C get the value 5, and then operand B get the value 4, then all stores would see the three changes in the same sequence. In a consistent execution, if one store saw the three changes in the given order, then all other stores would see operand B get the value 2 and then 4, but some might see operand C get the value 5 before seeing the two changes in value to B, others might see C change between the two value changes of B, and other stores might see C change last.

The rule of read synchronization expresses the idea that if two statements both read the same two operands, B and C, then if one statement reads operand B before the other statement reads operand B, then the one statement reads operand C before the other statement reads operand C. Read synchronization is a rule which would be expensive and pointless to implement. It arises as a formal variation on

THE RULE OF WRITE SYNCHRONIZATION (WS)

The intent of the rule of write synchronization is to express the idea that if statement L_1 writes into store S_a before statement L_2 writes into store S_a, then statement L_1 writes into store S_b before statement L_2 writes into store S_b (where S_a and S_b are any stores in the execution and L_1 and L_2 are any statements in any of the processes in the execution).

To form the graph set for an execution E under A(WS) perform the following steps:

1. For every pair of statements, L_1 and L_2, in the execution form two graphs. In the first graph draw an arc labeled $<_{WS}$ from each write event in L_1 to the write event in L_2 with the same store component. In the second graph draw an arc labeled $<_{WS}$ from each write event in L_2 to the write event in L_1 with the same store component.
2. Form the product of the pairs of graphs constructed in Step 1.
3. Delete from the product graph set all graphs containing a circuit. This diminished graph set constitutes the graph set for E under A(WS).

The transition template for WS is

$$(P, L, W, V, O, S) \quad <_{WS} \quad (-, -, W, -, -, =)$$

An arc labeled $<_{WS}$ occurs only between write events in different statements. The value components may be different. The operand components may be different. The store components are the same.

Theorem 8.1. WA $\Rightarrow$ WS.

Proof. Let E be any execution which obeys an architecture A_1 which includes the rule of write atomicity. Let G_1 be a circuit-free element of the graph set for E under A_1. For each arc labeled $<_{WA}$, relabel it $<_{WS}$ if it connects two write events with the same store component; otherwise delete it. Call the new graph G_2. Then G_2 is in the graph set for the execution under architecture A_2, which is identical to A_1 except that write atomicity is replaced by write synchronization. Since G_2 is constructed by deleting arcs from a circuit-free graph, by Lemma 3.3 it also is circuit-free. Consequently E obeys A_2. ■

An Execution Exhibiting a Failure to Be Write Synchronized (Theorem A39)

Consider the execution in Fig. 8.1.

```
Initially, A = B = X = Y = 0.

   P₁              P₂
L₁: A:= 1;      L₁: B:= 1;
L₂: Y:= B;      L₂: X:= A;

Terminally, A = B = 1, X = Y = 0.
```
Figure 8.1 A failure to be WS.

The following linear ordering of the events of the execution shows that the execution obeys A(CMP, POS).

P_1	P_2
	$(L_1, R, 1, 1, S_2)$
$(L_1, R, 1, 1, S_1)$	
$(L_1, W, 1, A, S_1)$	
$(L_2, R, 0, B, S_1)$	
	$(L_1, W, 1, B, S_1)$
	$(L_1, W, 1, B, S_2)$
	$(L_2, R, 0, A, S_2)$
$(L_1, W, 1, A, S_2)$	
	$(L_2, W, 0, X, S_1)$
	$(L_2, W, 0, X, S_2)$
$(L_2, W, 0, Y, S_1)$	
$(L_2, W, 0, Y, S_2)$	

Under architecture A(CMP, POS) every member of the graph set for the execution contains both of the following two paths:

$$(P_1, L_1, W, 1, A, S_1) <_{POS} (P_1, L_2, R, 0, B, S_1)$$
$$<_{CRW} (P_2, L_1, W, 1, B, S_1)$$

$$(P_2, L_1, W, 1, B, S_2) <_{POS} (P_2, L_2, R, 0, A, S_2)$$
$$<_{CRW} (P_1, L_1, W, 1, A, S_2)$$

Thus, if the execution occurs on a machine that is known to obey A(CMP, POS), the execution reveals a failure of the machine to be write synchronized since statement L_1 in process P_1 writes into S_1 before statement L_1 in process P_2 writes in S_1, but statement L_1 in process P_2 writes into S_2 before statement L_1 in process P_1 writes into S_2.

THE RULE OF CONSISTENCY (CON)

The intent of the rule of consistency is to express the idea that if statement L_1 writes into operand O in store S_a before statement L_2 writes into operand O in store S_a, then statement L_1 writes into operand O in store S_b before statement L_2 writes into operand O in store S_b.

Consistency is just the rule of write synchronization restricted to statements which write into the same operand. The transition templates are identical except that in any path $W_1 <_{CON} W_2$ the operand component is the same in W_1 and W_2, but not necessarily in the path $W_1 <_{WS} W_2$.

To form the graph set for an execution E under A(CON) perform the following steps:

1. For every pair of statements, L_1 and L_2, in E, with the same sink operand, form two graphs. In the first graph draw an arc labeled $<_{CON}$ from each write event in L_1 to the write event in L_2 with the same store component. In the second graph draw an arc labeled $<_{CON}$ from each write event in L_2 to the write event in L_1 with the same store component.
2. Form the product of the pairs of graphs constructed in Step 1.
3. Delete from the product graph set all graphs containing a circuit. This diminished graph set constitutes the graph set for E under A(CON).

The transition template for CON is

$$(P,L,W,V,O,S) \quad <_{CON} \quad (-,-,W,-,=,=)$$

An arc labeled $<_{CON}$ occurs only between write events in different statements. The value components may be different. The operand components are the same. The store components are the same.

The importance of consistency is given by the following theorem.

Theorem 8.2. If an execution obeys A(CMP, CON), then for each operand the terminal values of the operand are the same in all stores.

Proof. Let E be an execution that obeys A(CMP, CON). Choose any circuit-free element of the graph set for the execution under A(CMP, CON). For a given operand consider the set of write events for store S_1, for store S_2, and so on. (Observe that these are subsets of SOSS sets.) Each such set under $<_{CON}$ forms a complete graph and so by Lemma 3.6 there is a unique ordering of the events in each of the sets. Further, from the construction of the graph set, all the events which are last in the orderings belong to the same statement.

To see this, assume the contrary and let L_z be the statement whose write event is last in the ordering for S_1, say. By the assumption there are other write events in L_z for which there is an arc labeled $<_{CON}$ incident out from them, but there is none for the write event for S_1. This violates the definition of CON.

Consequently, the SOSS sequences for the given operand and the various stores all have as their last write event the write events for statement L_z. Thus, all copies of the given operand in the different stores have the same terminal value. ∎

Theorem 8.3. WS $\Rightarrow$ CON.

Proof. See Prob. 8.1.

An Execution Exhibiting a Failure to Be Consistent (Theorem A35)

Consider the execution in Fig. 8.2.

Initially, A = 0.

```
     P₁              P₂
L₁: A:= 1;    L₁: A:= 2;
```

Terminally, operand A in store S_1 = 2, and operand A in store S_2 = 1.

Figure 8.2 A failure to be CON.

The following linear ordering of the events of the execution shows that the execution obeys A(CMP).

```
           P₁                    P₂
    (L₁,R,1,1,S₁)
                          (L₁,R,2,2,S₂)
    (L₁,W,1,A,S₁)
                          (L₁,W,2,A,S₁)
                          (L₁,W,2,A,S₂)
    (L₁,W,1,A,S₂)
```

Under architecture A(CMP) every member of the graph set for the execution contains both of the following two paths:

$$(P_1,L_1,W,1,A,S_1) \;<_{\text{cww}}\; (P_2,L_1,W,2,A,S_1)$$

$$(P_2,L_1,W,2,A,S_2) \;<_{\text{cww}}\; (P_1,L_1,W,1,A,S_2)$$

Thus, if the execution occurs on a machine known to obey A(CMP), then the execution reveals a failure of the machine to be consistent since statement L_1 in process P_1 writes into operand A in S_1 before statement L_1 in process P_2 writes into operand A in S_1, but statement L_1 in process P_2 writes into operand A in S_2 before statement L_1 in process P_1 writes into operand A in S_2.

THE RULE OF READ SYNCHRONIZATION (RS)

Let L_1 and L_2 be two statements which both read operands O_1 and O_2. The intent of the rule of read synchronization is to express the idea that if statement L_1 reads operand O_1 before statement L_2 reads operand O_1, then statement L_1 reads operand O_2 before statement L_2 reads operand O_2.

To form the graph set for an execution E under A(RS) perform the following steps:

1. Let L_1 and L_2 be any two statements which both read a common set of operands, say, for example, the pair O_1 and O_2. For every such pair of statements in E, form two graphs. In the first graph draw an arc labeled $<_{RS}$ from the read event in L_1 for operand O_1 to the read event in L_2 for operand O_1 and from the read event in L_1 for operand O_2 to the read event in L_2 for operand O_2.

    In the second graph draw arcs labeled $<_{RS}$ from the read event in L_2 for operand O_1 to the read event in L_1 for operand O_1 and from the read event in L_2 for operand O_2 to the read event in L_1 for operand O_2.

    Repeat Step 1 for every pair of statements which read a common set of operands.
2. Form the product of the pairs of graphs constructed in Step 1.
3. Delete from the product graph set all graphs containing a circuit. This diminished graph set constitutes the graph set for E under A(RS).

The transition template for RS is

$$(P, L, R, V, O, S) \quad <_{RS} \quad (-, -, R, -, =, -)$$

An arc labeled $<_{RS}$ occurs only between read events in different statements. The value components may be different. The store components may be different. The operand components are the same.

Theorem 8.4. RA $\Rightarrow$ RS.

Proof. See Prob. 8.1.

An Execution Exhibiting a Failure to Be Read Synchronized (Theorem A41)

Consider the execution in Fig. 8.3.

Initially, A = B = X = Y = 0.

P_1	P_2	P_3
L_1: A:= 1;	L_1: X:= A + B;	L_1: Y:= A + B;
L_2: A:= 2;		
L_3: B:= 4;		
L_4: B:= 8;		

Terminally, A = 2, B = 8, X = 8, Y = 2.

Figure 8.3 A failure to be RS.

The following linear ordering of the events of the execution shows that the execution obeys A(CMP, WO).

P_1	P_2	P_3
	$(L_1, R, 0, A, S_2)$	
$(L_1, R, 1, 1, S_1)$		
$(L_1, W, 1, A, S)$		
$(L_2, R, 2, 2, S_1)$		
$(L_2, W, 2, A, S)$		
		$(L_1, R, 2, A, S_3)$
		$(L_1, R, 0, B, S_3)$
$(L_3, R, 4, 4, S_1)$		
$(L_3, W, 4, B, S)$		
$(L_4, R, 8, 8, S_1)$		
$(L_4, W, 8, B, S)$		
	$(L_1, R, 8, B, S_2)$	
	$(L_1, W, 8, X, S)$	
		$(L_1, W, 2, Y, S)$

Under architecture A(CMP, WO) every member of the graph set for the execution contains both of the following two paths:

$$(P_2, L_1, R, 0, A, S_2) \quad <_{CRW} \quad (P_1, L_1, W, 1, A, S_2)$$
$$<_{WO} \quad (P_1, L_2, W, 2, A, S_3)$$
$$<_{CWR} \quad (P_3, L_1, R, 2, A, S_3)$$

$$(P_3, L_1, R, 0, B, S_3) \quad <_{CRW} \quad (P_1, L_3, W, 4, B, S_3)$$
$$<_{WO} \quad (P_1, L_4, W, 8, B, S_2)$$
$$<_{CWR} \quad (P_2, L_1, R, 8, B, S_2)$$

Thus, if the execution occurs on a machine that is known to obey A(CMP, WO), then the execution reveals a failure of the machine to be read synchronized since P_2 reads A before P_3 reads A, but P_3 reads B before P_2 reads B.

PROBLEMS

8.1. Prove:
  (a) WS $\Rightarrow$ CON (Theorem 8.3).
  (b) RA $\Rightarrow$ RS (Theorem 8.4).

8.2. How many elements does the graph set for the following execution have under A(RS)?

P_1	P_2	P_3	P_4
L_1: A:= 1;	L_1: B:= 4;	L_1: C:= A + B;	L_1: D:= A + B;
L_2: B:= 2;	L_2: A:= 8;		

9

The Rules of Intrastatement Order

Suppose a machine is built in which each statement makes its result visible first to processor 1, then to processor 2, and so on. To model this requires a rule that prescribes, in each statement, an arc from the write event for store S_1 to the write event for store S_2, and from the write event for store S_2 to the write event for store S_3, and so on. This is the function of the write-in-canonical-order rules, both AWC (for absolute) and RWC (for relative).

Suppose also a machine is built in which each statement fetches operands in a predefined order, say from lower memory addresses to higher. To model this requires a rule that prescribes, in each statement, an arc from one read event to another read event, in accordance with the predefined order. This is the function of the read-in-canonical-order rules, both ARC (for absolute) and RRC (for relative).

THE RULE OF ABSOLUTE WRITE CANONICAL ORDER (AWC)

The intent of the rule of absolute write canonical order is to express the idea that all statements write into the n stores in the same order: $S_1, S_2, \ldots, S_n$ (for example).

To form the graph set for an execution E under A(AWC) perform the following step:

The Rule of Absolute Write Canonical Order (AWC)

For each statement, draw an arc labeled $<_{AWC}$ from the write event with store component S_i to all write events with store component S_j, where S_j follows S_i in the canonical order. This graph constitutes the graph set for E under A(AWC).

The transition template for AWC is

$$(P,L,W,V,O,S) \quad <_{AWC} \quad (=,=,W,=,=,-)$$

An arc labeled $<_{AWC}$ occurs only between write events within the same statement. Such events always have the same value and operand components.

A Violation of Atomicity?

The canonical order rules define that a path of the form $E_1 < E_2 < E_3$ occurs among the read (write) events of a statement. Does this mean that an execution which obeys A(AWC) cannot also obey A(WA)? The answer is that an execution can obey both. An execution fails to obey A(WA) if there is an event *not in the atomic set* which can be shown to occur between members of the atomic set. In the preceding path, E_2 is a member of the atomic set and so there is no incompatibility between AWC and WA.

In fact, it is possible to show that WA $\Rightarrow$ AWC. The proof is quite different from that for similar results such as PO $\Rightarrow$ RO.

Theorem 9.1. WA $\Rightarrow$ AWC.

Proof. Let A_1 be any architecture which includes WA. Let A_2 be the architecture which includes the same set of rules as A_2 except that WA is omitted, and AWC is included. Let E be any execution that obeys architecture A_1. Choose any circuit-free element of the graph set for E under A_1. Draw arcs labeled $<_{AWC}$ in the canonical order among the write events for each statement. The new arcs by themselves do not create any circuits. The new arcs in conjunction with any old arcs do not extend a path into a circuit. (If any did, the path would show the execution was not write atomic, contrary to assumption.) Delete from the graph the arcs labeled $<_{WA}$. Then by Lemma 3.3 the resulting graph is circuit-free. By construction it occurs in the graph set for E under A_2. Since E was arbitrary, WA $\Rightarrow$ AWC. ∎

An Execution Exhibiting a Failure to Be Absolute Write Canonically Ordered (Theorem A43)

Consider the execution in Fig. 9.1.

Initially, A = B = X = Y = Z = 0.

P_1
L_1: A := 1;

P_2
L_1: X := B;
L_2: Y := A;

P_3
L_1: Z := A;
L_2: B := 1;

Terminally, A = B = X = Z = 1, Y = 0.

Figure 9.1 A failure to be AWC.

The following linear ordering of the events of the execution shows that the execution obeys A(CMP, RO).

P_1
$(L_1, R, 1, 1, S_1)$
$(L_1, W, 1, A, S_1)$
$(L_1, W, 1, A, S_3)$

P_3
$(L_1, R, 1, A, S_3)$
$(L_1, W, 1, Z, S)$
$(L_2, R, 1, 1, S_3)$
$(L_2, W, 1, B, S)$

P_2
$(L_1, R, 1, B, S_2)$
$(L_1, W, 1, X, S)$
$(L_2, R, 0, A, S_2)$
$(L_2, W, 0, Y, S)$

P_1
$(L_1, W, 1, A, S_2)$

Under architecture A(CMP, RO) every member of the graph set for the execution contains the following path. The path shows that statement L_1 in process P_1 writes into store S_3 before writing into store S_2.

$(P_1, L_1, W, 1, A, S_3)$ $<_{CWR}$ $(P_3, L_1, R, 1, A, S_3)$
$<_{RO}$ $(P_3, L_2, R, 1, 1, S_3)$
$<_{SRW}$ $(P_3, L_2, W, 1, B, S_2)$
$<_{CWR}$ $(P_2, L_1, R, 1, B, S_2)$
$<_{RO}$ $(P_2, L_2, R, 0, A, S_2)$
$<_{CRW}$ $(P_1, L_1, W, 1, A, S_2)$

Consequently, if the execution occurs on a machine that is known to obey A(CMP, RO), then the execution reveals a failure of the machine to obey AWC.

THE RULE OF ABSOLUTE READ CANONICAL ORDER (ARC)

The intent of the rule of absolute read canonical order is to express the idea that all statements read global operands in the same order. Since the order is arbitrary, the order A, B, C, ..., may be chosen without loss of generality. The predefined order can be thought of as representing the location of operands in storage, the size of operands (say, smallest first), and so on.

To form the graph set for an execution E under A(ARC) perform the following step:

Within each statement order the read events according to the canonical order of operands: A, B, C, ... Draw an arc labeled $<_{ARC}$ from (each of) the read event(s) whose operand component appears first in the canonical order to (each of) the read event(s) whose operand component appears later in the canonical order. Repeat for each subsequent event. This graph constitutes the graph set for E under A(ARC).

There is one complication involving ARC that is absent from AWC, namely, repeated operands. The care taken in defining the graph set for ARC is due to the need to handle the case of the statement

$$X := A + A + B + B + B;$$

In this example there will be six arcs labeled $<_{ARC}$, one from each of the read events for operand A to each of the read events for operand B.

The transition template for ARC is

$$(P, L, R, V, O, S) \quad <_{ARC} \quad (=, =, R, -, -, =)$$

An arc labeled $<_{ARC}$ occurs only between read events within the same statement. Such events always reference the same store, namely, the store associated with the process in which the read events occur. The value components of the events may differ. The operand components of the events may differ.

Theorem 9.2. RA $\Rightarrow$ ARC.

Proof. See Prob. 9.1.

An Execution Exhibiting a Failure to Be Absolute Read Canonically Ordered (Theorem A46)

Consider the execution in Fig. 9.2.

```
                    Initially, A = B = X = 0.

                         P₁              P₂
                    L₁: X:= A + B;   L₁: B:= 2;
                                     L₂: A:= 1;
```

Figure 9.2 A failure to be ARC.   Terminally, A = 1, B = 2, X = 1.

The following linear ordering of the events of the execution shows that the execution obeys A(CMP, WO).

$$
\begin{array}{ll}
P_1 & P_2 \\
(L_1, R, 0, B, S_1) & \\
 & (L_1, R, 2, 2, S_2) \\
 & (L_1, W, 2, B, S) \\
 & (L_2, R, 1, 1, S_2) \\
 & (L_2, W, 1, A, S) \\
(L_1, R, 1, A, S_1) & \\
(L_1, W, 1, X, S) & \\
\end{array}
$$

Under architecture A(CMP, WO) every member of the graph set for the execution contains the following path. The path shows that statement L_1 in process P_1 reads operand B before reading operand A.

$$
\begin{array}{ll}
(P_1, L_1, R, 0, B, S_1) & <_{CRW} \quad (P_2, L_1, W, 2, B, S_1) \\
 & <_{WO} \quad (P_2, L_2, W, 1, A, S_1) \\
 & <_{CWR} \quad (P_1, L_1, R, 1, A, S_1) \\
\end{array}
$$

Consequently, if the execution occurs on a machine that is known to obey A(CMP, WO), then the execution reveals a failure of the machine to obey ARC.

THE RULE OF RELATIVE WRITE CANONICAL ORDER (RWC)

The intent of the rule of relative write canonical order is to express the idea that all statements write into the n stores in the same order, where the order is not predefined, but may be apparent from internal evidence within the execution.

To form the graph set for an execution E under A(RWC) perform the following steps:

1. If there are n stores in the execution, construct the fact(n) linear orderings of the stores.
2. Choose one of the orderings constructed in Step 1. Draw arcs labeled $<_{RWC}$ among the write events within each statement, according to the chosen linear ordering. The graph thus constructed is one element of the graph set for the execution under A(RWC).
3. Perform Step 2 once for each of the orderings constructed in Step 1. The result is a graph set with fact(n) elements.

The transition template for RWC is

$$(P, L, W, V, O, S) \quad <_{RWC} \quad (=, =, W, =, =, -)$$

The template is the same as for AWC.

The Rule of Relative Write Canonical Order (RWC)

Theorem 9.3. AWC $\Rightarrow$ RWC.

Proof. See Prob. 9.1.

An Execution Exhibiting a Failure to Be Relative Write Canonically Ordered (Theorem A45)

Consider the execution in Fig. 9.3.

Initially, $A = B = C = D = S = T = U = V = X = Y = 0$

P_1	P_2	P_3	P_4
L_1: $A := 1$;	L_1: $B := 1$;	L_1: $U := A$;	L_1: $S := C$;
		L_2: $C := 1$;	L_2: $V := A$;
		L_3: $T := D$;	L_3: $X := B$;
		L_4: $Y := B$;	L_4: $D := 1$;

Terminally, $A = B = C = D = S = T = U = X = 1$, $V = Y = 0$.

Figure 9.3 A failure to be RWC.

Under architecture A(CMP, RO) every member of the graph set for the execution contains both of the following two paths. The first path shows that statement L_1 in process P_1 writes into store S_3 before it writes into store S_4. The second path shows that statement L_1 in process P_2 writes into store S_4 before it writes into store S_3.

$(P_1, L_1, W, 1, A, S_3)$ $<_{CWR}$ $(P_3, L_1, R, 1, A, S_3)$
$<_{RO}$ $(P_3, L_2, R, 1, 1, S_3)$
$<_{SRW}$ $(P_3, L_2, W, 1, C, S_4)$
$<_{CWR}$ $(P_4, L_1, R, 1, C, S_4)$
$<_{RO}$ $(P_4, L_2, R, 0, A, S_4)$
$<_{CRW}$ $(P_1, L_1, W, 1, A, S_4)$

$(P_2, L_1, W, 1, B, S_4)$ $<_{CWR}$ $(P_4, L_3, R, 1, B, S_4)$
$<_{RO}$ $(P_4, L_4, R, 1, 1, S_4)$
$<_{SRW}$ $(P_4, L_4, W, 1, D, S_3)$
$<_{CWR}$ $(P_3, L_3, R, 1, D, S_3)$
$<_{RO}$ $(P_3, L_4, R, 0, B, S_3)$
$<_{CRW}$ $(P_2, L_1, W, 1, B, S_3)$

Consequently, if the execution occurs on a machine that is known to obey A(CMP, RO), then the execution reveals a failure of the machine to obey RWC.

The following linear ordering of the events of the execution shows that the execution obeys A(CMP, RO).

P_1	P_2	P_3	P_4
$(L_1,R,1,1,S_1)$			
	$(L_1,R,1,1,S_2)$		
$(L_1,W,1,A,S_1)$			
$(L_1,W,1,A,S_2)$			
$(L_1,W,1,A,S_3)$			
		$(L_1,R,1,A,S_3)$	
		$(L_1,W,1,U,S)$	
		$(L_2,R,1,1,S_3)$	
		$(L_2,W,1,C,S)$	
			$(L_1,R,1,C,S_4)$
			$(L_1,W,1,S,S)$
			$(L_2,R,0,A,S_4)$
			$(L_2,W,0,V,S)$
$(L_1,W,1,A,S_4)$			
	$(L_1,W,1,B,S_1)$		
	$(L_1,W,1,B,S_2)$		
	$(L_1,W,1,B,S_4)$		
			$(L_3,R,1,B,S_4)$
			$(L_3,W,1,X,S)$
			$(L_4,R,1,1,S_4)$
			$(L_4,W,1,D,S)$
		$(L_3,R,1,D,S_3)$	
		$(L_3,W,1,T,S)$	
		$(L_4,R,0,B,S_3)$	
		$(L_4,W,0,Y,S)$	
	$(L_1,W,1,B,S_3)$		

THE RULE OF RELATIVE READ CANONICAL ORDER (RRC)

The intent of the rule of relative read canonical order is to express the idea that all statements read from the set of operands in the same order, where the order is not predefined, but may be apparent from internal evidence within the execution.

To form the graph set for an execution E under A(RRC) perform the following steps:

1. If there are n distinct source operands in the execution, construct the fact(n) linear orderings of the distinct operands.
2. Choose one of the orderings constructed in Step 1. Draw arcs labeled $<_{RRC}$ among the read events within each statement, according to the chosen linear ordering. The graph thus constructed is one element of the graph set for the execution under A(RRC). Repeated operands within a statement are handled as with ARC.

The Rule of Relative Read Canonical Order (RRC)

3. Perform Step 2 once for each of the orderings constructed in Step 1. The result is a graph set with fact(n) elements.

The transition template for RRC is

$$(P,L,R,V,O,S) \quad <_{RRC} \quad (=,=,R,-,-,=)$$

The template is the same as for ARC.

Theorem 9.4. ARC $\Rightarrow$ RRC.

Proof. See Prob. 9.1.

An Execution Exhibiting a Failure to Be Relative Read Canonically Ordered (Theorem A48)

Consider the execution in Fig. 9.4.

Initially, A = B = X = Y = 0.

```
    P₁              P₂              P₃                  P₄
L₁: A:= 1;      L₁: B:= 4;      L₁: X:= A + B;      L₁: Y:= A + B;
L₂: B:= 2;      L₂: A:= 8;
```

Terminally, A = 8, B = 2, X = 2, Y = 8.

Figure 9.4 A failure to be RRC.

The following linear ordering of the events of the execution shows that the execution obeys A(CMP, WO).

```
        P₁                    P₂                    P₃                      P₄
                                            (L₁,R,0,A,S₃)
                                                                    (L₁,R,0,B,S₄)
(L₁,R,1,1,S₁)
(L₁,W,1,A,S)
                        (L₁,R,4,4,S₂)
                        (L₁,W,4,B,S)
                        (L₂,R,8,8,S₂)
                        (L₂,W,8,A,S)
(L₂,R,2,2,S₁)
(L₂,W,2,B,S)
                                            (L₁,R,2,B,S₃)
                                                                    (L₁,R,8,A,S₄)
                                            (L₁,W,2,X,S)
                                                                    (L₁,W,8,Y,S)
```

Under architecture A(CMP, WO) every member of the graph set for the execution contains both of the following two paths. The first path shows that statement L_1 in process P_3 reads operand A before operand B. The second path shows that statement L_1 in process P_4 reads operand B before operand A.

$$(P_3,L_1,R,0,A,S_3) <_{CRW} (P_1,L_1,W,1,A,S_3)$$
$$<_{WO} (P_1,L_2,W,2,B,S_3)$$
$$<_{CWR} (P_3,L_1,R,2,B,S_3)$$

$$(P_4,L_1,R,0,B,S_4) <_{CRW} (P_2,L_1,W,4,B,S_4)$$
$$<_{WO} (P_2,L_2,W,8,A,S_4)$$
$$<_{CWR} (P_4,L_1,R,8,A,S_4)$$

Consequently, if the execution occurs on a machine that is known to obey A(CMP, WO), then the execution reveals a failure of the machine to obey RRC.

PROBLEM

9.1. Prove:
    (a) RA $\Rightarrow$ ARC (Theorem 9.2).
    (b) AWC $\Rightarrow$ RWC (Theorem 9.3).
    (c) ARC $\Rightarrow$ RRC (Theorem 9.4).

10

The Structure of Architectures

In the preceding chapters, the rules of architecture were defined for an elementary model of a multiprocessing computer system. In order to illustrate each rule an example was presented which showed how a failure to obey the rule could be observed. The format of the example showed two architectures, A_1 and A_2, such that the execution obeyed A_1, but did not obey A_2. Thus, the effect of the example was to prove two architectures to be distinguishable, that is, the execution showed that it would be impossible to build a machine according to architecture A_1 and to offer it as architecture A_2. The execution would enable a programmer to reveal the deception.

The following chapters address the opposite problem. Suppose two architectures are indistinguishable, that is, suppose no program exists which can obtain an answer under one of the architectures which it provably cannot obtain under the other architecture. How is it possible to prove the two architectures to be indistinguishable?

Before addressing these concerns in the next several chapters it is appropriate to pause and to collect some general ideas and results on architectures.

THE ARCHITECTURES AN EXECUTION DOES/DOES NOT OBEY

A given execution divides the set of all architectures into two subsets: those architectures which the execution obeys, and those architectures which the execution does not obey. The execution distinguishes each of the architectures in the former group from each of the architectures in the latter group.

THE EXECUTIONS THAT DO/DO NOT OBEY A GIVEN ARCHITECTURE

Any given architecture divides the set of all executions into a pair of subsets: the first subset is the set of executions that obey the architecture; the second is the set of executions that do not obey the architecture. Two distinguishable architectures divide the set of all executions into two distinct pairs of sets. Two indistinguishable architectures divide the set of all executions into the same pair of subsets.

Identifying an architecture with the set of executions that obey the architecture provides a natural way to prove that indistinguishability is an equivalence relation on architectures.

Theorem 10.1. Let A, B, and C be architectures. Then

1. $A \Leftrightarrow A$,
2. if $A \Leftrightarrow B$, then $B \Leftrightarrow A$,
3. if $A \Leftrightarrow B$ and $B \Leftrightarrow C$, then $A \Leftrightarrow C$.

Proof. See Prob. 10.1.

The phrase "logical correctness of architectures" is used to cover several current areas of research in computer architecture. The concept of equivalence classes of architectures is useful in illuminating the issues in these areas.

Proving that two architectures are (are not) indistinguishable can be viewed as proving that the two architectures are (are not) in the same equivalence class. More generally, such work can be seen as proving that two equivalence classes are (are not) indistinguishable. Work in this area is mathematical and uncontentious.

A second major area involves deciding which equivalence class is to be the standard against which others are to be evaluated. The idea of sequential consistency, which may be taken to be equal to {CMP, UPO, PO, WA}, is now the unquestioned standard. This need not remain the case. In data base systems the standard is that of transaction atomicity. Both standards are based on a common sense understanding of what is achievable and what is necessary to make a system usable in a specific environment. Discussion of this issue can be impassioned.

A sequentially consistent machine is slow. Program order requires all operations to be done in order; write atomicity requires that every write operation be completed before the next instruction is fetched. A third major area of research aims to find architectures which in general are weaker than sequential consistency, but which allow programmers the function to achieve sequential consistency, or more, where required.

The Unique Importance of the Rule of Computation

SETS OF RULES VERSUS SETS OF EXECUTIONS

Theorem 10.2. If the set of rules for architecture A_2 is contained in the set of rules for architecture A_1, then $A_1 \Rightarrow A_2$. For example, $A(R_1, R_2, \ldots, R_n) \Rightarrow A(R_2, \ldots, R_n)$.

Proof. Choose any circuit-free member of the graph set for an execution E under architecture A_1. Delete arcs due to rules found in A_1 which are not in A_2. By Lemma 3.3 the graph remains circuit-free. The new graph is in the graph set for architecture A_2. Consequently, E obeys A_2. ∎

If the set of rules for architecture A_2 is properly included in the set of rules for architecture A_1, then $A_1 \Rightarrow A_2$, and then (usually) the set of executions that obey A_1 is properly contained in the set of executions that obey A_2. An exception occurs when the architectures are indistinguishable. Then the two sets of executions are identical. For example, {CMP, WS} is properly included in {CMP, WS, WA}, but the set of executions obeying A(CMP, WS, WA) is identical to the set obeying A(CMP, WS). (See Theorem 12.1 in Chap. 12.)

THE GRAPH OF RULES X,Y SUCH THAT X ⇒ Y

Theorem 10.3. If $X \rightarrow Y$ in Fig. 10.1, then $X \Rightarrow Y$.

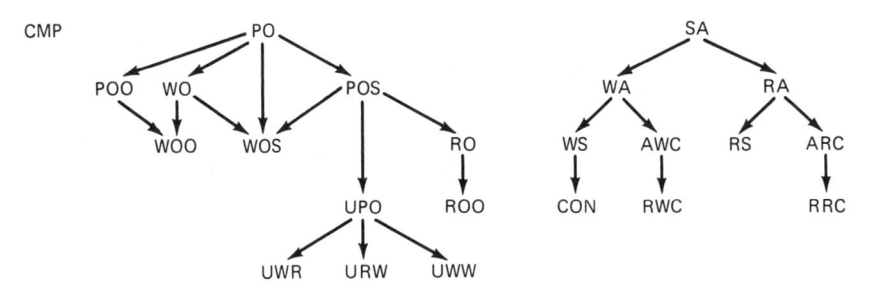

Figure 10.1 A graph of rules R_1, R_2 such that $R_1 \Rightarrow R_2$.

Proof. Each arc in this graph was the subject of a theorem in Chaps. 5 through 9.

THE UNIQUE IMPORTANCE OF THE RULE OF COMPUTATION

Theorem 10.4. Every circuit contains an arc labeled $<_{CWR}$, $<_{CRW}$, or $<_{CWW}$.

Proof. Let E be any execution. Construct the following linearly ordered graph G for the events of E. First come the events for process 1, then process 2, and so on. Within each process first come the events for statement 1, then statement 2, and so forth. Within each statement first come the read events for the statement and then the write events. Arrange the read events within each statement in a linear order consistent with the order defined by ARC or RRC. Within each set of write events arrange the write events in a linear order consistent with the order defined by AWC or RWC. This ordering obeys SRW, UPO, PO, and SA and all their subsidiary rules. Since it is linearly ordered, it is circuit-free. Hence, if a circuit exists in a graph for an execution, then it must contain an arc with either a $<_{CWR}$, $<_{CRW}$, or $<_{CWW}$ label. ∎

Theorem 10.4 shows that nothing can be proven about an architecture without making use of the rules of computation.

THE PRODUCT OF ARCHITECTURES

Theorem 10.5 expresses, not a new insight, but instead the result of deliberately requiring each architecture rule to have the effect of defining a graph set on the events of each execution, independently of any other rule.

Theorem 10.5. If R_1, R_2, ..., R_n are distinct rules, then $A(R_1, R_2, ..., R_n) = A(R_1) * A(R_2) * ... * A(R_n)$.

Proof. Each rule defined in Chaps. 5 through 9 generates a graph set for every execution independently of any other rule. For each execution E the graph set for E under $A(R_1, R_2, ..., R_n)$ is equal to the product of the graph sets for each separate rule. ∎

Note, however, that in Chap. 15 the discussion of conditional rules suggests that it may be desirable to define rules that do not obey Theorem 10.5.

PROBLEM

10.1. Carry out the proof of Theorem 10.1.

11

Out-of-Order Read Operations

The fact that some architectures can be proven to be indistinguishable holds out the hope that for every simple architecture A_1 it will be possible to discover an indistinguishable architecture A_2 which is faster than A_1, though possibly more complex. Then a machine can be built to obey the rules of A_2, but presented as obeying A_1, thus appearing to be both fast and simple.

A SIMPLE EXAMPLE OF INDISTINGUISHABLE ARCHITECTURES

Theorem 11.1 is obvious and yields no insight into how to build a machine. Its value is to offer practice in the ways of proving two architectures to be indistinguishable.

Theorem 11.1. A(CMP, RO, SA) ⇔ A(CMP, PO, SA).

Proof. ⇐: follows from PO ⇒ RO.
⇒: If E obeys A(CMP, RO, SA), then the graph set for E under A(CMP, RO, SA) is partly circuit-free. Choose some circuit-free element of the graph set. Consider the events for a single process. Every statement contains at least one read event. Between every two read events in different statements in the same process there is an arc labeled $<_{RO}$. If $r_1 <_{RO} r_2$, then since the graph is circuit-free, there is an arc labeled $<_{SA}$ from every event in the statement containing r_1 to every event in the statement containing r_2. But this ensures that under A(CMP, RO, PO, SA) adjacent to every arc labeled $<_{PO}$ is another arc labeled $<_{SA}$. Thus, the arcs labeled

$<_{PO}$ introduce no new circuits. Hence, if E obeys A(CMP, RO, SA), it obeys A(CMP, RO, PO, SA) and so it obeys A(CMP, PO, SA). ■

Can Theorem 11.1 be modified to show that other rules can be added to both architectures? For example, is it true that A(CMP, RO, SA, RWC) ⇔ A(CMP, PO, SA, RWC)? The following generalization of Theorem 11.1 shows that almost any combination of rules can be added to both architectures. Let A be any architecture not containing RO, PO, or SA. Let $A_1 = A * A(RO) * A(SA)$ and $A_2 = A * A(PO) * A(SA)$. Then $A_1 \Leftrightarrow A_2$. (Proof: See Prob. 11.3.)

OUT-OF-ORDER READS ON A MULTIPROCESSOR

In 1986 Bradly Frey [FREY86] saw that operands could be fetched out of order from a cache on a multiprocessing system without the fact being detected providing the following condition was met. Suppose E_1 and E_2 are two read events, where E_2 reads operand A, such that E_1 occurs in a program before E_2. Then E_2 can occur before E_1 during execution of the program providing no write into the cache occurs for operand A after E_2 occurs and before E_1 occurs. The heart of the proof is contained in Lemma 11.1.

Lemma 11.1. Let A be an architecture which includes the rules CMP, RO, and WO, but not the rule of RS. Let E be any execution under architecture A. Let C_1 be any circuit in a graph in the graph set for E under A, such that C_1 has no arcs labeled $<_{xa}$. If the circuit is of the form

$$R_1 < R_2 < W_3 < \ldots < R_1$$

where R_1 and R_2 are read events, W_3 is a write event, and $R_1 <_{RO} R_2$, then $R_2 <_{CRW} W_3$.

Briefly, the lemma says that under the given conditions in any circuit after an arc labeled $<_{RO}$, if the next arc leads to a write event, then either this next arc is labeled $<_{CRW}$ or adjacent to this next arc is an arc labeled $<_{CRW}$.

TRANSITION TEMPLATES

Transition templates were given for each architecture rule defined in Chaps. 5 through 9. The templates are collected and listed here.

$$(P,L,R,V,O,S) <_{SRW} (=,=,W,-,-,-)$$
$$(P,L,W,V,O,S) <_{CWR} (-,-,R,=,=,=)$$
$$(P,L,R,V,O,S) <_{CRW} (-,-,W,-,=,=)$$
$$(P,L,W,V,O,S) <_{CWW} (-,-,W,-,=,=)$$
$$(P,L,W,V,O,S) <_{UWR} (=,-,R,-,=,=)$$
$$(P,L,R,V,O,S) <_{URW} (=,-,W,-,=,=)$$
$$(P,L,W,V,O,S) <_{UWW} (=,-,W,-,=,=)$$

Proof of Lemma 11.1

$$
\begin{array}{lll}
(P,L,R,V,O,S) & <_{RO} & (=,-,R,-,-,=) \\
(P,L,R,V,O,S) & <_{ROO} & (=,-,R,-,=,=) \\
(P,L,W,V,O,S) & <_{WO} & (=,-,W,-,-,-) \\
(P,L,W,V,O,S) & <_{WOO} & (=,-,W,-,=,-) \\
(P,L,W,V,O,S) & <_{WOS} & (=,-,W,-,-,=) \\
(P,L,-,V,O,S) & <_{PO} & (=,-,R,-,-,-) \\
(P,L,-,V,O,S) & <_{PO} & (=,-,W,-,-,-) \\
(P,L,-,V,O,S) & <_{POO} & (=,-,R,-,=,-) \\
(P,L,-,V,O,S) & <_{POO} & (=,-,W,-,=,-) \\
(P,L,-,V,O,S) & <_{POS} & (=,-,R,-,-,=) \\
(P,L,-,V,O,S) & <_{POS} & (=,-,W,-,-,=) \\
(P,L,-,V,O,S) & <_{RA} & (-,-,-,-,-,-) \\
(P,L,R,V,O,S) & =_{RA} & (=,=,R,-,-,=) \\
(P,L,-,V,O,S) & <_{WA} & (-,-,-,-,-,-) \\
(P,L,W,V,O,S) & =_{WA} & (=,=,W,=,=,\#) \\
(P,L,-,V,O,S) & <_{SA} & (-,-,-,-,-,-) \\
(P,L,-,V,O,S) & =_{SA} & (=,=,R,-,-,-) \\
(P,L,-,V,O,S) & =_{SA} & (=,=,W,-,-,-) \\
(P,L,R,V,O,S) & <_{RS} & (-,-,R,-,=,-) \\
(P,L,R,V,O,S) & <_{ARC} & (=,=,R,-,-,=) \\
(P,L,R,V,O,S) & <_{RRC} & (=,=,R,-,-,=) \\
(P,L,W,V,O,S) & <_{WS} & (-,-,W,-,-,=) \\
(P,L,W,V,O,S) & <_{CON} & (-,-,W,-,=,=) \\
(P,L,W,V,O,S) & <_{AWC} & (=,=,W,=,=,\#) \\
(P,L,W,V,O,S) & <_{RWC} & (=,=,W,=,=,\#) \\
\end{array}
$$

An equals sign (=) shows where a component is the same in the right-hand event as in the left-hand event. A number sign (#) shows where the component must be different (though this is not used anywhere in the proof). A dash (–) indicates that the component is not defined. Action components are filled in with an "R" for a read event or with a "W" for a write event or with a dash (–) where the action is either a read event or a write event.

The original transition template for $<_{PO}$ in Chap. 6 did not specify the action component. It is necessary now to include two transition templates for $<_{PO}$, one with an "R" for the action component, and one with a "W". Since every event is either a read event or a write event, no information is gained or lost by the change. The same change has also been made for $<_{POO}$, $<_{POS}$, and $=_{SA}$.

PROOF OF LEMMA 11.1

The proof starts with an arbitrary read event (P, L, R, V, O, P), shown on line 0, and called E_2 in the proof. (Since this is a read event, the store component has the same value as the process component.) The proof has the form of a tree structure with E_2 as the root node. In the next level of the tree each of the 32 transition templates are considered, one at a time. The left-hand event of the transition template is applied to E_2. If the action components fit, then a new event E_3 is constructed. If not, then the transition template is ignored and the next one is considered.

For example, in line 1 the template for $<_{SRW}$ is considered. Since E_2 is a read event and the left-hand event of the template is a read event, there is a match and so the template is used to create the second event. The second event will have the same process and statement components as E_2, but of course will be a write event, not a read event. The path in circuit C_1 from E_3 back to E_2 shows that SRW is violated, contrary to the assumption that the architecture includes CMP.

In line 2 the transition template for CRW is compared with E_2. Since the template requires that the left-hand event be a write event and since E_2 is a read event, the template does not match. The comment at the right-hand end of line 2 notes that a read event cannot occur at the beginning of an arc labeled $<_{CRW}$.

In line 3 the arc labeled $<_{CRW}$ is explicitly anticipated by the Lemma.

In lines 4 and 5 the templates do not match.

Line 6 is similar to line 1. In line 1 E_3 was in the same statement as E_2. Here, E_3 is not in the same statement; it is in a subsequent statement in the same process as the statement containing E_2. Now the path in the circuit from E_3 back to E_2 shows that WO is violated, which is contrary to the assumption that the architecture includes WO.

In line 8 if $E_2 <_{RO} E_3$ in the original circuit

$$E_1 < E_2 < E_3 < \ldots < E_1$$

then the original circuit can be replaced by the shorter circuit

$$E_1 <_{RO} E_3 < \ldots < E_1$$

and the proof can start over with the shorter circuit. Obviously, this substitution can be made only a finite number of times.

In line 19 the template for $<_{RA}$ is considered. This template is explicitly excluded from the statement of the lemma.

The full search tree for the proof is as follows:

```
0 (P,L,R,V,O,P) . . .
    1    <SRW   (P,L,W,-,-,-)   3. SRW violated.
    2    <CWR   (-,-,-,-,-,-)   1. R <CWR -.
    3    <CRW   (-,-,W,-,0,P)   6. CRW.
    4    <CWW   (-,-,-,-,-,-)   1. R <CWW -.
    5    <UWR   (-,-,-,-,-,-)   1. R <UWR -.
    6    <URW   (P,-,W,-,0,P)   4. WO violated.
    7    <UWW   (-,-,-,-,-,-)   1. R <UWW -.
    8    <RO    (P,-,R,-,-,P)   5. Start over.
    9    <ROO   (P,-,R,-,0,P)   5. Start over.
   10    <WO    (-,-,-,-,-,-)   1. R <WO -.
   11    <WOO   (-,-,-,-,-,-)   1. R <WOO -.
   12    <WOS   (-,-,-,-,-,-)   1. R <WOS -.
   13    <PO    (P,-,R,-,-,P)   5. Start over.
   14    <PO    (P,-,W,-,-,-)   4. WO violated.
```

15	$<_{POO}$	(P,−,R,−,O,P)	5. Start over.
16	$<_{POO}$	(P,−,W,−,O,−)	4. WO violated.
17	$<_{POS}$	(P,−,R,−,−,P)	5. Start over.
18	$<_{POS}$	(P,−,W,−,−,P)	4. WO violated.
19	$<_{RA}$	(−,−,−,−,−,−)	2. Excluded.
20	$=_{RA}$	(P,L,R,−,−,P)	5. Start over.
21	$<_{WA}$	(−,−,−,−,−,−)	2. Excluded.
22	$=_{WA}$	(−,−,−,−,−,−)	1. R $=_{WA}$ −.
23	$<_{SA}$	(−,−,−,−,−,−)	2. Excluded.
24	$=_{SA}$	(P,L,R,−,−,P)	5. Start over.
25	$=_{SA}$	(P,L,W,−,−,−)	3. SRW violated.
26	$<_{RS}$	(−,−,R,−,O,−)	2. Excluded.
27	$<_{ARC}$	(P,L,R,−,−,P)	5. Start over.
28	$<_{RRC}$	(P,L,R,−,−,P)	5. Start over.
29	$<_{WS}$	(−,−,−,−,−,−)	1. R $<_{WS}$ −.
30	$<_{CON}$	(−,−,−,−,−,−)	1. R $<_{CON}$ −.
31	$<_{AWC}$	(−,−,−,−,−,−)	1. R $<_{AWC}$ −.
32	$<_{RWC}$	(−,−,−,−,−,−)	1. R $<_{RWC}$ −.

Explanation

1. R $<$xxx −. A read event cannot have an arc labeled $<$xxx incident out of it.
2. Excluded. Arcs labeled $<_{RS}$, $<_{RA}$, $<_{WA}$, and $<_{SA}$ are excluded from the lemma.
3. SRW violated. W_3 is a write event in the same statement as R_2. The path from W_3 to R_1 and the path $R_1 <_{SRW} W_k$, for any write event W_k in the same statement as R_1, shows that the execution does not obey the subrule of SRW, contrary to the definition of architecture A.
4. WO violated. W_3 is a write event in the same or later statement in the same process as R_2. The path from W_3 to R_1 and the path $R_1 <_{SRW} W_k$, for any write event W_k in the same statement as R_1, shows that the execution is not write ordered, contrary to the definition of architecture A.
5. Start over. The search has found a sequence of the form $R_2 <$xxx R_3, where R_3 is in the same process as R_1 and R_2. Therefore, $R_1 <_{RO} R_3$, and so the search can start over with R_3 in place of R_2. Since a process has finite length, this can occur at most a finite number of times.
6. CRW. The path showing a failure to obey RO has an arc labeled $<_{CRW}$ following the arc labeled $<_{RO}$. ■

WARP ARCHITECTURES

In a machine with a conventional architecture the rules prevent certain sequences of events from occurring. In a machine with a warp architecture certain normally forbidden sequences of events are allowed to occur, but the subset of them (which are visibly pathological) are detected, and the evidence of their occurrence is obliterated.

The model of a warp architecture described in the following is obtained, first, by describing a large class of (mostly) read events and, second, by explicitly deleting the forbidden sequences. The model is constructed via a series of steps from a beginning architecture A_1, through A_2 and A_3, and finally to A_4. Adopt the notation that graph G_i occurs in graph set GS_i which represents some execution E under architecture A_i, $i = 1,2,3,4$.

Let A_1 be any architecture which includes at least the rules CMP, RO, and WO, but excludes the rule RS.

Let A_2 be identical to A_1, except that A_2 does not include RO.

Define a new rule, RUF, for Read-unordered-factorially. The graph set for an execution E under A(RUF) is formed as follows. Suppose there are k_1 read events in process P_1, k_2 in P_2, and so on. For each pair of read events R_1 and R_2 in P_1, in P_2, and so on, form the graph set

$$\{(\{R_1,R_2\},\{R_1 <_{RUF} R_2\}),(\{R_1,R_2\},\{R_2<_{RUF}R_1\})\}.$$

Take the product of all of these graph sets. The product graph set is the graph set for E under A(RUF).

Define architecture A_3 to be the same as A_2 but with RUF included, that is $A_3 = A_2 * A(RUF)$. Then by Lemma 3.5 $A_3 \Leftrightarrow A_2$.

GS_3 represents the reification of the nondeterminism implicit in moving from GS_1 to GS_2. The graphs in GS_1 are ordered by read order. The graphs in GS_2 are freed of this restriction. GS_3 makes explicit the freedom enjoyed in GS_2 over GS_1.

Define architecture A_4 as follows. The graph set for E under A_4 is the same as the graph set for E under A_3, except that some graphs are omitted. A graph G_3 in the graph set GS_3 for E under A_3 is not in the graph set GS_4 for E under A_4 if the following conditions occur among read events R_1 and R_2 and write event W_3: $R_2 <_{RUF} R_1$, where $R_1 <_{RO} R_2$ in G_1, and $R_2 <_{CRW} W_3$. Otherwise, G_3 occurs also in GS_4.

Corresponding to G_1 in GS_1, there is exactly one graph G_2 in GS_2 (since A(RO) contains only one graph). For each graph G_2 in GS_2 there are $2 ** (k_1 + k_2 + \ldots + k_n)$ graphs in GS_3. For each graph G_3 in GS_3 there is either zero or one corresponding graph in GS_4.

Theorem 11.2 (Frey's Theorem). For the architectures defined above $A_1 \Leftrightarrow A_4$.

Proof of $A_1 \Rightarrow A_4$. See Prob. 11.6.

Proof of $A_4 \Rightarrow A_1$. Assume not. Then there is an execution E which obeys A_4, but does not obey A_1. Let G_4 be any circuit-free element of GS_4. There is a unique element G_1 of GS_1, corresponding to G_4. Since E does not obey A_1, G_1 must contain a circuit C_1. By Lemma 7.2 it is fair to assume that the circuit contains no arcs labeled $<_{xa}$, though there may be arcs labeled $=_{xa}$. If the circuit does not contain an arc labeled $<_{RO}$, then the circuit exists in G_2, and in all the corresponding G_3 graphs and in all the corresponding G_4 graphs, contrary to the assumption. So assume the circuit in G_1 does contain an arc labeled $<_{RO}$. Lemma 11.1 can be applied since the circuit has no arcs labeled $<xa$. Hence, the circuit has the form

$$R_1 <_{RO} R_2 <_{CRW} W_3 < \ldots < R_1$$

In G_2 the circuit does not exist because of the absence of the arc labeled $<_{RO}$.

In GS_3 half the graphs corresponding to G_1 have a path $R_1 <_{RUF} R_2$ and so have the circuit also. The graphs in GS_4 corresponding to these graphs also have circuits and so cannot be the original graph G_4.

The other half of the graphs in GS_3 corresponding to G_1 meet the following condition: $R_2 <_{RUF} R_1$ and $R_2 <_{CRW} W_3$. By the definition of A_4, these graphs do not appear in GS_4. Thus, all the graphs in GS_4 corresponding to G_1 contain circuits, contrary to the choice of G_4 as being circuit-free. Consequently, $A_4 \Rightarrow A_1$. ∎

PROBLEMS

11.1. Prove A(CMP, WO, SA) ⇔ A(CMP, PO, SA).

11.2. Prove A(CMP, RO, SA) ⇔ A(CMP, WO, SA). Hint: use the results of Prob. 11.1 and Theorem 11.1.

11.3. Let A be any architecture not containing RO, PO, or SA. Let $A_1 = A * A(RO) * A(SA)$ and $A_2 = A * A(PO) * A(SA)$. Then $A_1 \Leftrightarrow A_2$. Prove.

Prove the following facts regarding architectures A_1, A_2, A_3, and A_4 used in the proof of Frey's Theorem.

11.4. $A_2 \Rightarrow A_1$.

11.5. $A_2 \Leftrightarrow A_3$.

11.6. Prove $A_1 \Rightarrow A_4$ in the first half of Frey's Theorem.

11.7. $A_3 \Rightarrow A_4$.

REFERENCES

The application of Frey's Theorem is an example of a technique that has been termed "Time Warp" [JEFF85] since events which have in fact occurred are made to appear as if they hadn't, as if time had been backed up and started over.

The IBM Corporation has sought patent protection, in the names of B. G. Frey and R. J. Pederson, for the use of Frey's Theorem in the design of a multiprocessor.

FREY86. B. FREY. Private communication. 1986.

JEFF85. D. R. JEFFERSON. Virtual Time. ACM Transactions on Programming Languages and Systems. 7 (3, July 1985). pp. 404–425.

12

Write Synchronized Is Write Atomic

A FUNDAMENTAL RESULT ON STORAGE HIERARCHIES

A second important theorem about indistinguishable architectures is the theorem that a write synchronized architecture is (in the absence of the rule of read synchronization) indistinguishable from a write atomic architecture.

First some preliminary results need to be proved.

Consider an execution which obeys an architecture which includes the rule WA, and consider a path in a graph in the graph set for the execution under the architecture. Read and write events may appear in arbitrary sequence in the path; the arcs from one event to the next in the path may be labeled with any of the rules in the architecture. However, for every two write events not in the same statement, from one write event in the path to the next write event there must appear, in addition to the other arcs, an arc labeled $<_{WA}$. This follows from the fact that the graph is circuit-free and the fact that (under a WA architecture) between every two write events, not in the same statement, there is a $<_{WA}$ arc in one direction or the other. This proves the following.

Lemma 12.1. Let E be an execution which obeys an architecture containing the rule WA. Let W_1 and W_2 be any two write events, not in the same statement, in a path in a circuit-free member of the graph set for execution E. If W_1 precedes W_2 in the path, then there is also an arc from W_1 to W_2 labeled $<_{WA}$.

Even though WS is a far weaker rule (in the sense of imposing fewer arcs) than WA, a similar situation is true in a path in a graph for an execution under a WS architecture. This is proven in Lemma 12.5. Some subsidiary results pave the way.

A Fundamental Result on Storage Hierarchies

Define $X(W_2, W_1)$ to be the write event which is in the same statement as write event W_2 and which has the same store component as write event W_1.

Lemma 12.2. Let W_1 and W_2 be write events, not in the same statement, in an execution which obeys an architecture which includes write synchronization. Then either (a) is true for every other write event W_* or (b) is true for every other write event W_*.

(a) $X(W_1, W_*) <_{WS} X(W_2, W_*)$
(b) $X(W_2, W_*) <_{WS} X(W_1, W_*)$

Proof. (a) and (b) simply restate the definition of write synchronization as the product of graph sets in terms of the X function. ∎

Lemma 12.3. If $W_1 <_{WS} X(W_2, W_1)$ and $W_2 <_{WS} X(W_3, W_2)$ in a graph in the graph set for a circuit-free execution which obeys WS, then $W_1 <_{WS} X(W_3, W_1)$.

Proof. $W_2 <_{WS} X(W_3, W_2) \Rightarrow X(W_2, W_2) <_{WS} X(W_3, W_2)$ since $X(W_2, W_2) = W_2$ (see Prob. 12.1a). Then $X(W_2, W_*) <_{WS} X(W_3, W_*)$ for any write event W_* by Lemma 12.2. In particular, $X(W_2, W_1) <_{WS} X(W_3, W_1)$. Thus, $W_1 <_{WS} X(W_2, W_1) <_{WS} X(W_3, W_1)$ and since the execution is circuit-free and obeys WS, $W_1 <_{WS} X(W_3, W_1)$. ∎

Let $E_1 < E_2 < E_3 < E_4$ be a path containing only write events in a circuit-free, write synchronized execution. If E_2 and E_3 are in the same statement, then it is false that $E_2 <_{WS} X(E_3, E_2)$. However, it is true that $E_1 <_{WS} X(E_3, E_1)$ and $E_2 <_{WS} X(E_4, E_2)$, as the following lemma shows.

Lemma 12.4. Let E_1, E_2, E_3, and E_4 be write events in a path in a circuit-free graph for a write synchronized execution such that

1. $E_1 <_{WS} X(E_2, E_1)$,
2. $E_2 <_{xxx} E_3$, for $<_{xxx}$ in $\{=_{WA}, =_{SA}, <_{AWC}, <_{ARC}\}$, that is, E_2 and E_3 are in the same statement,
3. $E_3 <_{WS} X(E_4, E_3)$,

Then $E_i <_{WS} X(E_j, E_i)$, for $0 < i < j < 5$ and E_i and E_j not in the same statement.

Proof.

1. $E_1 <_{WS} X(E_2, E_1)$ is given.
2. $X(E_2, E_1) = X(E_3, E_1)$ since E_2 and E_3 are in the same statement. Hence, $E_1 <_{WS} X(E_3, E_1)$.
3. $E_3 <_{WS} X(E_4, E_3) \Rightarrow X(E_3, E_3) <_{WS} X(E_4, E_3) \Rightarrow X(E_3, E_1) <_{WS} X(E_4, E_1)$, by Lemma 12.3. By the previous result $E_1 <_{WS} X(E_3, E_1)$. Since the graph is circuit-free, $E_1 <_{WS} X(E_4, E_1)$.

4. $E_3 = X(E_3,E_3) <_{WS} X(E_4,E_3)$ is given. By Lemma 12.3 $X(E_3,E_2) <_{WS} X(E_4,E_2)$. Then $E_2 = X(E_3,E_2) <_{WS} X(E_4,E_2)$ since E_2 and E_3 are in the same statement.
5. $E_3 <_{WS} X(E_4,E_3)$ is given. ∎

The major step in proving that a write synchronized system appears to be write atomic is Lemma 12.5. The lemma comes as close as possible to doing for write synchronization what Lemma 12.1 did for write atomicity.

Lemma 12.5. Let A_1 be any architecture which contains the rule WS. Let E be an execution which obeys A_1. Let $E_1 < E_2 < \ldots < E_n$ be a path in a graph for E under A (where the path is restricted to not contain any arcs labeled $<_{RS}$, $<_{RA}$, $<_{WA}$, or $<_{SA}$). Let W_1 and W_2 be any two write events, not in the same statement, in the path. If W_1 precedes W_2 in the path, then $W_1 <_{WS} X(W_2,W_1)$.

Lemma 12.5 says that under architecture A_1 the arcs in any path (in a circuit-free graph of an execution which obeys A_1) run in the same direction as the arcs labeled $<_{WS}$. Specifically, it says that if W_1 and W_2 occur in sequence in a path with zero or more intervening read events, and if W_1 and W_2 have the same store component, then no matter what label is on the arc, there is also an arc from W_1 to W_2 labeled $<_{WS}$.

If W_1 and W_2 have distinct store components (which is the interesting case), then Lemma 12.5 says that there is an arc labeled $<_{WS}$, not from W_1 to W_2, but from W_1 to the write event in the same statement as W_2 which has the same store component as W_1, that is, $X(W_2,W_1)$.

The proof, however, is not so simple as it was in the case of Lemma 12.1. There the proof depended solely on the nature of the WA rule. For Lemma 12.5 the proof depends on the nature of each rule occurring in the path.

The need to exclude read synchronization will be made clear subsequently.

The proof is based on an exhaustive search, from a starting write event E_1, along every possible arc, to another event E_2, and in the case that E_2 is a read event, along every possible arc to a third event E_3. The event E_1 is represented by (P, L, W, V, O, S), where P, L, V, O, and S are arbitrary process, line, value, operand, and store components. The components of events E_2 and E_3 are determined by the transition templates which were defined in Chaps. 5 through 9 and collected in Chap. 11.

There are many, many cases to consider. From the root node of the search tree there are 224 nodes only two arcs away. While many differ only irrelevantly, a mechanical search still has to consider each case. (For a listing of the full search tree see App. B.)

There are three cases that must be explicitly excluded in the statement of Lemma 12.5.

1. Across an arc labeled $<_{RS}$ the store component does not propagate. This flaw is irreparable and so RS has to be excluded in the statement of Theorem 12.1.

… Discussion of Part I of the Proof

2. No components of an event propagate across an arc labeled $<_{RA}$, $<_{WA}$, or $<_{SA}$. In these cases the flaw is not fatal to the proof of Theorem 12.1, since Lemma 7.2 ensures that arcs labeled $<xa$ can essentially be ignored.
3. Finally, Lemma 12.5 is not true from one write event to another write event in the same statement, obviously, since there are no arcs labeled $<_{WS}$ between events within the same statement. However, Lemma 12.4 shows that Lemma 12.5 is true for any two write events in a path which are not in the same statement.

DISCUSSION OF PART I OF THE PROOF

The proof starts with an arbitrary write event (P,L,W,V,O,S), shown on line W00 (following), and called E_1 in the proof. The proof has the form of a tree structure with E_1 as the root node. In the next level of the tree each of the 32 transition templates are considered, one at a time. The left-hand event of the transition template is applied to E_1. If the action components fit, then a new event E_2 is constructed. If not, then the transition template is ignored and the next one is considered.

For example, in line W01 the template for $<_{SRW}$ is considered. Since E_1 is a write event and the left-hand event of the template is a read event, there is no match and the template is ignored. The comment at the right-hand end of line W01 notes that a write event cannot have an arc labeled $<_{SRW}$ incident out of it.

If the left-hand event of the template is a write event, as in line W02, then the template is used to create a new event E_2 at the second level of the tree. For example, when the template for $<_{CWR}$

$$(-,-,W,-,-,-) \quad <_{CWR} \quad (-,-,R,=,=,=)$$

is compared with E_1, both E_1 and the left-hand event in the template are seen to be write events, and so a new event, E_2, is constructed. E_2 is required by the template to be a read event with the same value, operand, and store components as E_1.

One more item of information can be deduced about E_2. The model requires that reads always occur from the store associated with the process. In the proof it is convenient simply to use the same symbol for both process and store components in a read event. Unification of symbols could proceed in either of two directions; E_2 could be represented by (P,-,R,V,O,P) or by (S,-,R,V,O,S); the latter was more convenient.

The note, "Not determined.", at the right-hand end of line W02 indicates that the conditions do not exist for concluding the truth of the lemma at this point in the path and so the path must be continued along each of the next possible arcs to subsequent events. Cases such as this are handled in Part II of the proof.

In line W04 of the proof the template for $<_{CWW}$ requires that E_2 be a write event with the same operand and store components as E_1. Since the execution is assumed to obey write synchronization and to be circuit-free, there must also be an arc labeled $<_{WS}$ from E_1 to E_2. Hence, $E_1 <_{WS} E_2 = X(E_2,E_1)$.

By the definition of write order, if $E_i <_{WO} E_j$, then $E_i <_{WO} E_k$ for all other write events E_k in the same statement as E_j. Consequently, if $E_i <_{WO} E_j$, then $E_i <_{WS} X(E_j,E_i)$. The comment in line W10 summarizes this as $E_1 <$ all (E_2).

Line W19 shows that nothing may be known about an event with an arc labeled $<_{RA}$ incident into it. Therefore, the lemma fails to hold along such arcs.

Line W22 illustrates the case of two events in the same statement occurring in sequence in the path. Lemma 12.5 fails for two such events, but Lemma 12.4 shows that Lemma 12.5 still holds for write events surrounding the two events in the same statement.

Part I of the Proof

```
W00  (P,L,W,V,O,S)
W01   <SRW    (-,-,-,-,-,-)      1. W <SRW -.
W02   <CWR    (S,-,R,V,O,S)      6. Not determined.
W03   <CRW    (-,-,-,-,-,-)      1. W <CRW -.
W04   <CWW    (-,-,W,-,O,S)      4. E1 <WS E2.
W05   <UWR    (S,-,R,-,O,S)      6. Not determined.
W06   <URW    (-,-,-,-,-,-)      1. W <URW -.
W07   <UWW    (P,-,W,-,O,S)      4. E1 <WS E2.
W08   <RO     (-,-,-,-,-,-)      1. W <RO -.
W09   <ROO    (-,-,-,-,-,-)      1. W <RO -.
W10   <WO     (P,-,W,-,-,-)      5. E1 < all(E2).
W11   <WOO    (P,-,W,-,=,-)      5. E1 < all(E2).
W12   <WOS    (P,-,W,-,-,S)      4. E1 <WS E2.
W13   <PO     (S,-,R,-,-,S)      6. Not determined.
W14   <PO     (P,-,W,-,-,-)      5. E1 < all(E2).
W15   <POO    (S,-,R,-,O,S)      6. Not determined.
W16   <POO    (P,-,W,-,O,-)      5. E1 < all(E2).
W17   <POS    (S,-,R,-,-,S)      6. Not determined.
W18   <POS    (P,-,W,-,-,S)      4. E1 <WS E2.
W19   <RA     (-,-,-,-,-,-)      2b. Fail.
W20   =RA     (-,-,-,-,-,-)      1. W =RA -.
W21   <WA     (-,-,-,-,-,-)      2b. Fail.
W22   =WA     (P,L,W,V,O,-)      2c. Fail.
W23   <SA     (-,-,-,-,-,-)      2b. Fail.
W24   =SA     (S,L,R,-,-,S)      6. Not determined.
W25   =SA     (P,L,W,-,-,-)      2c. Fail.
W26   <RS     (-,-,-,-,-,-)      1. W <RS -.
W27   <ARC    (-,-,-,-,-,-)      1. W <ARC -.
W28   <RRC    (-,-,-,-,-,-)      1. W <RRC -.
W29   <WS     (-,-,W,-,-,S)      4. E1 <WS E2.
W30   <CON    (-,-,W,-,O,S)      4. E1 <WS E2.
W31   <AWC    (P,L,W,V,O,-)      2c. Fail.
W32   <RWC    (P,L,W,V,O,-)      2c. Fail.
                                 End of Part I.
```

Explanations. The following explanations amplify on the short notes in the right-hand column. Explanation number 3 applies only to the second half of the proof.

1. R (W) $<$xxx $-$. A read (write) event cannot have an arc labeled $<$xxx incident out of it.
2a. Fail. The lemma fails irreparably on arcs labeled $<_{RS}$.
2b. Fail. Arcs labeled $<_{RA}$, $<_{WA}$, and $<_{SA}$ are excluded from the lemma (but see Lemma 7.2).
2c. Fail. Arcs labeled $=_{WA}$, $=_{SA}$, $<_{AWC}$, and $<_{RWC}$ are excluded from the lemma (but see Lemma 12.4).
3. P–R–P $<$ P–R–P. Two read events in sequence in a path have the same process and store components.
4. $E_1 <_{WS} E_i$. There is a path from E_1 to E_i. The two write events have the same store component. Since the execution is write synchronized and circuit-free, there is also an arc labeled $<_{WS}$ from E_1 to E_i. Hence, $E_1 <_{WS} X(E_i,E_1)$.
5. $E_i <$xxx all(E_j). By the definition of $<$xxx if $E_i <$xxx E_j, then $E_i <$xxx E_k, where E_k is any other write event in the statement containing E_j. In particular, $E_i <_{WS} X(E_i,E_j)$.
6. Not Determined. There is insufficient information in the event either to prove or to disprove the lemma at this event in the path. Therefore, continue the search at the next level down in the tree.

DISCUSSION OF PART II OF THE PROOF

The six read events encountered in Part I of the proof all had the same process and store components as E_1. (In some cases other components were also the same as those for E_1, but this is immaterial.) From each of the six read events the search tree can be extended as shown next.

The second part of the proof starts with event E_2 being a read event with process and store components equal to those for E_1. In line R01 the template for $<_{SRW}$ is applied to E_2. By the definition of SRW there is an arc labeled $<_{SRW}$ from E_2 to all write events in the statement containing E_3. Hence $E_1 <$xxx $E_2 <_{SRW} X(E_3,E_1)$. Since the execution is assumed to obey write synchronization and to be circuit-free, $E_1 <_{WS} X(E_3,E_1)$.

In line R02 the template for $<_{CWR}$ does not match E_2's being a read event.

In line R03 the template for $<_{CRW}$ results in E_3 being a write event with the same store component as E_1. Since $E_1 <$xxx $E_2 <_{CRW} E_3$ and since the execution obeys WS and is circuit-free, it must be that $E_1 <_{WS} E_3$.

In line R08 the template for RO requires that E_3 be a read event with the same process and store components as E_2. This condition is true for all cases where E_3 is a read event (see lines R13, R15, R17, R20, R24, R27, and R28). Thus, if the search is continued down to event E_4, then the same analysis applied going from E_3

to E_4 will show that the read events at the E_4 level will still have the same process and store components as E_1. Similarly, on down through an indefinite number of levels of consecutive read events.

Part II of the Proof

R00	$<$xxx	$(S,-,R,-,-,S)$	
R01	$<_{SRW}$	$(S,-,W,-,-,-)$	5. $E_2 <$ all(E_3).
R02	$<_{CWR}$	$(-,-,-,-,-,-)$	1. $R <_{CWR} -$.
R03	$<_{CRW}$	$(-,-,W,-,-,S)$	4. $E_1 <_{WS} E_3$.
R04	$<_{CWW}$	$(-,-,-,-,-,-)$	1. $R <_{CWW} -$.
R05	$<_{UWR}$	$(-,-,-,-,-,-)$	1. $R <_{UWR} -$.
R06	$<_{URW}$	$(S,-,W,-,-,S)$	4. $E_1 <_{WS} E_3$.
R07	$<_{UWW}$	$(-,-,-,-,-,-)$	1. $R <_{UWW} -$.
R08	$<_{RO}$	$(S,-,R,-,-,S)$	3. P–R–P $<$ P–R–P.
R09	$<_{ROO}$	$(S,-,R,-,-,S)$	3. P–R–P $<$ P–R–P.
R10	$<_{WO}$	$(-,-,-,-,-,-)$	1. $R <_{WO} -$.
R11	$<_{WOO}$	$(-,-,-,-,-,-)$	1. $R <_{WOO} -$.
R12	$<_{WOS}$	$(-,-,-,-,-,-)$	1. $R <_{WOS} -$.
R13	$<_{PO}$	$(S,-,R,-,-,S)$	3. P–R–P $<$ P–R–P.
R14	$<_{PO}$	$(S,-,W,-,-,-)$	5. $E_2 <$ all(E_3).
R15	$<_{POO}$	$(S,-,R,-,-,S)$	3. P–R–P $<$ P–R–P.
R16	$<_{POO}$	$(S,-,W,-,-,-)$	5. $E2 <$ all(E_3).
R17	$<_{POS}$	$(S,-,R,-,-,S)$	3. P–R–P $<$ P–R–P.
R18	$<_{POS}$	$(S,-,W,-,-,S)$	4. $E_1 <_{WS} E_3$.
R19	$<_{RA}$	$(-,-,-,-,-,-)$	2b. Fail.
R20	$=_{RA}$	$(S,-,R,-,-,S)$	3. P–R–P $<$ P–R–P.
R21	$<_{WA}$	$(-,-,-,-,-,-)$	2b. Fail.
R22	$=_{WA}$	$(-,-,-,-,-,-)$	1. $R =_{WA} -$.
R23	$<_{SA}$	$(-,-,-,-,-,-)$	2b. Fail.
R24	$=_{SA}$	$(S,-,R,-,-,S)$	3. P–R–P $<$ P–R–P.
R25	$=_{SA}$	$(S,-,W,-,-,-)$	5. $E_2 <$ all(E_3).
R26	$<_{RS}$	$(-,-,R,-,-,-)$	2a. Fail.
R27	$<_{ARC}$	$(S,-,R,-,-,S)$	3. P–R–P $<$ P–R–P.
R28	$<_{RRC}$	$(S,-,R,-,-,S)$	3. P–R–P $<$ P–R–P.
R29	$<_{WS}$	$(-,-,-,-,-,-)$	1. $R <_{WS} -$.
R30	$<_{CON}$	$(-,-,-,-,-,-)$	1. $R <_{CON} -$.
R31	$<_{AWC}$	$(-,-,-,-,-,-)$	1. $R <_{AWC} -$.
R32	$<_{RWC}$	$(-,-,-,-,-,-)$	1. $R <_{RWC} -$.

End of Part II.

CONCLUSION OF THE PROOF

In a write synchronized execution let $W_1 < W_2 < \ldots < W_n$ be a path consisting only of write events which contains no arcs labeled $<_{RS}$, $<_{RA}$, $<_{WA}$, or $<_{SA}$.

If the path contains no two events from the same statement, then Part I shows that $W_i <_{WS} X(W_j, W_i)$ for $0 < i = j - 1 < n$.

Repeated application of Lemma 12.3 shows that $W_i <_{ws} X(W_j,W_i)$ for $0 < i < j < n$.

If the path contains events from the same statement, then Lemma 12.4 shows that $W_i <_{ws} X(W_j,W_i)$ for $0 < i < j < n$ and W_i and W_j not in the same statement.

Where $W < R$ occurs in the path, Part I shows that R has the same store component as W. Part II shows that if $R_1 < R_2$ occurs, then both read events have the same store component. Consequently, all the events in the path $R_1 < R_2 < \ldots < R_n$ have the same store component.

Part II also shows that if $R <xxx W$ occurs, then either W has the same store component as R, or there is an arc labeled $<xxx$ from R to each of the write events in the statement containing event W. Hence, in a path such as $W_1 < R_1 < \ldots < R_k < W_2$, one of the following two conditions is true:

1. W_1 and W_2 have the same store component, so $W_1 <_{ws} W_2 = X(W_2,W_1)$.
2. $W_1 < R_1 < \ldots < R_k < X(W_2,W_1)$. Since the execution is circuit-free, $W_1 <_{ws} X(W_2,W_1)$.

Combining these results yields the statement of Lemma 12.5. ∎

A SMALL GENERALIZATION

The definition of statement atomicity requires that all statements in an execution be treated as being executed atomically. Thus, when an arc labeled $=_{SA}$ was encountered in the preceding proof, it would have been possible to argue that the presence of such an arc required that Lemma 12.5 be true since SA ⇒ WA.

A deliberate choice was made to avoid the easy argument and to argue instead as if statement atomicity applied only to the statement containing the event from which the arc labeled $=_{SA}$ emanated. The intent was to allow the proof to remain valid even in a more general case in which statement atomicity is defined to apply only to specific statements.

WRITE SYNCHRONIZED IS WRITE ATOMIC

Theorem 12.1 (WSISWA). Let A be any architecture which does not contain RS, WS, or WA. Let $A_1 = A * A(WS)$ and $A_2 = A * A(WA)$. Then $A_1 \Leftrightarrow A_2$.

Proof of $\leq$. Follows from WA ⇒ WS.

Proof of ⇒. Define $A_3 = A * A(WS) * A(WA)$ and assume the theorem is false, that is, assume that A_1 and A_2 are distinguishable. Then there is an execution E that obeys A_1, but which does not obey A_2. If E does not obey A_2, then it also does not obey A_3. This means that every member of the graph set for E under A_1 occurs (multiple times) in the graph set for E under A_3 with additional arcs labeled $<_{WA}$. Choose a circuit-free member, G_1, of the graph set for E under A_1. Choose any one, G_3, of the members of the graph set for E under A_3 obtained by adding arcs labeled $<_{WA}$. G_3 contains a circuit since all members of the graph set for E under A_3 contain circuits. Call the circuit C_1. C_1 includes an arc labeled $<_{WA}$ since G_1 is circuit-free and G_3 is identical to G_1 except for additional arcs labeled $<_{WA}$. There may also be arcs labeled $<_{RA}$ and $<_{SA}$. Then by Lemma 7.2 there is another circuit C2, not containing arcs labeled $<_{WA}$, $<_{RA}$, and $<_{SA}$, but possibly containing arcs labeled $=_{WA}$, $=_{RA}$, or $=_{SA}$. The circuit has the form

$$W_1 < E_2 < E_3 < \ldots < W_n < W_1$$

where W_1 and W_n are write events in the same statement.

Repeated application of Lemma 12.5 to the circuit yields

$$W_1 <_{WS} X(W_n, W_1) <_{WS} X(W_1, W_1) = W_1.$$

This is a contradiction since the graph under A(WS) is circuit-free. Hence, the assumption that A_1 and A_2 are distinguishable is false, that is, A_1 and A_2 are indistinguishable. ∎

THE PROBLEM WITH READ SYNCHRONIZATION

If A_1 and A_2 include the rule of RS, then it is possible to distinguish A_1 and A_2. A corollary to Theorem A31 shows how.

Corollary to Theorem A31. $A(CMP, RS, WS) \neg \Rightarrow A(CMP, RS, WA)$.

Proof. Consider the following execution.

```
Initially, A = B = X = Y = 0.

        P1                  P2                  P3              P4
L1: X:= A + B;    L1: Y:= A + B;    L1: A:= 1;    L1: B:= 2;

Terminally, A = 1, B = 2, X = 1, and Y = 2.
```

Since the execution obeys RS, every element of the graph set for the execution contains either one or the other of the following two pairs of paths.

$(P_1, L_1, R, 1, A, S_1)$ $<_{RS}$ $(P_2, L_1, R, 0, A, S_2)$
$(P_1, L_1, R, 0, B, S_1)$ $<_{RS}$ $(P_2, L_1, R, 2, B, S_2)$

$(P_2, L_1, R, 0, A, S_2)$ $<_{RS}$ $(P_1, L_1, R, 1, A, S_1)$
$(P_2, L_1, R, 2, B, S_2)$ $<_{RS}$ $(P_1, L_1, R, 0, B, S_1)$

Therefore, under architecture A(CMP, RS, WS) every member of the graph set for the execution contains one or the other of the following two paths.

A Source of Performance Improvement

$(P_3, L_1, W, 1, A, S_1)$ $<_{CWR}$ $(P_1, L_1, R, 1, A, S_1)$
$<_{RS}$ $(P_2, L_1, R, 0, A, S_2)$
$<_{CRW}$ $(P_3, L_1, W, 1, A, S_2)$

$(P_4, L_1, W, 2, B, S_2)$ $<_{CWR}$ $(P_2, L_1, R, 2, B, S_2)$
$<_{RS}$ $(P_1, L_1, R, 0, B, S_1)$
$<_{CRW}$ $(P_4, L_1, W, 2, B, S_1)$

The first path shows a path between two write events in the same statement, namely, statement L_1 in process P_3. The second path does the same for two events in statement L_1 in process P_4. Each path shows that the member of the graph set in which the path occurs does not obey WA. Since one path or the other occurs in every element of the graph set for the execution, the execution does not obey A(CMP, RS, WA).

Under architecture A(CMP, RS, WS) there is an element of the graph set for the execution that is circuit-free (though not WA).

P_1	P_2	P_3	P_4
		$(L_1, R, 1, 1, S_3)$	
			$(L_1, R, 2, 2, S_4)$
		$(L_1, W, 1, A, S_1)$	
$(L_1, R, 1, A, S_1)$			
$(L_1, R, 0, B, S_1)$			
	$(L_1, R, 0, A, S_2)$		
		$(L_1, W, 1, A, S_2)$	
		$(L_1, W, 1, A, S_3)$	
		$(L_1, W, 1, A, S_4)$	
			$(L_1, W, 2, B, S)$
	$(L_1, R, 2, B, S_2)$		
$(L_1, W, 1, X, S)$			
	$(L_1, W, 2, Y, S)$		

Read synchronization is the only rule in the model which allows one to deduce that a write synchronized system is not write atomic. Fortunately, abstaining from assuming read synchronization is not a burden since in most systems there is no natural way to implement this principle and hence no temptation on the part of a user to assume it is true. However, the lesson of this execution is to warn that it can be as important to know what rules are excluded from an architecture as it is to know what rules are included. For example, a machine can be built to be in fact both read and write synchronized, but advertised as being write atomic and not read synchronized, and no program can detect the difference.

A SOURCE OF PERFORMANCE IMPROVEMENT

In Chap. 13 Theorem 12.2 will be seen to offer a potentially significant performance improvement.

Theorem 12.2. Let A be any architecture not containing POS, PO, WS, RS, or WA. Let $A_1 = A * A(POS) * A(WS)$ and $A_2 = A(PO) * A(WA)$. Then $A_1 \Leftrightarrow A_2$.

Proof. By Theorem 12.1 A_1 is indistinguishable from $A_3 = A * A(POS) * A(WA)$. Since PO $\Rightarrow$ POS, it remains only to show that an execution that obeys A_3 also obeys A_2. Let process P_i have store S_i. Then POS guarantees that all the read events and the write events with store S_i occur in program order. Since every statement contains a write event with store component S_i, WA guarantees that all events in P_i occur in program order. ∎

PROBLEMS

12.1. Let W_1 and W_2 be write events in an execution that is write synchronized. Prove each of the following statements.
(a) $X(W_1, W_1) = W_1$.
(b) If W_1 and W_2 are in the same statement, then $X(W_2, W_1) = W_1$.
(c) W_1 and $X(W_2, W_1)$ have the same store components.
(d) If W_1 and W_2 have the same store components, then $X(W_2, W_1) = W_2$.

12.2. Let W_1 and W_2 be write events in distinct statements in an execution which obeys WS. Prove that if $W_1 <_{WS} X(W_2, W_1)$, then $X(W_1, W_2) <_{WS} W_2$.

12.3. Prove: $X(X(W_1, W_2), W_3) = X(W_1, W_3)$.

12.4. Prove $X[W_1, X(W_2, W_3)] = X(W_1, W_3)$.

12.5. Theorem 12.1 says that an architecture which includes write synchronization but not read synchronization is indistinguishable from an architecture which is write atomic. Is there a corresponding theorem that an architecture which includes read synchronization but not write synchronization is indistinguishable from an architecture which is read atomic? (Hint. Ask what an execution which is vacuously read synchronized would look like and then examine the proof of Theorem A32.)

12.6. Theorem 12.1 says that a write synchronized system appears to be write atomic, no matter how many processes are in the system. If the number of processes is restricted, then can a system appear to be write atomic by obeying a weaker rule than write synchronization? For example, suppose a machine has only two processors and obeys the rule of consistency. Will the machine appear to be write atomic?

(Hint. Use the following execution to show that $A(CMP, RO, CON) \neg \Rightarrow A(CMP, RO, WA)$, even on a system consisting of only two processes.

Initially, A = B = X = Y = 0.

P_1	P_2
L_1: A:= 1;	L_1: X:= B;
L_2: B:= A;	L_2: Y:= A;

Terminally, A = B = X = 1, Y = 0.)

13

Ring-shaped Systems

The utility of Theorem 12.1 can be seen most clearly in a ring-shaped system in which $n + 1$ processors each communicate only with the next processor in the sequence $P_0, P_1, P_2, \ldots, P_n, P_0$.

A RING-SHAPED SYSTEM

Let $P_0, P_1, P_2, \ldots, P_n$ be a group of processors connected in a ring. Each processor communicates with other processors only by sending messages to its successor in the sequence $P_0, P_1, P_2, \ldots, P_n, P_0$.

Each processor P_i has a separate memory unit, or store S_i. Each store contains a copy of all of the operands that can be read or written by any of the processors.

Messages sent around the ring are of two types: data messages and control messages. Data messages are represented by write events as in the previous chapters.

Control messages are messages sent between a processor and the supervisor processor, P_0. Control messages are represented by short, imperative statements. Of course, the functions of P_0 could be incorporated into the functions of any of the other processors.

Messages need not remain in first-in-first-out order around the ring except where explicitly noted.

RING ARCHITECTURE 1: NOT CONSISTENT

When a processor changes the value of a operand, it sends a data message around the ring to tell the other processors to change the value of the operand as recorded in the other processors' stores.

Execution 1

Processor P_2 sets A equal to 1. Operand A is changed in value from 0 (its initial value) to 1 in the store for each processor in the system, cyclically, around the ring. Eventually, A becomes equal to 1 in all stores.

```
             Initially, A = 0 in each store.

    P₁           P₂           P₃       P₄
              L₁: A:= 1;

             Terminally, A = 1 in each store.
```

Here, the events of the execution are shown with the events belonging to a common processor listed in a column (the processor format).

```
    P₁                P₂                    P₃           P₄
              (P₂,L₁,R,1,1,S₂)
              (P₂,L₁,W,1,A,S₂)
              (P₂,L₁,W,1,A,S₃)
              (P₂,L₁,W,1,A,S₄)
              (P₂,L₁,W,1,A,S₁)
```

The events of the execution can also be written in the following format in which events belonging to a common store are listed in a single column (the store format). Both formats are used in subsequent examples. (In contrast to the executions in the preceding chapters events here are shown with the process component included. This is necessary in order to keep track of the events in the store format.)

```
    S₁                S₂                    S₃                 S₄
              (P₂,L₁,R,1,1,S₂)
              (P₂,L₁,W,1,A,S₂)
                              (P₂,L₁,W,1,A,S₃)
                                                  (P₂,L₁,W,1,A,S₄)
(P₂,L₁,W,1,A,S₁)
```

There is a period of time when A is equal to 0 in some stores and equal to 1 in other stores. However, nothing more than the passage of time and the completion of the current statement is required for A to acquire the same value in all stores.

Ring Architecture 1: Not Consistent

Execution 2

Processor P_2 sets A equal to 1 at the same time that processor P_3 sets B equal to 2. The two changes can be made at the same time. Eventually, both operands will have acquired a new value in all stores in the system.

Initially, A = 0 and B = 0 in each store.

P_1	P_2	P_3	P_4
	L_1: A:= 1;	L_1: B:= 2;	

Terminally, A = 1 and B = 2 in each store.

P_1	P_2	P_3	P_4
	$(P_2,L_1,R,1,1,S_2)$	$(P_3,L_1,R,2,2,S_3)$	
	$(P_2,L_1,W,1,A,S_2)$	$(P_3,L_1,W,2,B,S_3)$	
	$(P_2,L_1,W,1,A,S_3)$	$(P_3,L_1,W,2,B,S_4)$	
	$(P_2,L_1,W,1,A,S_4)$	$(P_3,L_1,W,2,B,S_1)$	
	$(P_2,L_1,W,1,A,S_1)$	$(P_3,L_1,W,2,B,S_2)$	

S_1	S_2	S_3	S_4
	$(P_2,L_1,R,1,1,S_2)$	$(P_3,L_1,R,2,2,S_3)$	
	$(P_2,L_1,W,1,A,S_2)$	$(P_3,L_1,W,2,B,S_3)$	
		$(P_2,L_1,W,1,A,S_3)$	
$(P_3,L_1,W,2,B,S_1)$			$(P_3,L_1,W,2,B,S_4)$
$(P_2,L_1,W,1,A,S_1)$	$(P_3,L_1,W,2,B,S_2)$		$(P_2,L_1,W,1,A,S_4)$

Execution 3

Processor P_2 sets A to 1 and processor P_3 sets A to 2.

Initially, A = B = 0 in each store.

P_1	P_2	P_3	P_4
	L_1: A:= 1;	L_1: A:= 2;	

Terminally, A = 1 in S_1, S_3, and S_4; A = 2 in S_2.

P_1	P_2	P_3	P_4
	$(P_2,L_1,R,1,1,S_2)$	$(P_3,L_1,R,2,2,S_3)$	
	$(P_2,L_1,W,1,A,S_2)$	$(P_3,L_1,W,2,A,S_3)$	
	$(P_2,L_1,W,1,A,S_3)$	$(P_3,L_1,W,2,A,S_4)$	
	$(P_2,L_1,W,1,A,S_4)$	$(P_3,L_1,W,2,A,S_1)$	
	$(P_2,L_1,W,1,A,S_1)$	$(P_3,L_1,W,2,A,S_2)$	

S_1	S_2	S_3	S_4
	$(P_2,L_1,R,1,1,S_2)$	$(P_3,L_1,R,2,A,S_3)$	
	$(P_2,L_1,W,1,A,S_2)$	$(P_3,L_1,W,2,A,S_3)$	
		$(P_2,L_1,W,1,A,S_3)$	$(P_3,L_1,W,2,A,S_4)$
$(P_3,L_1,W,2,A,S_1)$			
			$(P_2,L_1,W,1,A,S_4)$
$(P_2,L_1,W,1,A,S_1)$	$(P_3,L_1,W,2,A,S_2)$		

In contrast to the situation in executions 1 and 2, the failure of an operand to have the same terminal value in all stores in the execution is not transitory; the difference will persist until A is written into again. This execution exhibits a failure to obey the architecture rule of consistency (CON).

To avoid this problem one can require the system to be write atomic. This approach is taken in Ring Architecture 2.

RING ARCHITECTURE 2: WRITE ATOMIC

For processor P_i to set operand O to value V, P_i sends a control message of the form "P_i: set O=V" to processor P_0 and then waits for a control message from P_0 that P_i may resume. Whenever P_0 receives one or more such control messages, P_0 selects one of the control messages, queues the other(s), and then, for the selected control message, sends a data message around the ring to tell processors P_1, $P_2, \ldots, P_n$ to change the value of operand O to the value V. When one data message completes, P_0 sends a resume control message to the originator of the data message and then sends off the next pending data message, if any. Control messages are shown only in the listing of events in the store format.

Execution 4

Processor P_2 sends a message to P_0 to set A equal to one. Processor P_3 sends a message to P_0 to set A equal to two. P_0 receives both messages and chooses one or the other of them to send around the ring. When the data message comes back to P_0, P_0 sends a control message to the processor that it may resume. Then it handles the request for the other processor.

Initially, A = 0 in each store.

P_1	P_2	P_3	P_4
	L_1: A:= 1;	L_1: A:= 2;	
	L_2: U:= V;	L_2: X:= Y;	

Terminally, A = 2 in each store.

P_1	P_2	P_3	P_4
	$(P_2,L_1,R,1,1,S_2)$		
		$(P_3,L_1,R,2,2,S_3)$	

Ring Architecture 3: Write Synchronized

	$(P_2, L_1, W, 1, A, S_1)$		
	$(P_2, L_1, W, 1, A, S_2)$		
	$(P_2, L_1, W, 1, A, S_3)$		
	$(P_2, L_1, W, 1, A, S_4)$		
	$(P_2, L_2, R, 0, V, S_2)$		
		$(P_3, L_1, W, 2, A, S_1)$	
		$(P_3, L_1, W, 2, A, S_2)$	
		$(P_3, L_1, W, 2, A, S_3)$	
		$(P_3, L_1, W, 2, A, S_4)$	
		$(P_3, L_2, R, 0, Y, S_3)$	

S_1	S_2	S_3	S_4
	P_2: set A = 1.		
	P_2 waits.	P_2: set A = 1.	
		P_3: set A = 2.	P_2: set A = 1.
		P_3 waits.	P_3: set A = 2.
$(P_2, L_1, W, 1, A, S_1)$			
	$(P_2, L_1, W, 1, A, S_2)$		
		$(P_2, L_1, W, 1, A, S_3)$	
			$(P_2, L_1, W, 1, A, S_4)$
P_2: resume.			
	(P_2 continues.)		
	$(P_2, L_2, R, 0, V, S_2)$		
$(P_3, L_1, W, 2, A, S_1)$			
	$(P_3, L_1, W, 2, A, S_2)$		
		$(P_3, L_1, W, 2, A, S_3)$	
			$(P_3, L_1, W, 2, A, S_4)$
P_3: resume.			
	P_3: resume.		
		(P_3 continues.)	
		$(P_3, L_2, R, 0, Y, S_3)$	

Ring Architecture 2 is write atomic; the problem of inconsistent results cannot occur. There is a performance penalty paid to achieve write atomicity. Each processor waits for messages to make two or more traversals of the ring: the set control message from P_i to P_0, the data message around the ring, and the resume control message from P_0 back to P_i. In the preceding execution P_2 waited for two traversals and P_3 waited for three.

Generally, in the case of simultaneous messages, the first process will wait for messages to make two traversals of the ring, the second will wait for three, the third four, and so on. If there are k simultaneous messages, the average waiting time will be $(2 + 3 + \ldots + k + 1)/k = (k + 3)/2$

RING ARCHITECTURE 3: WRITE SYNCHRONIZED

Ring Architecture 3 is the same as Ring Architecture 2, except that it is write synchronized, instead of write atomic. Specifically, data messages may be sent around the ring simultaneously, provided only that they arrive in the same relative order at each processor.

Execution 5

Processors P_2 and P_3 both send control messages to P_0. P_0 sends two data messages to all processors to change the value of A. The data messages have to stay in order on the ring, but otherwise they can proceed asynchronously around the ring. When each data message returns to P_0, P_0 sends the originator a control message telling it that it may proceed.

Initially, A = 0 in each store.

P_1	P_2	P_3	P_4
	L_1: A:= 1;	L_1: A:= 2;	
	L_2: U:= V;	L_2: X:= Y;	

Terminally, A = 2 in each store.

P_1	P_2	P_3	P_4
	$(P_2,L_1,R,1,A,S_2)$		
		$(P_3,L_1,R,2,A,S_3)$	
	$(P_2,L_1,W,1,A,S_1)$		
	$(P_2,L_1,W,1,A,S_2)$	$(P_3,L_1,W,2,A,S_1)$	
	$(P_2,L_1,W,1,A,S_3)$	$(P_3,L_1,W,2,A,S_2)$	
	$(P_2,L_1,W,1,A,S_4)$	$(P_3,L_1,W,2,A,S_3)$	
	$(P_2,L_2,R,0,V,S_2)$	$(P_3,L_1,W,2,A,S_4)$	
		$(P_3,L_2,R,0,Y,S_3)$	

S_1	S_2	S_3	S_4
	$(P_2,L_1,R,1,1,S_2)$		
	P_2: set A = 1.	$(P_3,L_1,R,2,2,S_3)$	
	P_2 waits.	P_2: set A = 1.	
$(P_2,L_1,W,1,A,S_1)$		P_3: set A = 2.	P_2: set A = 1.
$(P_3,L_1,W,2,A,S_1)$	$(P_2,L_1,W,1,A,S_2)$	P_3 waits.	P_3: set A = 2.
	$(P_3,L_1,W,2,A,S_2)$	$(P_2,L_1,W,1,A,S_3)$	
$(P_2$: resume.		$(P_3,L_1,W,2,A,S_3)$	$(P_2,L_1,W,1,A,S_4)$
P_3: resume.	P_2: resume.		$(P_3,L_1,W,2,A,S_4)$
	P_3: resume.		
	$(P_2$ continues.)	P_3: resume.	
	$(P_2,L_2,R,0,V,S_2)$	$(P_3$ continues.)	
		$(P_3,L_2,R,0,Y,S_3)$	

Ring Architecture 3 allows each processor to wait for two, and only two, traversals, no matter how many processors seek to write operands at the same time.

By Theorem 12.1, Ring Architecture 2 and Ring Architecture 3 are indistinguishable.

RING ARCHITECTURE 4: PROGRAM ORDERED BY STORE

Let Ring Architecture 4 be the same as Ring Archtecture 3 except that P_0 never sends off a resume message. Instead processor P_i, when it has sent off a control message and then receives the corresponding data message, interprets the data message as a resume control message.

Execution 6

P_2 sends a message to P_0 to change the value of A. P_0 sends off a message around the ring, as before, but now when P_2 receives the message to change the value of A, P_2 may proceed with accessing the next operand. Thus, P_2 waits for a message to make only one full circuit on the ring, not two full circuits.

Initially, A = 0 in each store.

P_1	P_2	P_3	P_4
	L_1: A:= 1;	L_1: A:= 2;	
	L_2: U:= V;	L_2: X:= Y;	

Terminally, A = 2 in each store.

P_1	P_2	P_3	P_4
	$(P_2,L_1,R,1,1,S_2)$		
		$(P_3,L_1,R,2,2,S_3)$	
	$(P_2,L_1,W,1,A,S_1)$		
	$(P_2,L_1,W,1,A,S_2)$	$(P_3,L_1,W,2,A,S_1)$	
	$(P_2,L_2,R,0,V,S_2)$		
	$(P_2,L_1,W,1,A,S_3)$	$(P_3,L_1,W,2,A,S_2)$	
	$(P_2,L_1,W,1,A,S_4)$	$(P_3,L_1,W,2,A,S_3)$	
		$(P_3,L_2,R,0,Y,S_3)$	
		$(P_3,L_1,W,2,A,S_4)$	

S_1	S_2	S_3	S_4
	$(P_2,L_1,R,1,1,S_2)$		
	P_2: set A = 1.	$(P_3,L_1,R,2,2,S_3)$	
	P_2 waits.	P_2: set A = 1.	
		P_3: set A = 2.	P_2: set A = 1.
$(P_2,L_1,W,1,A,S_1)$		P_3 waits.	P_3: set A = 2.
$(P_3,L_1,W,2,A,S_1)$	$(P_2,L_1,W,1,A,S_2)$		
	(P_2 continues.)		
	$(P_2,L_2,R,0,V,S_2)$		
	$(P_3,L_1,W,2,A,S_2)$	$(P_2,L_1,W,1,A,S_3)$	
		$(P_3,L_1,W,2,A,S_3)$	$(P_2,L_1,W,1,A,S_4)$
		(P_3 continues.)	
		$(P_3,L_2,R,0,Y,S_3)$	
			$(P_3,L_1,W,2,A,S_4)$

In this architecture a processor has to wait for a message to make only one traversal of the ring before the processor is allowed to access the next operand.

Ring Architecture 4 is not program ordered. However, it is program ordered by store (POS), that is, events with a common processor and store occur in program order. By Theorem 12.2 this architecture is both write atomic and program ordered, that is, Ring Architecture 4 is also indistinguishable from Ring Architecture 2.

PROBLEMS

13.1. Discuss. The system described in this chapter is too slow. It is impossible to have to wait for every store operation to make a full cycle around the ring. This forces the CPUs to run at IO speeds. To speed up the system, data must be separated into two categories, local and global. Stores on local data take place in the node containing the data and nowhere else. Only stores on global data have to cycle around the ring. A program that stores into global data should be treated differently from a program that stores only into local data. It should be called asynchronously, as if it were an IO device: request an operation and continue processing and then later check whether or not the operation has completed.

13.2. Theorems A24 and A28 are based on the same execution, presented in both proofs in the process format. Rewrite the executions in both proofs in the store format. Draw a line connecting every pair of write events from the same statement. What is different about the connecting lines in the two cases? What does the difference reveal?

13.3. Dijkstra [DIJK74] described a set of processes arranged in a ring, but interacting in quite a different way from that described in this chapter. For each process there is a separate store. Each variable occurs in only one store. Each process writes only into its own store, but can read variables in its own store and in the stores of each of its two neighbors. How is write atomicity achieved in this system?

REFERENCES

The material in this chapter originally appeared in [COLL84].

COLL84. W. W. COLLIER. Write Atomicity in Distributed Systems. Technical Report TR 00.3304, IBM Corporation, Poughkeepsie, N.Y., Oct. 19, 1984.

DIJK74. E. W. DIJKSTRA. Self-Stabilizing Systems in Spite of Distributed Control. Communications of the ACM, 17, 11 (Nov. 1974), pp. 643–644.

14

A Model of a Shared Memory Multiprocessor

The basic model developed in the preceding chapters can be extended to model a shared memory multiprocessor. To do so with the rigor of the basic model would require recapitulating all of Chaps. 5 through 9. For now it is enough to describe a multiprocessing system briefly and colloquially, to indicate how it can be modeled, and to illustrate how to reason about the model.

A TYPICAL SHARED MEMORY MULTIPROCESSOR

In a (greatly simplified) shared memory multiprocessor there are n processors, each with its own cache, and main storage. An operand may or may not appear in any given cache. If present, it may be flagged as either read-only or exclusive. An operand may be flagged exclusive in at most one cache; it can be flagged read-only in any number of caches; if flagged exclusive in any cache, it cannot be flagged read-only in any other cache.

When processor P_1 executes

$$A := B;$$

the machine checks to see if operand B is flagged exclusive or read-only in P_1's cache. If it is, execution continues. If not, the machine checks to see if operand B is held exclusive in any other cache. If B is found in the cache for Processor 2, say, the value of B in P_2's cache is copied to P_1's cache; the copy in P_2's cache is flagged read-only; and the copy of B in P_1's cache is flagged read-only.

If operand B is flagged read-only in any cache, the value of B in main storage is fetched to P_1's cache, and B is flagged read-only in P_1's cache.

If operand B does not exist in any other cache, then the value of B in main storage is fetched to P_1's cache, and B is flagged read-only in P_1's cache.

Operand A is flagged not-here in all caches except P_1's where it is flagged exclusive.

When a cache becomes full from lines being fetched into it, some lines are chosen to be erased from the cache and possibly to be written back to main storage.

THE MP MODEL

In the MP model events, statements, and rules are more complex than in the basic model, that is, the model of the preceding chapters.

Each event consists of seven components. The new component is called a flag. A flag denotes the status of an operand in a store (= a cache). The flag component is E for an operand flagged exclusive, R for an operand flagged read-only, and N for an operand flagged not-here. The flag component is defined to be the fifth component of an event. In the MP model the operand and store components are the sixth and seventh components, respectively, of an event.

The value component for an event flagged as either E or R is an integer (as in the basic model). For an event flagged as not-here the value is undefined, indicated by a dash (–).

A statement consists of one read event for each source operand, n source write events (for n the number of processes) for each source operand, one read event for the sink operand, and then n sink write events for the sink operand. For the statement A: = B + C; there are 3 read events and $3 * n$ write events. The source read and write events represent the fetching of the value of the source operands and the resetting of the flags for the source operands. The sink read and write events represent the reading of the flag for the sink operand and the storing of the value for the sink operand.

The action component is R_1 (W_1) for a source read (write) event. The action component is R_2 (W_2) for a sink read (write) event.

As an example, consider the following execution.

```
             Initially, A = 0, B = 1.

                 P₁                    P₂
            L₁:  A:= B;

             Terminally, A = 1, B = 1.
```

$$P_1 \qquad\qquad P_2$$
$$(L_1, R1, -, N, B, S_1)$$
$$(L_1, W1, 1, R, B, S_1)$$
$$(L_1, W1, -, N, B, S_2)$$
$$(L_1, R2, -, N, A, S_1)$$
$$(L_1, W2, 1, E, A, S_1)$$
$$(L_1, W2, -, N, A, S_2)$$

There is a read event (R_1) for operand B, followed by two write (W_1) events for operand B. The read event represents the interrogation of the flag for operand B. The write events represent the rewriting of the value and the flag of operand B in zero or more of the caches in the system.

In P_1 if B is flagged as exclusive or read-only, its flag and value are left unchanged. If B is flagged as not-here, it becomes flagged as read-only and the value recorded for B in some other cache is written into the cache for P_1. In P_2 if B is flagged as exclusive, it is flagged as read-only and its value is left unchanged. If B is flagged as read-only or not-here, its value and flag are left unchanged.

There is a read event (R_2) for operand A, followed by two write (W_2) events for operand A. The read event represents the interrogation of the flag of operand A. (If the operand is a literal, or if the flag is either exclusive or not-here, then R_2 also represents reading the value of the operand.) The write events represent the rewriting of the value and the flag of operand A in one or more of the caches in the system.

In P_1 if A is flagged as exclusive, its flag is left unchanged. If A is flagged as read-only or not-here, it is flagged as exclusive. The sum of the values in the W_1 events in the statement are written into A.

In P_2 A is flagged as not-here.

The possible changes in the setting of flags for operands A and B in the execution that follows are shown in Fig. 14.1. The "From" column shows the beginning states of the flags for operands in stores S_1 and S_2. The "To" column shows the ending state. The column headed "Data From" shows the source from which a new value of an operand is received.

SHORTCUTS

As in the basic model, the intent is to capture a specific, limited slice of detail, in this case, the reading and writing of operand values and operand flags into caches. For the sake of simplicity some shortcuts are taken.

1. Each cache (store) is treated as if it contained a value and a flag for every operand. To model an operand being absent from a cache, the operand is flagged not-here and the value is set to null, represented by a dash (–).
2. Caches are assumed never to get full. This obviates modeling what might appear to be the arbitrary and spontaneous flagging of an operand as not-here.

P_1 P_2
L_1: A := B;

Change in the flag for A.				Change in the flag for B.				Data
From		To		From		To		From
S_1	S_2	S_1	S_2	S_1	S_2	S_1	S_2	
NH	NH	EX	NH	NH	NH	RO	NH	S_0
NH	RO	EX	NH	NH	RO	RO	RO	S_0
NH	EX	EX	NH	NH	EX	RO	RO	S_2
RO	NH	EX	NH	RO	NH	RO	NH	—
RO	RO	EX	NH	RO	RO	RO	RO	—
EX	NH	EX	NH	EX	NH	EX	NH	—

EX = exclusive, RO = read-only, NH = not-here.

Figure 14.1 Before and after status of flags.

3. Processor P0 is treated as only a source, never a sink. Since castouts from caches to main storage (S0) are not modeled, there are no write events representing a write operation into store S0.

4. In the basic model the statement C: = A + B; was modeled via two read events and several write events. The addition of A and B was not explicitly represented. Such an operation can be called interstitial, since it is understood to occur in between the events that are explicitly modeled in the system.

In a real MP system when a processor finds an operand is not in a cache, it sends out a query to the other processors for the operand and receives back the value and the flag for the operand. In the MP model this function is treated as interstitial, since it is understood to occur between the R_1 and W_1 events and between the R_2 and W_2 events. It is required of the query and the response that they not change the values and flags of operands.

ARCHITECTURE RULES IN THE MP MODEL

Let the term "write set" refer to (1) the set of all W_1 events in a statement, and (2) the set of all W_2 events in a statement. If an execution has n statements, then the execution has $2 * n$ write sets.

The Rule of Write Atomicity

The write sets are atomic sets. The graph set for write atomicity is constructed as before.

The Rule of Write Synchronization

The graph set for write synchronization is constructed as before except that it is constructed between every pair of write sets, instead of between the write events in every pair of statements.

The Order Rules

The definition of program order does not change. There is an arc from e_1 to e_2, labeled $<_{PO}$, if e_1 and e_2 are in the same process and the line number for e_1 is less than the line number for e_2. The rules UWR, URW, UWW, RO, ROO, WO, WOO, WOS, POO, and POS are treated similarly.

The Rule of Computation

The rule for generating arcs labeled $<_{CWR}$, $<_{CRW}$, and $<_{CWW}$ is considerably more complex than in the basic model.

Initially, all operands are in P0, flagged exclusive, and flagged not-here in all other caches. Thereafter, every write set has the following effect on one nonliteral operand. The operand is flagged exclusive in one cache and not-here in all other caches. Or, the operand is flagged read-only in one or more caches and not-here in all other caches.

In the basic model all potential orderings of the events were considered and some were eliminated. Then values were assigned to the events according to a straightforward rule, and if the values matched the terminal values of the operands specified in the execution, then the ordering of the events was included in the graph set for CMP. In the MP model not only values, but also the flags, of the operands have to be assigned. (See Prob. 14.1.)

In place of the rule for the existence of arcs labeled $<_{SRW}$ in the basic model, there are rules for arcs labeled as follows:

From each R_1 event to each W_1 event in the same statement there is an arc labeled $<_{SRW1}$.

From each W_1 event to each R_2 event in the same statement there is an arc labeled $<_{SWR}$.

From each R_2 event to each W_2 event in the same statement there is an arc labeled $<_{SRW2}$.

For example, for the statement
A: = B + C;
the events composing the statement have arcs labeled as shown in Fig. 14.2.

TRANSITION TEMPLATES

The transition templates for the rules defined for the MP model are

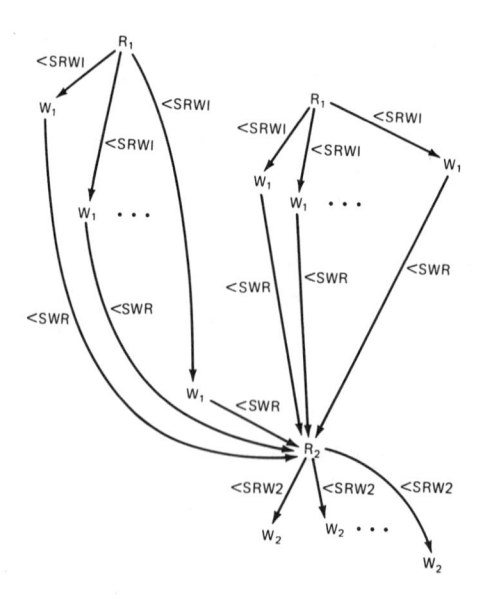

$$
\begin{array}{lll}
(P,L,R1,V,F,O,S) & <_{SRW1} & (=,=,W1,-,-,-,-) \\
(P,L,W1,V,F,O,S) & <_{SWR} & (=,=,R2,-,-,-,-) \\
(P,L,R2,V,F,O,S) & <_{SRW2} & (=,=,W2,-,-,-,-) \\
(P,L,W-,V,F,O,S) & <_{CWR} & (-,-,R-,=,-,=,=) \\
(P,L,R-,V,F,O,S) & <_{CRW} & (-,-,W-,-,-,=,=) \\
(P,L,W-,V,F,O,S) & <_{CWW} & (-,-,W-,-,-,=,=) \\
(P,L,W-,V,F,O,S) & <_{UWR} & (=,-,R-,-,-,=,=) \\
(P,L,R-,V,F,O,S) & <_{URW} & (=,-,W-,-,-,=,=) \\
(P,L,W-,V,F,O,S) & <_{UWW} & (=,-,W-,-,-,=,=) \\
(P,L,R-,V,F,O,S) & <_{RO} & (=,-,R-,-,-,-,=) \\
(P,L,R-,V,F,O,S) & <_{ROO} & (=,-,R-,-,-,=,=) \\
(P,L,W-,V,F,O,S) & <_{WO} & (=,-,W-,-,-,-,-) \\
(P,L,W-,V,F,O,S) & <_{WOO} & (=,-,W-,-,-,=,-) \\
(P,L,W-,V,F,O,S) & <_{WOS} & (=,-,W-,-,-,-,=) \\
(P,L,-,V,F,O,S) & <_{PO} & (=,-,R-,-,-,-,-) \\
(P,L,-,V,F,O,S) & <_{PO} & (=,-,W-,-,-,-,-) \\
(P,L,-,V,F,O,S) & <_{POO} & (=,-,R-,-,-,=,-) \\
(P,L,-,V,F,O,S) & <_{POO} & (=,-,W-,-,-,=,-) \\
(P,L,-,V,F,O,S) & <_{POS} & (=,-,R-,-,-,-,=) \\
(P,L,-,V,F,O,S) & <_{POS} & (=,-,W-,-,-,-,=) \\
(P,L,-,V,F,O,S) & <_{WA} & (-,-,-,-,-,-,-) \\
(P,L,W-,V,F,O,S) & =_{WA} & (=,=,W-,=,-,=,\#) \\
(P,L,-,V,F,O,S) & <_{SA} & (-,-,-,-,-,-,-) \\
(P,L,-,V,F,O,S) & =_{SA} & (=,=,R-,-,-,-,-) \\
(P,L,-,V,F,O,S) & =_{SA} & (=,=,W-,-,-,-,-) \\
(P,L,W-,V,F,O,S) & <_{WS} & (-,-,W-,-,-,-,=) \\
\end{array}
$$

Figure 14.2. Arcs between events within a statement.

AN EXECUTION SHOWING INTERACTIONS BETWEEN PROCESSORS

Initially, A = 1, B = 2.

P_1 P_2
L_1: A:= B; L_1: B:= A;

Terminally, A = 2, B = 1.

P_1 P_2
$(L_1, R1, -, N, B, S_1)$
$(L_1, W1, 2, R, B, S_1)$
$(L_1, W1, -, N, B, S_2)$
$\qquad\qquad\qquad (L_1, R1, -, N, A, S_2)$
$\qquad\qquad\qquad (L_1, W1, -, N, A, S_1)$
$\qquad\qquad\qquad (L_1, W1, 1, R, A, S_2)$
$(L_1, R2, -, N, A, S_1)$
$(L_1, W2, 2, E, A, S_1)$
$(L_1, W2, -, N, A, S_2)$
$\qquad\qquad\qquad (L_1, R2, -, N, B, S_2)$
$\qquad\qquad\qquad (L_1, W2, -, N, B, S_1)$
$\qquad\qquad\qquad (L_1, W2, 1, E, B, S_2)$

P_1 does not get the current value of A from store S_2, but rather uses the value in the preceding W_1 write events as the value to be written. The purpose of the R_2 event is to interrogate the flag for the operand. When the operand is found not to be flagged exclusive, the W_2 events write not-here flags for the operand in all other caches.

A Write Synchronized Execution

Initially, A = 0.

P_1 P_2
L_1: A:= 1; L_1: A:= 2;

Terminally, A = 1.

If the execution is write synchronized, then one of the ways the events might be interleaved is as follows:

P_1 $\qquad\qquad$ P_2
$(L_1, R1, -, R, 1, S_1)$
$\qquad\qquad\qquad$ $(L_1, R1, -, R, 2, S_2)$
$(L_1, W1, =, =, 1, S_1)$
$\qquad\qquad\qquad$ $(L_1, W1, =, =, 2, S_1)$
$(L_1, W1, =, =, 1, S_2)$
$\qquad\qquad\qquad$ $(L_1, W1, =, =, 2, S_2)$
$(L_1, R2, -, N, A, S_1)$
$\qquad\qquad\qquad$ $(L_1, R2, -, N, A, S_2)$
$(L_1, W2, 1, E, A, S_1)$
$\qquad\qquad\qquad$ $(L_1, W2, -, N, A, S_1)$
$(L_1, W2, -, N, A, S_2)$
$\qquad\qquad\qquad$ $(L_1, W2, 2, E, A, S_2)$

If the W_2 events violate write synchronization, then either both caches can be left holding A flagged as exclusive

P_1 $\qquad\qquad$ P_2
$\qquad\qquad\qquad$ $(L_1, W2, -, N, A, S_1)$
$(L_1, W2, 1, E, A, S_1)$
$(L_1, W2, -, N, A, S_2)$
$\qquad\qquad\qquad$ $(L_1, W2, 2, E, A, S_2)$

or both caches can be left holding A flagged not-here

P_1 $\qquad\qquad$ P_2
$(L_1, W2, 1, E, A, S_1)$
$\qquad\qquad\qquad$ $(L_1, W2, -, N, A, S_1)$
$\qquad\qquad\qquad$ $(L_1, W2, 2, E, A, S_2)$
$(L_1, W2, -, N, A, S_2)$

Deadlock and Livelock

Deadlock and livelock are potential dangers in any system in which processes share data. Deadlock occurs when process P_1 waits to use data held by process P_2; process P_2 waits to use data held by process P_3; . . . ; and process P_n waits to use data held by process P_1. Since there is no possibility of holding onto one operand while waiting for another in the MP model, there is no possibility of deadlock.

In the general case of interacting processes it can happen that two or more processes signal an intent to use some datum, see that other processes have the same intent, and so back off to try again later. Livelock occurs when the cycle of try and back off, try and back off, occurs repeatedly.

What is to prevent livelock in the MP model in, for example, the following execution in which two statements both access the same operand as both source operand and as sink operand?

Phantom Events

Initially, A = 0.

P_1 P_2
L_1: A:= A + 1; L_1: A:= A + 1;

Terminally, A = 1.

P_1	P_2
$(L_1, R1, -, N, A, S_1)$	
	$(L_1, R1, -, N, A, S_2)$
$(L_1, W1, 0, R, A, S_1)$	
$(L_1, W1, -, N, A, S_2)$	
	$(L_1, W1, 0, R, A, S_1)$
	$(L_1, W1, 0, R, A, S_2)$
$(L_1, R1, 1, R, 1, S_1)$	
	$(L_1, R1, 1, R, 1, S_2)$
$(L_1, W1, =, =, 1, S_1)$	
$(L_1, W1, =, =, 1, S_2)$	
	$(L_1, W1, =, =, 1, S_1)$
	$(L_1, W1, =, =, 1, S_2)$
$(L_1, R2, -, R, A, S_1)$	
$(L_1, W2, 1, E, A, S_1)$	
$(L_1, W2, -, N, A, S_2)$	
	$(L_1, R2, -, N, A, S_2)$
	$(L_1, W2, -, N, A, S_1)$
	$(L_1, W2, 1, E, A, S_2)$

A closer look at executions in the MP model shows that, not only is there not a case in which an event has to be repeated (equivalent to backing up), there is not even a case in which a process has to wait. The worst that can happen is that a flag can be set to not-here or read-only so that subsequent W_2 events have to rewrite the flag for the operand in other stores. A flag may be set to not-here so that more work has to be done than if the flag were set to exclusive or not-here, but the progress of subsequent write events is never impeded.

PHANTOM EVENTS

If, in an actual machine, processor P_i reads a sink operand and finds that it is flagged exclusive, then there is no reason for the machine to write into other caches; the operand is required not to exist in any other cache than S_i.

If, in the MP model, process P_i reads a sink operand and finds that it is flagged exclusive, then the model still requires that there be W_2 events for each of the other caches. Such events, required by the model, but unnecessary in real machines, are called phantom events.

Phantom events can play an important role in the architecture and high-level design of a system. For example, in a later section it is shown that in the MP model, just as in the basic model, a write synchronized architecture is indistinguishable from a write atomic architecture. The proof is much simpler when phantom events are defined to exist than it would be if they were absent.

Phantom events may also guide the high level design of real systems. For example, suppose that write operations into operands A, B, and C are to occur in a write synchronized fashion. Represent this by

$$
\begin{array}{ccc}
S_1 & S_2 & S_3 \\
A & A & A \\
B & B & B \\
C & C & B
\end{array}
$$

Suppose some of the events are phantom events, represented by lower case letters.

$$
\begin{array}{ccc}
S_1 & S_2 & S_3 \\
A & A & a \\
b & B & B \\
C & c & C
\end{array}
$$

The real events on S_1 must occur in the order of first A, then C, but the reason for this ordering is due to the ordering of events A and B on S_2 and event B and C on S_3. Keeping the phantom events in mind may assist in preserving the correct sequence of events and may help avoid events occurring out of order, as in

$$
\begin{array}{ccc}
S_1 & S_2 & S_3 \\
C & & \\
A & A & \\
 & B & B \\
 & & C
\end{array}
$$

There are other places where phantom events occur. When a literal operand is read as a source operand, none of the W_1 events need be implemented. When a source operand is read which is flagged either read-only or not-here, the W_1 write events to other caches will change neither the value nor the flag for the operand in the other caches. Therefore, such writes can be treated as phantom events.

In subsequent executions phantom events are shown as having value and read components equal to "=."

THE RELAXATION OF CENSIER AND FEAUTRIER

In a CF machine, that is, a machine which obeys Censier and Feautrier's rule for achieving cache coherence, every fetch operation from an operand is required to see the latest value written into the operand. To ensure adherence to the rule of CF, a real processor might send out invalidate signals at the start of a write operation and wait for responses from other processors before continuing the write operation. This guarantees that any subsequent read event sees the most recent write operation. The following execution shows how CF can be unnecessarily stringent.

The Relaxation of Censier and Feautrier

Initially, A = B = C = 0.

P_1 P_2
L_1: A:= 2; L_1: A:= 1;
L_2: B:= A; L_2: C:= A;

Terminally, A = B = 2, C = 1.

The events in the execution could occur in the following statement atomic order and at the same time calculate the given terminal values.

P_1 P_2
  L_1: A:= 1;
  L_2: C:= A;
L_1: A:= 2;
L_2: B:= A;

Therefore, the execution obeys at least both CF and write atomicity.

Now consider the following write synchronized sequence of events for the execution. CF is strongly violated. P_1 writes into operand A in L_1 without waiting for A to be flagged not-here in S_2. A is flagged exclusive in both caches for some considerable time. And P_1 and P_2 both read operand A during the time that A is flagged exclusive, and each obtains a distinct value. None-the-less, since the sequence is write synchronized, it is certain to appear to be write atomic.

```
         P_1                       P_2
                          (L_1, R1, 1, R, 1, S_2)
                          (L_1, W1, =, =, 1, S_1)
                          (L_1, W1, =, =, 1, S_2)
                          (L_1, R2, -, E, A, S_2)
                          (L_1, W2, -, N, A, S_1)
                          (L_1, W2, 1, E, A, S_2)   ← P_2 flags A exclusive.
(L_1, R1, 2, R, 2, S_1)
(L_1, W1, =, =, 2, S_1)
(L_1, W1, =, =, 2, S_2)
(L_1, R2, -, N, A, S_1)
(L_1, W2, 2, E, A, S_1)                             ← P_1 flags A exclusive.
(L_2, R1, 2, E, A, S_1)                             ← P_1 reads 2 from A.
(L_2, W1, =, =, A, S_1)
(L_2, R2, -, N, B, S_1)
(L_2, W2, 2, E, B, S_1)
                          (L_2, R1, 1, E, A, S_2)   ← P_2 reads 1 from A.
                          (L_2, W1, =, =, A, S_1)
(L_1, W2, -, N, A, S_2)
(L_2, W1, =, =, A, S_2)
(L_2, W2, -, N, B, S_2)
                          (L_2, W1, =, =, A, S_2)
                          (L_2, R2, -, R, C, S_2)
                          (L_2, W2, 1, N, C, S_1)
                          (L_2, W2, 1, E, C, S_2)
```

THE ANALOGUE OF LEMMA 12.5 IN THE MP MODEL

For the MP model also, a write synchronized system (which is not read synchronized) appears to be write atomic.

Theorem 14.1. Let A be an architecture consisting of a subset of the rules in the set {CMP, UWR, URW, UWW, PO, POO, POS, RO, ROO, WO, WOO, WOS, SA}. Let A_1 and A_2 be two architectures such that $A_1 = A * A(WS)$ and $A_2 = A * A(WA)$. Then $A_1 \Leftrightarrow A_2$.

Proof. The proof reduces to verifying the analog of Lemma 12.5.

WOO (P, L, W–, V, F, O, S)

W01	$<_{SRW1}$	(–,–, –,–,–, –,–)	1. $W <_{SRW1}$ –
W02	$<_{SWR}$	(S,L,R2,–,–, –,S)	6. Not determined.
W03	$<_{SRW2}$	(–,–, –,–,–, –,–)	1. $W <_{SRW2}$ –.
W04	$<_{CWR}$	(S,–,R–,V,–, 0,S)	6. Not determined.
W05	$<_{CRW}$	(–,–, –,–,–, –,–)	1. $W <_{CRW}$ –.
W06	$<_{CWW}$	(–,–,W–,–,–, 0,S)	4. $E_1 <_{WS} E_2$.
W07	$<_{UWR}$	(S,–,R–,–,–, 0,S)	6. Not determined.
W08	$<_{URW}$	(–,–, –,–,–, –,–)	1. $W <_{URW}$ –.
W09	$<_{UWW}$	(P,–,W–,–,–, 0,S)	4. $E_1 <_{WS} E_2$.
W10	$<_{RO}$	(–,–, –,–,–, –,–)	1. $W <_{RO}$ –.
W11	$<_{ROO}$	(–,–, –,–,–, –,–)	1. $W <_{ROO}$ –.
W12	$<_{WO}$	(P,–,W–,–,–, –,–)	5. $E_1 < all(E_2)$.
W13	$<_{WOO}$	(P,–,W–,–,–, =,–)	5. $E_1 < all(E_2)$.
W14	$<_{WOS}$	(P,–,W–,–,–, –,S)	4. $E_1 <_{WS} E_2$.
W15	$<_{PO}$	(S,–,R–,–,–, –,S)	6. Not determined.
W16	$<_{PO}$	(P,–,W–,–,–, –,–)	5. $E_1 < all(E_2)$.
W17	$<_{POO}$	(S,–,R–,–,–, 0,S)	6. Not determined.
W18	$<_{POO}$	(P,–,W–,–,–, 0,–)	5. $E_1 < all(E_2)$.
W19	$<_{POS}$	(S,–,R–,–,–, –,S)	6. Not determined.
W20	$<_{POS}$	(P,–,W–,–,–, –,S)	4. $E_1 <_{WS} E_2$.
W21	$<_{WA}$	(–,–, –,–,–, –,–)	2b. Fail.
W22	$=_{WA}$	(P,L,W–,V,–, 0,–)	2c. Fail.
W23	$<_{SA}$	(–,–, –,–,–, –,–)	2b. Fail.
W24	$=_{SA}$	(S,L,R–,–,–, –,S)	6. Not determined.
W25	$=_{SA}$	(P,L,W–,–,–, –,–)	2c. Fail.
W26	$<_{WS}$	(–,–,W–,–,–, –,S)	4. $E_1 <_{WS} E_2$.
R00		(S,–,R–,–,–, –,S)	6. Not determined.
R01	$<_{SRW1}$	(S,–,W1,–,–, –,–)	5. $E_2 < all(E_3)$.
R02	$<_{SWR}$	(–,–, –,–,–, –,–)	1. $R– <_{SWR}$ –.
R03	$<_{SRW2}$	(S,–,W2,–,–, –,–)	5. $E_2 < all(E_3)$.
R04	$<_{CWR}$	(–,–, –,–,–, –,–)	1. $R– <_{CWR}$ –.
R05	$<_{CRW}$	(–,–,W–,–,–, –,S)	4. $E_1 <_{WS} E_3$.
R06	$<_{CWW}$	(–,–, –,–,–, –,–)	1. $R– <_{CWW}$ –.
R07	$<_{UWR}$	(–,–, –,–,–, –,–)	1. $R– <_{UWR}$ –.
R08	$<_{URW}$	(S,–,W–,–,–, –,S)	4. $E_1 <_{WS} E_3$.
R09	$<_{UWW}$	(–,–, –,–,–, –,–)	1. $R– <_{UWW}$ –.

R10	$<_{RO}$	(S,−,R−,−,−,−,S)	3. P−R−P < P−R−P.
R11	$<_{ROO}$	(S,−,R−,−,−,−,S)	3. P−R−P < P−R−P.
R12	$<_{WO}$	(−,−, −,−,−,−,−)	1. R− $<_{WO}$ −.
R13	$<_{WOO}$	(−,−, −,−,−,−,−)	1. R− $<_{WOO}$ −.
R14	$<_{WOS}$	(−,−, −,−,−,−,−)	1. R− $<_{WOS}$ −.
R15	$<_{PO}$	(S,−,R−,−,−,−,S)	3. P−R−P < P−R−P.
R16	$<_{PO}$	(S,−,W−,−,−,−,−)	5. E_2 < all(E_3).
R17	$<_{POO}$	(S,−,R−,−,−,−,S)	3. P−R−P < P−R−P.
R18	$<_{POO}$	(S,−,W−,−,−,−,−)	5. E_2 < all(E_3).
R19	$<_{POS}$	(S,−,R−,−,−,−,S)	3. P−R−P < P−R−P.
R20	$<_{POS}$	(S,−,W−,−,−,−,S)	4. E_1 $<_{WS}$ E_3.
R21	$<_{WA}$	(−,−, −,−,−,−,−)	2b. Fail.
R22	$=_{WA}$	(−,−, −,−,−,−,−)	1. R− $=_{WA}$ −.
R23	$<_{SA}$	(−,−, −,−,−,−,−)	2b. Fail.
R24	$=_{SA}$	(S,−,R−,−,−,−,S)	3. P−R−P < P−R−P.
R25	$=_{SA}$	(S,−,W−,−,−,−,−)	5. E_2 < all(E_3).
R26	$<_{WS}$	(−,−, −,−,−,−,−)	1. R− $<_{WS}$ −.

Explanations

1. R (W) <xxx −. A read (write) event cannot have an arc labeled <xxx incident out of it.
2a. Fail. The lemma fails irreparably on arcs labeled $<_{RS}$.
2b. Fail. Arcs labeled $<_{RA}$, $<_{WA}$, and $<_{SA}$ are excluded from the lemma (but see Lemma 7.2).
2c. Fail. Arcs labeled $=_{WA}$, $=_{SA}$, $<_{AWC}$, and $<_{RWC}$ are excluded from the lemma (but see Lemma 12.4).
3. P−R−P < P−R−P. Two read events in sequence in a path have the same process and store components.
4. E_1 $<_{WS}$ E_i. There is a path from E_1 to E_i. The two write events have the same store component. Since the execution is write synchronized and circuit-free, there is also an arc labeled $<_{WS}$ from E_1 to E_i. Hence, E_1 $<_{WS}$ $X(E_i, E_1)$.
5. E_i <xxx all(E_j). By the definition of <xxx if E_i <xxx E_j, then E_i <xxx E_k, where E_k is any other write event in the statement containing E_j. In particular, E_i $<_{WS}$ $X(E_i, E_j)$.
6. Not Determined. There is insufficient information in the event either to prove or to disprove the lemma at this event in the path. Therefore continue the search at the next level down in the tree.

PROBLEMS

*14.1. Define the CMP rule for the MP model. Ignore literals.

*14.2. Can you see a failure to be WA among the W_1 events of a statement? If so, show how. If not, prove that it cannot be seen.

*14.3. Define two forms of read atomicity among the read events within a statement. RA_1 refers only to the R_1 events. RA_2 refers to both R_1 and R_2 events. Can the two cases be distinguished, that is, can you demonstrate an execution that obeys RA_1, but demonstrably does not obey RA_2? If so, do. Else prove.

15

Future Work

THE LIMITS ON DISOBEYING RULES

Suppose a machine obeys some complex architecture such as A(CMP, RO, WO, WS, AWC, RRC). When the time comes for the machine to execute a program, one could argue that the machine does not have to obey A(CMP, RO, WO, WS, AWC, RRC); it only has to generate, via any conceivable mechanism, an answer that falls into the set of correct answers. This prompts the following question: what are the limits on violating the rules of an architecture? One answer is supplied by a machine which obeys the Principle of Totally Unconstrained Implementation (PTUI).

The PTUI computer is table driven. Rather than actually doing any real computation, the PTUI computer simply reads in a program and its input data and looks them up in a table. It then randomly selects one of several answers in the table entry and prints the answer out. If there is no entry for the program and its input data, PTUI prints out the message "MEMORY OVERFLOW" and stops.

What is the architecture of PTUI? It clearly has nothing to do with its hardware implementation. A change in the contents of the table converts PTUI from a machine that obeys A(CMP, PO, SA) to a machine that obeys A(RRC, RS), from a machine that prints out "sensible" answers to a machine that generates garbage, all without soldering a single circuit.

The point of the PTUI computer is that there are no rules that the implementation of a computer absolutely has to follow. It may be efficient to implement the rules in some cases, to implement a logically indistinguishable set of rules in other cases, and in yet other cases to violate the rules, but to recover when the violation could be detected. The three cases are illustrated by CMP in Chap. 5, the WSISWA

Theorem in Chap. 12, and Frey's Theorem in Chap. 11. The next two sections and the problem set look at some further ways the rules might be relaxed.

CONDITIONAL RULES

Consider the execution in Fig. 15.1.

```
Initially, A = B = C = D = 0.

       P₁                    P₂
L₁: A:= 1;             L₁: C:= 3;
L₂: B:= 2;             L₂: D:= 4;

Terminally, A = 1, B = 2, C = 3, D = 4.
```

Figure 15.1 Example of the utility of conditional rules.

The execution in Fig. 15.1 computes the correct answers whether it obeys A(CMP) or A(CMP, PO, WA) or something in between. It seems wasteful to require the write events in the execution to be write atomic (or even WS) when there is obviously no interaction among the events of the statements. Thus, the question arises whether or not it is possible to require an execution to be WA only when, in some sense, it counts.

Define a new rule, called Conditional Write Atomicity (CWA). Let GS_1 be the graph set for an execution E under some architecture A_1. Then the graph set for E under $A_1 * A(CWA)$ is constructed by taking each graph G_1 in GS_1 and adding arcs labeled $<_{CWA}$ in the following fashion. If $E_1 < W_2$ in G_1, where W_2 is a write event and $<$ represents an arc with any label, then for all write events W_j in the same statement as W_2, $E_1 <_{CWA} W_j$. Similarly with $W_1 < E_2$.

All rules up until now were defined in such a way that they commuted; $A(R_1) * A(R_2) = A(R_2) * A(R_1)$. Further, the empty set $\emptyset$ acted as an identity; $\emptyset * R = R * \emptyset = R$. For the rule CWA commutativity no longer holds. Assume that $R_1 * R_2$ means that R_1 is applied to the events of an execution and then R_2 is applied to the graphs in the resulting graph set. Then $\emptyset * CWA = \emptyset$, not CWA. And CWA * CMP, for example, is CMP, not CMP * CWA.

Under A(CMP, PO, WA) the events of the preceding execution are far more tightly structured than under A(CMP, PO, CWA) in the following sense. In the graphs in a graph set for an execution E under A(CMP, PO, WA) there are arcs from an event X not in an atomic write set to every event which is in an atomic write set. Under A(CMP, PO, CWA) there are arcs, labelled CWA, from X to the events in the atomic write set only if there is an adjacent path from X to some event in the atomic write set. (The argument can be repeated for arcs from the events in the atomic set to X.)

Rules on Global Events versus Rules on All Events

To avoid ambiguity in the meaning of architectures containing one or more conditional rules, require that the conditional rules be applied only to the graph set for the nonconditional rules.

Conjecture 15.1. For any architecture A, A * A(CWA) ⇔ A * A(WA).

***Proof of* ⇐.** Let G_2 be any element of GS_2, the graph set for an execution E under A * A(WA). Let S be a write atomic set, and let x be any node not in the atomic set. If there is no path from x to any members of S other than arcs labelled $<_{WA}$, then delete the arcs labelled $<_{WA}$ from the graph. Relabel with $<_{CWA}$ the remaining arcs labeled $<_{WA}$. Then the resulting graph is a member of GS_1, the graph set for E under A * A(CWA). Consequently, if GS_2 is partly circuit-free, then so is GS_1. ■

***Proof of* ⇒.** Open.

Of course, what is needed to make Conjecture 15.1 useful is a result linking CWA and CWS, conditional write synchronization.

Conjecture 15.2. For any architecture A which does not include read synchronization, A * A(CWS) ⇔ A * A(CWA).

RULES ON GLOBAL EVENTS VERSUS RULES ON ALL EVENTS

The circuits in the proofs of the theorems in App. A all contain events whose operands are global, not local. It is clear that CMP and UPO have to be defined on both local and global data. Could it be, however, that the other rules need to be defined only on global operands?

Consider, for example, program order. PO required all events within a process to be ordered by $<_O$. Define PO+ to be program order restricted to events for global operands: $E_1 <_{PO+} E_2$ if $E_1 <_{PO} E_2$ and if the operand components of E_1 and E_2 are both global operands.

Here is a conjecture that says that given that an architecture has to be UPO, then it suffices to be PO+ in order to appear to be PO.

Conjecture 15.3. For any architecture A, A * A(UPO, PO+) ⇔ A * A(PO).

***Proof of* ⇐.** PO ⇒ UPO. PO ⇒ PO+.

***Proof of* ⇒.** Open.

Similar conjectures may hold for many of the rules other than CMP and UPO. For example, under the definition of WS there can be an arc from an event on a local or global operand in one process to an event on a local or global operand in a different process. That only WS+ is necessary is suggested by the fact that circuits in the proofs in App. A show only events with a global operand connected by arcs labeled $<_{WS}$.

PROBLEMS

15.1. The PTUI Computer Company's newest machine generates only write atomic answers. However, the architecture for the machine says that the machine does not obey the rule of write atomicity. Can any program detect that the machine does not obey its architecture?

*15.2. Prove Conjecture 15.1.

*15.3. Prove Conjecture 15.2.

*15.4. Prove Conjecture 15.3.

*15.5. Many of the theorems in App. A prove that an execution does not belong to an architecture of the form $A(CMP, R_w, R_r)$, where R_w is a rule involving write events and R_r is a rule involving read events. Why does this pattern recur so often?

*15.6. Is it possible to prove $A(CMP) \neg \Rightarrow A(CMP, ARC)$? Or $A(CMP) \neg \Rightarrow A(CMP, WS)$? If so, do. If not, prove it to be impossible.

15.7. Extend the definition of CMP to include the rule CRR which generates arcs labeled $<_{CRR}$ as follows. For any execution E under $A(CMP)$ let R_1 and R_2 be any two read events occurring in a SOSS sequence with no intervening write event. Then the graph $(\{R_1, R_2\}, \{R_1 < R_2, R_2 < R_1\})$ is contained in the graph set for E under $A(CRR)$.

Let A_1 be any architecture which does not contain CRR. Let $A_2 = A_1 * A(CRR)$. Prove that $A_1 \Leftrightarrow A_2$. (Hint. Use Lemma 3.5.)

*15.8. Addition, a commutative operator, was the only operator defined to connect source operands. Would a noncommutative operator be more effective in detecting differences between architectures? In the following execution there is no way that a failure to be write ordered can be observed.

Initially, A = B = X = 0.

P_1
L_1: X:= A + B;

P_2
L_1: A:= 1;
L_2: B:= 1;

Terminally, A = B = X = 1.

However, if the noncommutative operator of concatenation, ||, is used, it is possible to see a failure to be write ordered.

Initially, A = B = X = 0.

P_1
L_1: X:= A||B;

P_2
L_1: A:= 1;
L_2: B:= 1;

Terminally, A = B = 1, X = 0||1.

On the other hand the same acuity of perception is achievable with distinct literal operands.

Initially, $A = B = X = 0$.

$$
\begin{array}{ll}
P_1 & P_2 \\
L_1: X := A + B; & L_1: A := 1; \\
& L_2: B := 2;
\end{array}
$$

Terminally, $A = 1, B = X = 2$.

Does a noncommutative operator ever allow architectures to be distinguished which could not be distinguished with a commutative operator and distinct values of literal operands?

Appendix A

Distinguishable Architectures

Two architectures are distinct if there is an execution that obeys one of the architectures but not the other. The theorems below distinguish pairs of architectures. The theorems have the form $A(X,Y) \neg \Rightarrow A(X,Y,Z)$ where X, Y, and Z are architectural rules. In each proof an execution is shown which obeys $A(X,Y)$, but does not obey $A(X,Y,Z)$.

The theorems are grouped so that all executions which fail to obey a given rule are listed together. For example, the theorems which show that an execution is not write atomic are listed together (A28, A29, A30, and A31). The order of the groups parallels the order in which the rules are presented in the text.

To find all the theorems which describe a failure to obey a given rule may require the use of the tree structure in Chap. 10 to identify which architectures imply which other architectures. For example, there are only two theorems in the list which explicitly describe a failure to be write atomic, but there are nine other theorems which implicitly describe a failure to be write atomic. Since WA $\Rightarrow$ CON, WA $\Rightarrow$ WS, WS $\Rightarrow$ AWC, and WS $\Rightarrow$ RWC, the theorems which exhibit a failure to be CON, WS, AWC, and RWC also describe failures to be write atomic.

Corollaries can be formed for many of the theorems. Rule R can be added to $A(X,Y) \neg \Rightarrow A(X,Y,Z)$ to form the theorem $A(X,Y,R) \neg \Rightarrow A(X,Y,R,Z)$ if the linear ordering of events showing an execution obeys $A(X,Y)$ also obeys $A(R)$. Most such corollaries offer no new insight. Occasionally, a corollary is stated either because it is not entirely obvious or because it is discussed in the text.

Appendix A

REFERENCES

Theorems A29 is from [DUBO86], cited in Chap. 2. Theorem A4 is from [SMIT72]. Theorems A24 and A28 are new. The rest are from [COLL84], cited in Chap. 2.

SMIT72. R. M. SMITH. Private communication. 1972.

1. Theorem A1.   A(CMP) $\neg \Rightarrow$ A(CMP,UWR).
2. Theorem A2.   A(CMP) $\neg \Rightarrow$ A(CMP,URW).
3. Theorem A3.   A(CMP) $\neg \Rightarrow$ A(CMP,UWW).

4. Theorem A4.   A(CMP) $\neg \Rightarrow$ A(CMP,PO).
5. Theorem A5.   A(CMP) $\neg \Rightarrow$ A(CMP,PO).
6. Theorem A6.   A(CMP) $\neg \Rightarrow$ A(CMP,WO).
7. Theorem A7.   A(CMP,RO) $\neg \Rightarrow$ A(CMP,RO, WO).
8. Theorem A8.   A(CMP,POS) $\neg \Rightarrow$ A(CMP,POS,WO).
9. Theorem A9.   A(CMP,SA) $\neg \Rightarrow$ A(CMP,SA, WO).
10. Theorem A10. A(CMP,RS) $\neg \Rightarrow$ A(CMP,RS, WO).
11. Theorem A11. A(CMP,ARC) $\neg \Rightarrow$ A(CMP,ARC,WO).
12. Theorem A12. A(CMP,RRC) $\neg \Rightarrow$ A(CMP,RRC,WO).
13. Theorem A13. A(CMP) $\neg \Rightarrow$ A(CMP,   RO).
14. Theorem A14. A(CMP,WO) $\neg \Rightarrow$ A(CMP,WO, RO).
15. Theorem A15. A(CMP,SA) $\neg \Rightarrow$ A(CMP,SA, RO).
16. Theorem A16. A(CMP,WA) $\neg \Rightarrow$ A(CMP,WA, RO).
17. Theorem A17. A(CMP,CON) $\neg \Rightarrow$ A(CMP,CON,RO).
18. Theorem A18. A(CMP,WS) $\neg \Rightarrow$ A(CMP,WS, RO).
19. Theorem A19. A(CMP,AWC) $\neg \Rightarrow$ A(CMP,AWC,RO).
20. Theorem A20. A(CMP,RWC) $\neg \Rightarrow$ A(CMP,RWC,RO).
21. Theorem A21. A(CMP,WO) $\neg \Rightarrow$ A(CMP,WO, POS).
22. Theorem A22. A(CMP,WS) $\neg \Rightarrow$ A(CMP,WS, POS).
23. Theorem A23. A(CMP,CON) $\neg \Rightarrow$ A(CMP,CON,POS).
24. Theorem A24. A(CMP,WA) $\neg \Rightarrow$ A(CMP,WA, WOS).

25. Theorem A25. A(CMP) $\neg \Rightarrow$ A(CMP,SA).
26. Theorem A26. A(CMP,WO) $\neg \Rightarrow$ A(CMP,WO, SA).
27. Theorem A27. A(CMP,RO) $\neg \Rightarrow$ A(CMP,RO, SA).
28. Theorem A28. A(CMP,WOS) $\neg \Rightarrow$ A(CMP,WOS,WA).
29. Theorem A29. A(CMP,RO) $\neg \Rightarrow$ A(CMP,RO, WA).
30. Theorem A30. A(CMP,RA) $\neg \Rightarrow$ A(CMP,RA, WA).
31. Theorem A31. A(CMP,RS) $\neg \Rightarrow$ A(CMP,RS, WA).
32. Theorem A32. A(CMP,WO) $\neg \Rightarrow$ A(CMP,WO, RA).
33. Theorem A33. A(CMP,WS) $\neg \Rightarrow$ A(CMP,WS, RA).
34. Theorem A34. A(CMP,WA) $\neg \Rightarrow$ A(CMP,WA, RA).

35. Theorem A35. A(CMP) $\neg \Rightarrow$ A(CMP,CON).
36. Theorem A36. A(CMP,RO) $\neg \Rightarrow$ A(CMP,RO, CON).
37. Theorem A37. A(CMP,POS) $\neg \Rightarrow$ A(CMP,POS,CON).

38. Theorem A38.	A(CMP,RO)	$\neg \Rightarrow$	A(CMP,RO, WS).
39. Theorem A39.	A(CMP,POS)	$\neg \Rightarrow$	A(CMP,POS,WS).
40. Theorem A40.	A(CMP,RA)	$\neg \Rightarrow$	A(CMP,RA, WS).
41. Theorem A41.	A(CMP,WO)	$\neg \Rightarrow$	A(CMP,WO, RS).
42. Theorem A42.	A(CMP,WA)	$\neg \Rightarrow$	A(CMP,WA, RS).
43. Theorem A43.	A(CMP,RO)	$\neg \Rightarrow$	A(CMP,RO, AWC).
44. Theorem A44.	A(CMP,ARC)	$\neg \Rightarrow$	A(CMP,ARC,AWC).
45. Theorem A45.	A(CMP,RO)	$\neg \Rightarrow$	A(CMP,RO, RWC).
46. Theorem A46.	A(CMP,WO)	$\neg \Rightarrow$	A(CMP,WO, ARC).
47. Theorem A47.	A(CMP,AWC)	$\neg \Rightarrow$	A(CMP,AWC,ARC).
48. Theorem A48.	A(CMP,WO)	$\neg \Rightarrow$	A(CMP,WO, RRC).

Theorem A1. $A(CMP) \neg \Rightarrow A(CMP, UWR)$.

Proof. Consider the following execution.

```
Initially, X = Y = 0.

        P₁
L₁: X:= 1;
L₂: Y:= X;

Terminally, X = 1, Y = 0.
```

Under architecture A(CMP,UWR) every member of the graph set for the execution contains the following circuit:

$$(P_1,L_1,W,1,X,S_1) <_{UWR} (P_1,L_2,R,0,X,S_1)$$
$$<_{CRW} (P_1,L_1,W,1,X,S_1)$$

Under architecture A(CMP) there is an element of the graph set for the execution which is circuit-free (though not UWR).

```
        P₁
(L₁,R,1,1,S₁)
(L₂,R,0,X,S₁)
(L₁,W,1,X,S₁)
(L₂,W,0,Y,S₁)
```

Theorem A2. $A(CMP) \neg \Rightarrow A(CMP, URW)$.

Proof. Consider the following execution.

Appendix A

```
Initially, X = Y = 0.

        P₁
L₁: Y:= X;
L₂: X:= 1;

Terminally, X = Y = 1.
```

Under architecture A(CMP,URW) every member of the graph set for the execution contains the following circuit:

$$(P_1, L_1, R, 1, X, S_1) \quad <_{URW} \quad (P_1, L_2, W, 1, X, S_1)$$
$$<_{CWR} \quad (P_1, L_1, R, 1, X, S_1)$$

Under architecture A(CMP) there is an element of the graph set for the execution which is circuit-free (though not URW).

```
        P₁
(L₂, R, 1, 1, S₁)
(L₂, W, 1, X, S₁)
(L₁, R, 1, X, S₁)
(L₁, W, 1, Y, S₁)
```

Theorem A3. A(CMP) ¬⇒ A(CMP, UWW).

Proof. Consider the following execution.

```
Initially, X = 0.

        P₁
L₁: X:= 2;
L₂: X:= 1;

Terminally, X = 2.
```

Under architecture A(CMP,UWW) every member of the graph set for the execution contains the following circuit:

$$(P_1, L_1, W, 2, X, S_1) \quad <_{UWW} \quad (P_1, L_2, W, 1, X, S_1)$$
$$<_{CWW} \quad (P_1, L_1, W, 2, X, S_1)$$

Under architecture A(CMP) there is an element of the graph set for the execution which is circuit-free (though not UWW).

```
        P₁
(L₁, R, 2, 2, S₁)
(L₂, R, 1, 1, S₁)
(L₂, W, 1, X, S₁)
(L₁, W, 2, X, S₁)
```

Theorem A4. $A(CMP) \neg \Rightarrow A(CMP, PO)$.

Proof. Consider the following execution.

$$\text{Initially, } A = B = X = Y = 0.$$

$$\begin{array}{ll} P_1 & P_2 \\ L_1: Y := B; & L_1: X := A; \\ L_2: A := 1; & L_2: B := 1; \end{array}$$

$$\text{Terminally, } A = B = X = Y = 1.$$

Under architecture $A(CMP,PO)$ every member of the graph set for the execution contains the following circuit:

$$\begin{array}{ll} (P_1, L_1, R, 1, B, S_1) & <_{PO} \quad (P_1, L_2, W, 1, A, S_2) \\ & <_{CWR} \quad (P_2, L_1, R, 1, A, S_2) \\ & <_{PO} \quad (P_2, L_2, W, 1, B, S_1) \\ & <_{CWR} \quad (P_1, L_1, R, 1, B, S_1) \end{array}$$

Under architecture $A(CMP)$ there is an element of the graph set for the execution which is circuit-free (though not PO).

$$\begin{array}{ll} P_1 & P_2 \\ & (L_2, R, 1, 1, S_2) \\ & (L_2, W, 1, B, S) \\ (L_1, R, 1, B, S_1) & \\ (L_1, W, 1, Y, S) & \\ (L_2, R, 1, 1, S_1) & \\ (L_2, W, 1, A, S) & \\ & (L_1, R, 1, A, S_2) \\ & (L_1, W, 1, X, S) \end{array}$$

Theorem A5. $A(CMP) \neg \Rightarrow A(CMP, PO)$.

Proof. Consider the following execution.

$$\text{Initially, } A = B = X = Y = 0.$$

$$\begin{array}{ll} P_1 & P_2 \\ L_1: A := 1; & L_1: B := 1; \\ L_2: X := B; & L_2: Y := A; \end{array}$$

$$\text{Terminally, } A = B = 1, X = Y = 0.$$

Under architecture A(CMP,PO) every member of the graph set for the execution contains the following circuit:

$$(P_1,L_1,W,1,A,S_2) <_{PO} (P_1,L_2,R,0,B,S_1)$$
$$<_{CRW} (P_2,L_1,W,1,B,S_1)$$
$$<_{PO} (P_2,L_2,R,0,A,S_2)$$
$$<_{CRW} (P_1,L_1,W,1,A,S_2)$$

Under architecture A(CMP) there is an element of the graph set for the execution which is circuit-free (though not PO).

P_1 $\quad\quad\quad\quad P_2$

$(L_1,R,1,1,S_1)$
$(L_1,W,1,A,S_1)$
$(L_2,R,0,B,S_1)$

$\quad\quad\quad\quad (L_1,R,1,1,S_2)$
$\quad\quad\quad\quad (L_1,W,1,B,S)$
$\quad\quad\quad\quad (L_2,R,0,A,S_2)$
$\quad\quad\quad\quad (L_2,W,0,Y,S)$

$(L_1,W,1,A,S_2)$
$(L_2,W,0,X,S)$

Theorem A6. $A(CMP) \neg \Rightarrow A(CMP, WO)$.

Proof. Consider the following execution.

Initially, $A = B = 0$.

$\quad\quad P_1 \quad\quad\quad\quad P_2$
L_1: $A := 1$; $\quad L_1$: $B := 1$;
L_2: $B := 2$; $\quad L_2$: $A := 2$;

Terminally, $A = B = 1$.

Under architecture A(CMP,WO) every member of the graph set for the execution contains both of the following two circuits, $S_x = S_1$ and S_2:

$$(P_1,L_1,W,1,A,S_x) <_{WO} (P_1,L_2,W,2,B,S_x)$$
$$<_{CWW} (P_2,L_1,W,1,B,S_x)$$
$$<_{WO} (P_2,L_2,W,2,A,S_x)$$
$$<_{CWW} (P_1,L_1,W,1,A,S_x)$$

Under architecture A(CMP) there is an element of the graph set for the execution which is circuit-free (though not WO).

$$
\begin{array}{ll}
P_1 & P_2 \\
(L_1,R,1,1,S_1) & \\
& (L_1,R,1,1,S_2) \\
(L_2,R,2,2,S_1) & \\
& (L_2,R,2,2,S_2) \\
& (L_2,W,2,A,S) \\
(L_1,W,1,A,S) & \\
(L_2,W,2,B,S) & \\
& (L_1,W,1,B,S)
\end{array}
$$

Theorem A7. $A(CMP, RO) \neg \Rightarrow A(CMP, RO, WO)$.

Proof. Consider the following execution.

```
            Initially, A = B = X = Y = 0.

         P₁                   P₂
    L₁: A:= 1;           L₁: Y:= B;
    L₂: B:= 1;           L₂: X:= A;

            Terminally, A = B = Y = 1, X = 0.
```

Under architecture $A(CMP, RO, WO)$ every member of the graph set for the execution contains the following circuit:

$$
\begin{array}{lll}
(P_1,L_1,W,1,A,S_2) & <_{WO} & (P_1,L_2,W,1,B,S_2) \\
& <_{CWR} & (P_2,L_1,R,1,B,S_2) \\
& <_{RO} & (P_2,L_2,R,0,A,S_2) \\
& <_{CRW} & (P_1,L_1,W,1,A,S_2)
\end{array}
$$

Under architecture $A(CMP, RO)$ there is an element of the graph set for the execution which is circuit-free (though not WO).

$$
\begin{array}{ll}
P_1 & P_2 \\
(L_1,R,1,1,S_1) & \\
(L_2,R,1,1,S_1) & \\
(L_2,W,1,B,S) & \\
& (L_1,R,1,B,S_2) \\
& (L_1,W,1,Y,S) \\
& (L_2,R,0,A,S_2) \\
& (L_2,W,0,X,S) \\
(L_1,W,1,A,S) &
\end{array}
$$

Theorem A8. $A(CMP, POS) \neg \Rightarrow A(CMP, POS, WO)$.

Proof. Consider the following execution.

Appendix A

Initially, $A = B = X = 0$.

$$P_1 \qquad\qquad P_2$$
L_1: $A := 1$; $\qquad$ L_1: $B := 1$;
L_2: $X := B$; $\qquad$ L_2: $A := 2$;

Terminally, $A = 2$, $B = 1$, $X = 0$.

Under architecture A(CMP, WO, POS) every member of the graph set for the execution contains the following circuit:

$$(P_1, L_1, W, 1, A, S_1) <_{POS} (P_1, L_2, R, 0, B, S_1)$$
$$<_{CRW} (P_2, L_1, W, 1, B, S_1)$$
$$<_{WO} (P_2, L_2, W, 2, A, S_1)$$
$$<_{CWW} (P_1, L_1, W, 1, A, S_1)$$

Under architecture A(CMP, POS) there is an element of the graph set for the execution which is circuit-free (though not WO).

$$P_1 \qquad\qquad P_2$$
$(L_1, R, 1, 1, S_1)$
$(L_1, W, 1, A, S_1)$
$(L_2, R, 0, B, S_1)$
$(L_2, W, 0, X, S_1)$

$\qquad\qquad\qquad (L_1, R, 1, 1, S_2)$
$\qquad\qquad\qquad (L_1, W, 1, B, S)$
$\qquad\qquad\qquad (L_2, R, 2, 2, S_2)$
$\qquad\qquad\qquad (L_2, W, 2, A, S_1)$

$(L_1, W, 1, A, S_2)$
$\qquad\qquad\qquad (L_2, W, 2, A, S_2)$
$(L_2, W, 0, X, S_2)$

Theorem A9. A(CMP, SA) $\neg \Rightarrow$ A(CMP, SA, WO).

Proof. Consider the following execution.

Initially, $A = B = 0$.

$$P_1 \qquad\qquad P_2$$
L_1: $A := 1$; $\qquad$ L_1: $B := A$;
L_2: $B := 2$;

Terminally, $A = 1$, $B = 0$.

Under architecture A(CMP, WO, SA) every member of the graph set for the execution contains both of the following two circuits, corresponding to $S_x = S_1$ and $S_x = S_2$.

$$(P_1,L_1,W,1,A,S_2) \quad <_{WO} \quad (P_1,L_2,W,2,B,S_x)$$
$$<_{CWW} \quad (P_2,L_1,W,0,B,S_x)$$
$$=_{SA} \quad (P_2,L_1,R,0,A,S_2)$$
$$<_{CRW} \quad (P_1,L_1,W,1,A,S_2)$$

Under architecture A(CMP, SA) there is an element of the graph set for the execution which is circuit-free (though not WO).

$$
\begin{array}{ll}
P_1 & P_2 \\
(L_2,R,2,2,S_1) & \\
(L_2,W,2,B,S) & \\
& (L_1,R,0,A,S_2) \\
& (L_1,W,0,B,S) \\
(L_1,R,1,1,S_1) & \\
(L_1,W,1,A,S) & \\
\end{array}
$$

Theorem A10. $A(CMP, RS) \neg \Rightarrow A(CMP, RS, WO)$.

Proof. Consider the following execution.

Initially, A = B = X = Y = 0.

```
         P₁              P₂                P₃
L₁: A:= 1;      L₁: X:= A + B;    L₁: Y:= A + B;
L₂: A:= 2;
L₃: B:= 4;
L₄: B:= 8;
```

Terminally, A = 2, B = 8, X = 8, Y = 2.

Under architecture A(RS) every element of the graph set for the execution contains one of the following two pairs of paths:

$$(P_2,L_1,R,0,A,S_2) \quad <_{RS} \quad (P_3,L_1,R,2,A,S_3)$$
$$(P_2,L_1,R,8,B,S_2) \quad <_{RS} \quad (P_3,L_1,R,0,B,S_3)$$

$$(P_3,L_1,R,2,A,S_3) \quad <_{RS} \quad (P_2,L_1,R,0,A,S_2)$$
$$(P_3,L_1,R,0,B,S_3) \quad <_{RS} \quad (P_2,L_1,R,8,B,S_2)$$

Consequently, under architecture A(CMP, RS, WO) every member of the graph set for the execution contains one of the following two circuits:

$$(P_2,L_1,R,8,B,S_2) \quad <_{RS} \quad (P_3,L_1,R,0,B,S_3)$$
$$<_{CRW} \quad (P_1,L_3,W,4,B,S_3)$$
$$<_{WO} \quad (P_1,L_4,W,8,B,S_2)$$
$$<_{CWR} \quad (P_2,L_1,R,8,B,S_2)$$

Appendix A

$$(P_3, L_1, R, 2, A, S_3) \quad <_{RS} \quad (P_2, L_1, R, 0, A, S_2)$$
$$<_{CRW} \quad (P_1, L_1, W, 1, A, S_2)$$
$$<_{WO} \quad (P_1, L_2, W, 2, A, S_3)$$
$$<_{CWR} \quad (P_3, L_1, R, 2, A, S_3)$$

Under architecture A(CMP, RS) there is an element of the graph set for the execution which is circuit-free (though not WO).

P_1	P_2	P_3
	$(L_1, R, 0, A, S_2)$	
$(L_1, R, 1, 1, S_1)$		
$(L_1, W, 1, A, S)$		
$(L_2, R, 2, 2, S_1)$		
$(L_2, W, 2, A, S)$		
		$(L_1, R, 2, A, S_3)$
$(L_3, R, 4, 4, S_1)$		
$(L_4, R, 8, 8, S_1)$		
$(L_4, W, 8, B, S)$		
	$(L_1, R, 8, B, S_2)$	
	$(L_1, W, 8, X, S)$	
		$(L_1, R, 0, B, S_3)$
		$(L_1, W, 2, Y, S)$
$(L_3, W, 4, B, S)$		

Theorem A11. A(CMP, ARC) $\neg \Rightarrow$ A(CMP, ARC, WO).

Proof. Consider the following execution.

Initially, A = B = X = 0.

P_1	P_2
L_1: X:= A + B;	L_1: B:= 2;
	L_2: A:= 1;

Terminally, A = 1, B = 2, X = 1.

Under architecture A(CMP, WO, ARC) every member of the graph set for the execution contains the following circuit:

$$(P_1, L_1, R, 0, B, S_1) \quad <_{CRW} \quad (P_2, L_1, W, 2, B, S_1)$$
$$<_{WO} \quad (P_2, L_2, W, 1, A, S_1)$$
$$<_{CWR} \quad (P_1, L_1, R, 1, A, S_1)$$
$$<_{ARC} \quad (P_1, L_1, R, 0, B, S_1)$$

Under architecture A(CMP, WO, ARC) there is an element of the graph set for the execution which is circuit-free (though not WO).

P_1 P_2
                             $(L_1, R, 2, 2, S_2)$
                             $(L_2, R, 1, 1, S_2)$
                             $(L_2, W, 1, A, S)$
$(L_1, R, 0, B, S_1)$
$(L_1, R, 1, A, S_1)$
                             $(L_1, W, 2, B, S)$
$(L_1, W, 1, X, S)$

Theorem A12. A(CMP, RRC) $\neg \Rightarrow$ A(CMP, RRC, WO).

Proof. Consider the following execution.

Initially, A = B = X = Y = 0.

P_1 P_2 P_3 P_4
L_1: A:= 1; L_1: B:= 4; L_1: X:= A + B; L_1: Y:= A + B;
L_2: B:= 2; L_2: A:= 8;

Terminally, A = 8, B = 2, X = 2, Y = 8.

Under architecture A(RRC) every element of the graph set for the execution contains one of the following two pairs of paths:

$(P_3, L_1, R, 0, A, S_3)$ $<_{RRC}$ $(P_3, L_1, R, 2, B, S_3)$
$(P_4, L_1, R, 8, A, S_4)$ $<_{RRC}$ $(P_4, L_1, R, 0, B, S_4)$

$(P_3, L_1, R, 2, B, S_3)$ $<_{RRC}$ $(P_3, L_1, R, 0, A, S_3)$
$(P_4, L_1, R, 0, B, S_4)$ $<_{RRC}$ $(P_4, L_1, R, 8, A, S_4)$

Consequently, under architecture A(CMP, RRC, WO) every member of the graph set for the execution contains one of the following two circuits:

$(P_4, L_1, R, 8, A, S_4)$ $<_{RRC}$ $(P_4, L_1, R, 0, B, S_4)$
                              $<_{CRW}$ $(P_2, L_1, W, 4, B, S_4)$
                              $<_{WO}$ $(P_2, L_2, W, 8, A, S_4)$
                              $<_{CWR}$ $(P_4, L_1, R, 8, A, S_4)$

$(P_3, L_1, R, 2, B, S_3)$ $<_{RRC}$ $(P_3, L_1, R, 0, A, S_3)$
                              $<_{CRW}$ $(P_1, L_1, W, 1, A, S_3)$
                              $<_{WO}$ $(P_1, L_2, W, 2, B, S_3)$
                              $<_{CWR}$ $(P_3, L_1, R, 2, B, S_3)$

Under architecture A(CMP, RRC) there is an element of the graph set for the execution which is circuit-free (though not WO).

Appendix A

P_1	P_2	P_3	P_4
$(L_1,R,1,1,S_1)$			
$(L_2,R,2,2,S_1)$			
		$(L_1,R,0,A,S_3)$	
$(L_1,W,1,A,S)$			
	$(L_1,R,4,4,S_2)$		
	$(L_2,R,8,8,S_2)$		
	$(L_2,W,8,A,S)$		
			$(L_1,R,8,A,S_4)$
			$(L_1,R,0,B,S_4)$
			$(L_1,W,8,Y,S)$
	$(L_1,W,4,B,S)$		
$(L_2,W,2,B,S)$			
		$(L_1,R,2,B,S_3)$	
		$(L_1,W,2,X,S)$	

Theorem A13. A(CMP) $\neg \Rightarrow$ A(CMP, RO).

Proof. Consider the following execution.

$$\text{Initially, } A = X = Y = 0.$$

P_1	P_2
L_1: A:= 1;	L_1: X:= A;
	L_2: Y:= A;

$$\text{Terminally, } A = X = 1, Y = 0.$$

Under architecture A(CMP, RO) every member of the graph set for the execution contains the following circuit:

$$(P_1,L_1,W,1,A,S_2) <_{CWR} (P_2,L_1,R,1,A,S_2)$$
$$<_{RO} (P_2,L_2,R,0,A,S_2)$$
$$<_{CRW} (P_1,L_1,W,1,A,S_2)$$

Under architecture A(CMP) there is an element of the graph set for the execution which is circuit-free (though not RO).

P_1	P_2
	$(L_2,R,0,A,S_2)$
$(L_1,R,1,1,S_1)$	
$(L_1,W,1,A,S)$	
	$(L_1,R,1,A,S_2)$
	$(L_1,W,1,X,S)$
	$(L_2,W,0,Y,S)$

Theorem A14. $A(CMP, WO) \neg\Rightarrow A(CMP, WO, RO)$.

Proof. Consider the following execution.

        Initially, A = B = X = Y = 0.

                P_1 P_2
        L_1: A:= 1; L_1: Y:= B;
        L_2: B:= 1; L_2: X:= A;

        Terminally, A = B = Y = 1, X = 0.

Under architecture $A(CMP, RO, WO)$ every member of the graph set for the execution contains the following circuit:

$$
\begin{array}{rl}
(P_1, L_1, W, 1, A, S_2) & <_{WO} \quad (P_1, L_2, W, 1, B, S_2) \\
& <_{CWR} \quad (P_2, L_1, R, 1, B, S_2) \\
& <_{RO} \quad (P_2, L_2, R, 0, A, S_2) \\
& <_{CRW} \quad (P_1, L_1, W, 1, A, S_2)
\end{array}
$$

Under architecture $A(CMP, WO)$ there is an element of the graph set for the execution which is circuit-free (though not RO).

                P_1 P_2
                                     $(L_2, R, 0, A, S_2)$
        $(L_1, R, 1, 1, S_1)$
        $(L_1, W, 1, A, S)$
        $(L_2, R, 1, 1, S_1)$
        $(L_2, W, 1, B, S)$
                                     $(L_1, R, 1, B, S_2)$
                                     $(L_1, W, 1, Y, S)$
                                     $(L_2, W, 0, X, S)$

Theorem A15. $A(CMP, SA) \neg\Rightarrow A(CMP, SA, RO)$.

Proof. Consider the following execution.

        Initially, A = B = C = X = 0.

            P_1 P_2 P_3 P_4
        L_1: X:= A; L_1: A:= 1; L_1: B:= A; L_1: A:= 2;
        L_2: Y:= B;

        Terminally, A = 1, B = 2, X = 1, Y = 0.

Under architecture $A(CMP, RO, SA)$ every member of the graph set for the execution contains the following circuit:

Appendix A

$$(P_1,L_1,R,1,A,S_1) <_{RO} (P_1,L_2,R,0,B,S_1)$$
$$<_{CRW} (P_3,L_1,W,2,B,S_1)$$
$$=_{SA} (P_3,L_1,R,2,A,S_3)$$
$$<_{CRW} (P_2,L_1,W,1,A,S_3)$$
$$=_{SA} (P_2,L_1,W,1,A,S_1)$$
$$<_{CWR} (P_1,L_1,R,1,A,S_1)$$

Under architecture A(CMP, SA) there is an element of the graph set for the execution which is circuit-free (though not RO).

P_1	P_2	P_3	P_4
$(L_2,R,0,B,S_1)$			
$(L_2,W,0,Y,S)$			
			$(L_1,R,2,2,S_4)$
			$(L_1,W,2,A,S)$
		$(L_1,R,2,A,S_3)$	
		$(L_1,W,2,B,S)$	
	$(L_1,R,1,1,S_2)$		
	$(L_1,W,1,A,S)$		
$(L_1,R,1,A,S_1)$			
$(L_1,W,1,X,S)$			

Theorem A16. A(CMP, WA) $\neg \Rightarrow$ A(CMP, WA, RO).

Proof. Consider the following execution.

Initially, A = B = X = Y = 0.

P_1	P_2	P_3
L_1: A:= 1;	L_1: B:= A;	L_1: X:= B;
		L_2: Y:= A;

Terminally, A = B = X = 1, Y = 0.

Under architecture A(CMP, RO, WA) every member of the graph set for the execution contains the following circuit:

$$(P_1,L_1,W,1,A,S_2) <_{CWR} (P_2,L_1,R,1,A,S_2)$$
$$<_{SRW} (P_2,L_1,W,1,B,S_3)$$
$$<_{CWR} (P_3,L_1,R,1,B,S_3)$$
$$<_{RO} (P_3,L_2,R,0,A,S_3)$$
$$<_{CRW} (P_1,L_1,W,1,A,S_3)$$
$$=_{WA} (P_1,L_1,W,1,A,S_2)$$

Under architecture A(CMP, WA) there is an element of the graph set for the execution which is circuit-free (though not RO).

P_1 $\qquad\qquad\qquad$ P_2 $\qquad\qquad\qquad$ P_3
$\qquad\qquad\qquad\qquad\qquad\qquad\qquad\qquad\qquad$ $(L_2,R,0,A,S_3)$
$(L_1,R,1,1,S_1)$
$(L_1,W,1,A,S)$
$\qquad\qquad\qquad\qquad$ $(L_1,R,1,A,S_2)$
$\qquad\qquad\qquad\qquad$ $(L_1,W,1,B,S)$
$\qquad\qquad\qquad\qquad\qquad\qquad\qquad\qquad\qquad$ $(L_1,R,1,B,S_3)$
$\qquad\qquad\qquad\qquad\qquad\qquad\qquad\qquad\qquad$ $(L_1,W,1,X,S)$
$\qquad\qquad\qquad\qquad\qquad\qquad\qquad\qquad\qquad$ $(L_2,W,0,Y,S)$

Theorem A17. $A(\text{CMP, CON}) \neg \Rightarrow A(\text{CMP, CON, RO})$.

Proof. Consider the following execution.

$\quad$ Initially, $A = U = V = X = Y = 0$.

$\quad$ P_1 $\qquad$ P_2 $\qquad$ P_3 $\qquad$ P_4
$\quad$ L_1: $A:= 1$; $\quad$ L_1: $U:= A$; $\quad$ L_1: $X:= A$; $\quad$ L_1: $A:= 2$;
$\quad$ L_2: $A:= 3$; $\quad$ L_2: $V:= A$; $\quad$ L_2: $Y:= A$;

$\quad$ Terminally, $A = 3$, $U = 1$, $V = 2$, $X = 2$, $Y = 1$.

Under architecture $A(\text{CON})$ every element of the graph set for the execution contains one of the following two pairs of paths:

$\qquad\qquad$ $(P_1,L_1,W,1,A,S_2)$ $\quad <_{\text{CON}}$ $\quad (P_4,L_1,W,2,A,S_2)$
$\qquad\qquad$ $(P_1,L_1,W,1,A,S_3)$ $\quad <_{\text{CON}}$ $\quad (P_4,L_1,W,2,A,S_3)$

$\qquad\qquad$ $(P_4,L_1,W,2,A,S_2)$ $\quad <_{\text{CON}}$ $\quad (P_1,L_1,W,1,A,S_2)$
$\qquad\qquad$ $(P_4,L_1,W,2,A,S_3)$ $\quad <_{\text{CON}}$ $\quad (P_1,L_1,W,1,A,S_3)$

Hence, in every circuit-free element of the graph set for the execution under architecture $A(\text{CMP, CON})$ one of the following two pairs of paths occurs:

$\qquad\qquad$ $(P_1,L_1,W,1,A,S_2)$ $\quad <_{\text{CWR}}$ $\quad (P_2,L_1,R,1,A,S_2)$
$\qquad\qquad\qquad\qquad\qquad\qquad$ $<_{\text{CRW}}$ $\quad (P_4,L_1,W,2,A,S_2)$
$\qquad\qquad\qquad\qquad\qquad\qquad$ $<_{\text{CWR}}$ $\quad (P_2,L_2,R,2,A,S_2)$

$\qquad\qquad$ $(P_1,L_1,W,1,A,S_3)$ $\quad <_{\text{CWR}}$ $\quad (P_3,L_2,R,1,A,S_3)$
$\qquad\qquad\qquad\qquad\qquad\qquad$ $<_{\text{CRW}}$ $\quad (P_4,L_1,W,2,A,S_3)$
$\qquad\qquad\qquad\qquad\qquad\qquad$ $<_{\text{CWR}}$ $\quad (P_3,L_1,R,2,A,S_3)$

$\qquad\qquad$ $(P_4,L_1,W,2,A,S_2)$ $\quad <_{\text{CWR}}$ $\quad (P_2,L_2,R,2,A,S_2)$
$\qquad\qquad\qquad\qquad\qquad\qquad$ $<_{\text{CRW}}$ $\quad (P_1,L_1,W,1,A,S_2)$
$\qquad\qquad\qquad\qquad\qquad\qquad$ $<_{\text{CWR}}$ $\quad (P_2,L_1,R,1,A,S_2)$

$\qquad\qquad$ $(P_4,L_1,W,2,A,S_3)$ $\quad <_{\text{CWR}}$ $\quad (P_3,L_1,R,2,A,S_3)$
$\qquad\qquad\qquad\qquad\qquad\qquad$ $<_{\text{CRW}}$ $\quad (P_1,L_1,W,1,A,S_3)$
$\qquad\qquad\qquad\qquad\qquad\qquad$ $<_{\text{CWR}}$ $\quad (P_3,L_2,R,1,A,S_3)$

Appendix A

Consequently, under architecture A(CMP, CON, RO) every member of the graph set for the execution contains one of the following two circuits:

$$(P_3, L_2, R, 1, A, S_3) <_{CRW} (P_4, L_1, W, 2, A, S_3)$$
$$<_{CWR} (P_3, L_1, R, 2, A, S_3)$$
$$<_{RO} (P_3, L_2, R, 1, A, S_3)$$

$$(P_2, L_2, R, 2, A, S_2) <_{CRW} (P_1, L_1, W, 1, A, S_2)$$
$$<_{CWR} (P_2, L_1, R, 1, A, S_2)$$
$$<_{RO} (P_2, L_2, R, 2, A, S_2)$$

Under architecture A(CMP, CON) there is an element of the graph set for the execution which is circuit-free (though not RO).

P_1	P_2	P_3	P_4
$(L_1, R, 1, 1, S_1)$			
$(L_1, W, 1, A, S)$			
	$(L_1, R, 1, A, S_2)$		
	$(L_1, W, 1, U, S)$		
			$(L_1, R, 2, 2, S_4)$
			$(L_1, W, 2, A, S_1)$
			$(L_1, W, 2, A, S_2)$
		$(L_2, R, 1, A, S_3)$	
			$(L_1, W, 2, A, S_3)$
			$(L_1, W, 2, A, S_4)$
		$(L_1, R, 2, A, S_3)$	
		$(L_1, W, 2, X, S)$	
		$(L_2, W, 1, Y, S)$	
	$(L_2, R, 2, A, S_2)$		
	$(L_2, W, 2, V, S)$		
$(L_2, R, 3, 3, S_1)$			
$(L_2, W, 3, A, S)$			

Theorem A18. A(CMP, WS) $\neg \Rightarrow$ A(CMP, WS, RO).

Proof. Consider the following execution.

Initially, A = B = U = V = X = Y = 0.

P_1	P_2	P_3	P_4
L_1: A := 1;	L_1: U := A;	L_1: X := B;	L_1: B := 1;
	L_2: V := B;	L_2: Y := A;	

Terminally, A = B = U = X = 1, V = Y = 0.

Under architecture A(WS) every element of the graph set for the execution contains one of the following two pairs of paths:

$(P_1,L_1,W,1,A,S_2) <_{WS} (P_4,L_1,W,1,B,S_2)$
$(P_1,L_1,W,1,A,S_3) <_{WS} (P_4,L_1,W,1,B,S_3)$

$(P_4,L_1,W,1,B,S_2) <_{WS} (P_1,L_1,W,1,A,S_2)$
$(P_4,L_1,W,1,B,S_3) <_{WS} (P_1,L_1,W,1,A,S_3)$

Consequently, under architecture A(CMP, RO, WS) every member of the graph set for the execution contains one of the following two circuits:

$(P_1,L_1,W,1,A,S_3) <_{WS} (P_4,L_1,W,1,B,S_3)$
$ <_{CWR} (P_3,L_1,R,1,B,S_3)$
$ <_{RO} (P_3,L_2,R,0,A,S_3)$
$ <_{CRW} (P_1,L_1,W,1,A,S_3)$

$(P_4,L_1,W,1,B,S_2) <_{WS} (P_1,L_1,W,1,A,S_2)$
$ <_{CWR} (P_2,L_1,R,1,A,S_2)$
$ <_{RO} (P_2,L_2,R,0,B,S_2)$
$ <_{CRW} (P_4,L_1,W,1,B,S_2)$

Under architecture A(CMP, WS) there is an element of the graph set for the execution which is circuit-free (though not RO).

P_1	P_2	P_3	P_4
		$(L_2,R,0,A,S_3)$	
$(L_1,R,1,1,S_1)$			
$(L_1,W,1,A,S)$			
	$(L_1,R,1,A,S_2)$		
	$(L_1,W,1,U,S)$		
	$(L_2,R,0,B,S_2)$		
	$(L_2,W,0,V,S)$		
			$(L_1,R,1,1,S_4)$
			$(L_1,W,1,B,S)$
		$(L_1,R,1,B,S_3)$	
		$(L_1,W,1,X,S)$	
		$(L_2,W,0,Y,S)$	

Theorem A19. A(CMP, AWC) $\neg \Rightarrow$ A(CMP, AWC, RO).

Proof. Consider the following execution.

Initially, $A = B = X = Y = Z = 0$.

	P_1	P_2	P_3
	L_1: $A := 1$;	L_1: $X := B$;	L_1: $Z := A$;
		L_2: $Y := A$;	L_2: $B := 1$;

Terminally, $A = B = X = 1$, $Y = 0$, $Z = 1$.

Under architecture A(CMP, RO, AWC) every member of the graph set for the execution contains the following circuit:

$$(P_1, L_1, W, 1, A, S_3) <_{CWR} (P_3, L_1, R, 1, A, S_3)$$
$$<_{RO} (P_3, L_2, R, 1, 1, S_3)$$
$$<_{SRW} (P_3, L_2, W, 1, B, S_2)$$
$$<_{CWR} (P_2, L_1, R, 1, B, S_2)$$
$$<_{RO} (P_2, L_2, R, 0, A, S_2)$$
$$<_{CRW} (P_1, L_1, W, 1, A, S_2)$$
$$<_{AWC} (P_1, L_1, W, 1, A, S_3)$$

Under architecture A(CMP, AWC) there is an element of the graph set for the execution which is circuit-free (though not RO).

P_1	P_2	P_3
	$(L_2, R, 0, A, S_2)$	
$(L_1, R, 1, 1, S_1)$		
$(L_1, W, 1, A, S)$		
		$(L_1, R, 1, A, S_3)$
		$(L_1, W, 1, Z, S)$
		$(L_2, R, 1, 1, S_3)$
		$(L_2, W, 1, B, S)$
	$(L_1, R, 1, B, S_2)$	
	$(L_1, W, 1, X, S)$	
	$(L_2, W, 0, Y, S)$	

Theorem A20. A(CMP, RWC) $\neg \Rightarrow$ A(CMP, RWC, RO).

Proof. Consider the following execution.

Initially, $A = B = C = D = S = T = U = V = X = Y = 0$.

P_1	P_2	P_3	P_4
L_1: A:= 1;	L_1: B:= 1;	L_1: U:= A;	L_1: S:= C;
		L_2: C:= 1;	L_2: V:= A;
		L_3: T:= D;	L_3: X:= B;
		L_4: Y:= B;	L_4: D:= 1;

Terminally, $A = B = C = D = S = T = U = X = 1$, $V = 0$, $Y = 0$.

Under architecture A(RWC) every element of the graph set for the execution contains one of the following two pairs of paths:

$$(P_1, L_1, W, 1, A, S_3) <_{RWC} (P_1, L_1, W, 1, A, S_4)$$
$$(P_2, L_1, W, 1, B, S_3) <_{RWC} (P_2, L_1, W, 1, B, S_4)$$

$$(P_1, L_1, W, 1, A, S_4) <_{RWC} (P_1, L_1, W, 1, A, S_3)$$
$$(P_2, L_1, W, 1, B, S_4) <_{RWC} (P_2, L_1, W, 1, B, S_3)$$

Consequently, under architecture A(CMP, RWC, RO) every member of the graph set for the execution contains one of the following two circuits:

$(P_2, L_1, W, 1, B, S_3)$ $<_{RWC}$ $(P_2, L_1, W, 1, B, S_4)$
                         $<_{CWR}$ $(P_4, L_3, R, 1, B, S_4)$
                         $<_{RO}$ $(P_4, L_4, R, 1, 1, S_4)$
                         $<_{SRW}$ $(P_4, L_4, W, 1, D, S_3)$
                         $<_{CWR}$ $(P_3, L_3, R, 1, D, S_3)$
                         $<_{RO}$ $(P_3, L_4, R, 0, B, S_3)$
                         $<_{CRW}$ $(P_2, L_1, W, 1, B, S_3)$

$(P_1, L_1, W, 1, A, S_4)$ $<_{RWC}$ $(P_1, L_1, W, 1, A, S_3)$
                         $<_{CWR}$ $(P_3, L_1, R, 1, A, S_3)$
                         $<_{RO}$ $(P_3, L_2, R, 1, 1, S_3)$
                         $<_{SRW}$ $(P_3, L_2, W, 1, C, S_4)$
                         $<_{CWR}$ $(P_4, L_1, R, 1, C, S_4)$
                         $<_{RO}$ $(P_4, L_2, R, 0, A, S_4)$
                         $<_{CRW}$ $(P_1, L_1, W, 1, A, S_4)$

Under architecture A(CMP, RWC) there is an element of the graph set for the execution which is circuit-free (though not RO).

P_1	P_2	P_3	P_4
			$(L_2, R, 0, A, S_4)$
$(L_1, R, 1, 1, S_1)$			
$(L_1, W, 1, A, S)$			
		$(L_1, R, 1, A, S_3)$	
		$(L_1, W, 1, U, S)$	
		$(L_2, R, 1, 1, S_3)$	
		$(L_2, W, 1, C, S)$	
			$(L_1, R, 1, C, S_4)$
			$(L_1, W, 1, S, S)$
			$(L_2, W, 0, V, S)$
		$(L_4, R, 0, B, S_3)$	
	$(L_1, R, 1, 1, S_2)$		
	$(L_1, W, 1, B, S)$		
			$(L_3, R, 1, B, S_4)$
			$(L_3, W, 1, X, S)$
			$(L_4, R, 1, 1, S_4)$
			$(L_4, W, 1, D, S)$
		$(L_3, R, 1, D, S_3)$	
		$(L_3, W, 1, T, S)$	
		$(L_4, W, 0, Y, S)$	

Theorem A21.   A(CMP, WO) $\neg \Rightarrow$ A(CMP, WO, POS).

Proof. Consider the following execution.

Appendix A   167

                     Initially, A = B = X = 0.

                           P_1 P_2
                     L_1: A:= 1; L_1: B:= 1;
                     L_2: X:= B; L_2: A:= 2;

                     Terminally, A = B = 1, X = 0.

Under architecture A(CMP, WO, POS) every member of the graph set for the execution contains the following circuit:

$$(P_1,L_1,W,1,A,S_1) <_{POS} (P_1,L_2,R,0,B,S_1)$$
$$ <_{CRW} (P_2,L_1,W,1,B,S_1)$$
$$ <_{WO} (P_2,L_2,W,2,A,S_1)$$
$$ <_{CWW} (P_1,L_1,W,1,A,S_1)$$

Under architecture A(CMP, WO) there is an element of the graph set for the execution which is circuit-free (though not POS).

               P_1 P_2
         $(L_1,R,1,1,S_1)$
         $(L_2,R,0,B,S_1)$
                                     $(L_1,R,1,1,S_2)$
                                     $(L_1,W,1,B,S)$
                                     $(L_2,R,2,2,S_2)$
                                     $(L_2,W,2,A,S)$
         $(L_1,W,1,A,S)$
         $(L_2,W,0,X,S)$

Theorem A22.   A(CMP, WS) $\neg \Rightarrow$ A(CMP, WS, POS).

Proof. Consider the following execution.

                     Initially, A = B = X = Y = 0.

                           P_1 P_2
                     L_1: A:= 1; L_1: B:= 1;
                     L_2: Y:= B; L_2: X:= A;

                     Terminally, A = B = 1, X = Y = 0.

Under architecture A(WS) every element of the graph set for the execution contains one of the following two pairs of paths:

$$(P_1,L_1,W,1,A,S_1) <_{WS} (P_2,L_1,W,1,B,S_1)$$
$$(P_1,L_1,W,1,A,S_2) <_{WS} (P_2,L_1,W,1,B,S_2)$$

$$(P_2,L_1,W,1,B,S_1) <_{WS} (P_1,L_1,W,1,A,S_1)$$
$$(P_2,L_1,W,1,B,S_2) <_{WS} (P_1,L_1,W,1,A,S_2)$$

Consequently, under architecture A(CMP, WS, POS) every member of the graph set for the execution contains one of the following two circuits:

$$(P_1,L_1,W,1,A,S_2) \quad <_{WS} \quad (P_2,L_1,W,1,B,S_2)$$
$$<_{POS} \quad (P_2,L_2,R,0,A,S_2)$$
$$<_{CRW} \quad (P_1,L_1,W,1,A,S_2)$$

$$(P_2,L_1,W,1,B,S_1) \quad <_{WS} \quad (P_1,L_1,W,1,A,S_1)$$
$$<_{POS} \quad (P_1,L_2,R,0,B,S_1)$$
$$<_{CRW} \quad (P_2,L_1,W,1,B,S_1)$$

Under architecture A(CMP, WS) there is an element of the graph set for the execution which is circuit-free (though not POS).

P_1	P_2
	$(L_1,R,1,1,S_2)$
$(L_1,R,1,1,S_1)$	
$(L_2,R,0,B,S_1)$	
	$(L_1,W,1,B,S_1)$
	$(L_1,W,1,B,S_2)$
	$(L_2,R,0,A,S_2)$
$(L_1,W,1,A,S_1)$	
$(L_1,W,1,A,S_2)$	
	$(L_2,W,0,X,S_1)$
	$(L_2,W,0,X,S_2)$
$(L_2,W,0,Y,S_1)$	
$(L_2,W,0,Y,S_2)$	

Theorem A23. A(CMP, CON) $\neg \Rightarrow$ A(CMP, CON, POS).

Proof. Consider the following execution.

Initially, A = X = Y = 0.

P_1	P_2
L_1: A:= 1;	L_1: A:= 2;
L_2: X:= A;	L_2: Y:= A;
L_3: A:= 3;	

Terminally, A = 3, X = 2, Y = 1.

The function of the statement L_3: A:=3; is to obscure irrelevant information about which of the two statements, L_1: A:=1; or L_1: A:=2;, came first.

Under architecture A(CON) every element of the graph set for the execution contains one of the following two pairs of paths:

$$(P_1,L_1,W,1,A,S_1) \quad <_{CON} \quad (P_2,L_1,W,2,A,S_1)$$
$$(P_1,L_1,W,1,A,S_2) \quad <_{CON} \quad (P_2,L_1,W,2,A,S_2)$$

Appendix A

$$(P_2, L_1, W, 2, A, S_1) <_{CON} (P_1, L_1, W, 1, A, S_1)$$
$$(P_2, L_1, W, 2, A, S_2) <_{CON} (P_1, L_1, W, 1, A, S_2)$$

Hence, in every circuit-free element of the graph set for the execution under architecture A(CMP, CON) one of the following two paths occurs:

$$(P_1, L_1, W, 1, A, S_2) <_{CWR} (P_2, L_2, R, 1, A, S_2)$$
$$<_{CRW} (P_2, L_1, W, 2, A, S_2)$$

$$(P_2, L_1, W, 2, A, S_1) <_{CWR} (P_1, L_2, R, 2, A, S_1)$$
$$<_{CRW} (P_1, L_1, W, 1, A, S_1)$$

Consequently, under architecture A(CMP, CON, POS) every member of the graph set for the execution contains one of the following two circuits:

$$(P_2, L_2, R, 1, A, S_2) <_{CRW} (P_2, L_1, W, 2, A, S_2)$$
$$<_{POS} (P_2, L_2, R, 1, A, S_2)$$

$$(P_1, L_2, R, 2, A, S_1) <_{CRW} (P_1, L_1, W, 1, A, S_1)$$
$$<_{POS} (P_1, L_2, R, 2, A, S_1)$$

Under architecture A(CMP, CON) there is an element of the graph set for the execution which is circuit-free (though not POS).

P_1	P_2
	$(L_1, R, 2, 2, S_2)$
$(L_1, R, 1, 1, S_1)$	
$(L_1, W, 1, A, S)$	
	$(L_2, R, 1, A, S_2)$
	$(L_1, W, 2, A, S)$
$(L_2, R, 2, A, S_1)$	
$(L_2, W, 2, X, S)$	
	$(L_2, W, 1, Y, S)$
$(L_3, R, 3, 3, S_1)$	
$(L_3, W, 3, A, S)$	

Theorem A24. A(CMP, WA) $\neg \Rightarrow$ A(CMP, WA, WOS).

Proof. Consider the following execution.

Initially, A = B = 0.

P_1	P_2
L_1: A := 1;	L_1: B := 1;
L_2: B := 2;	L_2: A := 2;

Terminally, A = B = 1.

Under architecture A(CMP, WA, WOS) every member of the graph set for the execution contains the following circuit:

$$
\begin{array}{rl}
(P_1,L_1,W,1,A,S_1) & <_{WOS} \ (P_1,L_2,W,2,B,S_1) \\
& =_{WA} \ (P_1,L_2,W,2,B,S_2) \\
& <_{CWW} \ (P_2,L_1,W,1,B,S_2) \\
& <_{WOS} \ (P_2,L_2,W,2,A,S_2) \\
& =_{WA} \ (P_2,L_2,W,2,A,S_1) \\
& <_{CWW} \ (P_1,L_1,W,1,A,S_1)
\end{array}
$$

Under architecture A(CMP, WA) there is an element of the graph set for the execution which is circuit-free (though not WOS).

$$
\begin{array}{ll}
P_1 & P_2 \\
(L_1,R,1,1,S_1) & \\
 & (L_1,R,1,1,S_2) \\
(L_2,R,2,2,S_1) & \\
 & (L_2,R,2,2,S_2) \\
 & (L_2,W,2,A,S) \\
(L_1,W,1,A,S) & \\
(L_2,W,2,B,S) & \\
 & (L_1,W,1,B,S)
\end{array}
$$

Theorem A25. A(CMP) $\neg \Rightarrow$ A(CMP, SA).

Proof. Consider the following execution.

Initially, A = 0, B = 1.

$$
\begin{array}{ll}
P_1 & P_2 \\
L_1: \ A := B; & L_1: \ B := A;
\end{array}
$$

Terminally, A = 1 and B = 0.

Under architecture A(CMP, SA) every member of the graph set for the execution contains the following circuit:

$$
\begin{array}{rl}
(P_1,L_1,R,1,B,S_1) & <_{CRW} \ (P_2,L_1,W,0,B,S_1) \\
& =_{SA} \ (P_2,L_1,R,0,A,S_2) \\
& <_{CRW} \ (P_1,L_1,W,1,A,S_2) \\
& =_{SA} \ (P_1,L_1,R,1,B,S_1)
\end{array}
$$

Under architecture A(CMP) there is an element of the graph set for the execution which is circuit-free (though not SA).

$$\begin{array}{ll} P_1 & P_2 \\ (L_1,R,1,B,S_1) & \\ & (L_1,R,0,A,S_2) \\ (L_1,W,1,A,S) & \\ & (L_1,W,0,B,S) \end{array}$$

Other executions may be used to prove the same theorem.

Initially, A = 0.

$$\begin{array}{ll} P_1 & P_2 \\ L_1\text{: A: } = A + 1; & L_1\text{: A: } = A + 1; \end{array}$$

Terminally, A = 1.

This execution shows that the statement A: = A; is not necessarily invisible.

Initially, A = 0.

$$\begin{array}{ll} P_1 & P_2 \\ L_1\text{: A: } = 1; & L_1\text{: A: } = A; \end{array}$$

Terminally, A = 0.

Theorem A26. A(CMP, WO) $\neg \Rightarrow$ A(CMP, WO, SA).

Proof. Consider the following execution.

Initially, A = B = 0.

$$\begin{array}{ll} P_1 & P_2 \\ L_1\text{: A:= 1;} & L_1\text{: B:= A;} \\ L_2\text{: B:= 2;} & \end{array}$$

Terminally, A = 1, B = 0.

Under architecture A(CMP, WO, SA) every member of the graph set for the execution contains both of the following two circuits, corresponding to $S_x = S_1$ and $S_x = S_2$.

$$\begin{array}{rl} (P_1,L_1,W,1,A,S_2) & <_{WO} \quad (P_1,L_2,W,2,B,S_x) \\ & <_{CWW} \quad (P_2,L_1,W,0,B,S_x) \\ & =_{SA} \quad (P_2,L_1,R,0,A,S_2) \\ & <_{CRW} \quad (P_1,L_1,W,1,A,S_2) \end{array}$$

Under architecture A(CMP, WO) there is an element of the graph set for the execution which is circuit-free (though not SA).

P_1 P_2
              $(L_1,R,0,A,S_2)$
$(L_1,R,1,1,S_1)$
$(L_1,W,1,A,S)$
$(L_2,R,2,2,S_1)$
$(L_2,W,2,B,S)$
              $(L_1,W,0,B,S)$

Theorem A27. $A(CMP, RO) \neg \Rightarrow A(CMP, RO, SA)$.

Proof. Consider the following execution.

Initially, $A = B = X = Y = 0$.

P_1 P_2 P_3 P_4
L_1: $X := A$; L_1: $A := 1$; L_1: $B := A$; L_1: $A := 2$;
L_2: $Y := B$;

Terminally, $A = 1$, $B = 2$, $X = 1$, $Y = 0$.

Under architecture $A(CMP, RO, SA)$ every member of the graph set for the execution contains the following circuit:

$(P_1,L_1,R,1,A,S_1)$ $<_{RO}$ $(P_1,L_2,R,0,B,S_1)$
                     $<_{CRW}$ $(P_3,L_1,W,2,B,S_1)$
                     $=_{SA}$ $(P_3,L_1,R,2,A,S_3)$
                     $<_{CRW}$ $(P_2,L_1,W,1,A,S_3)$
                     $=_{SA}$ $(P_2,L_1,W,1,A,S_1)$
                     $<_{CWR}$ $(P_1,L_1,R,1,A,S_1)$

Under architecture $A(CMP, RO)$ there is an element of the graph set for the execution which is circuit-free (though not SA).

P_1 P_2 P_3 P_4
                                                          $(L_1,R,2,2,S_4)$
                                                          $(L_1,W,2,A,S)$
                                       $(L_1,R,2,A,S_3)$
                    $(L_1,R,1,1,S_2)$
                    $(L_1,W,1,A,S)$
$(L_1,R,1,A,S_1)$
$(L_1,W,1,X,S)$
$(L_2,R,0,B,S_1)$
$(L_2,W,0,Y,S)$
                                                          $(L_1,W,2,B,S)$

Theorem A28. A(CMP, WOS) $\neg \Rightarrow$ A(CMP, WOS, WA).

Proof. Consider the following execution.

$$\text{Initially, } A = B = 0.$$

$$\begin{array}{ll} P_1 & P_2 \\ L_1\colon A := 1; & L_1\colon B := 1; \\ L_2\colon B := 2; & L_2\colon A := 2; \end{array}$$

$$\text{Terminally, } A = B = 1.$$

Under architecture A(CMP, WA, WOS) every member of the graph set for the execution contains the following circuit:

$$\begin{array}{ll}
(P_1, L_1, W, 1, A, S_1) & <_{WOS} \;\; (P_1, L_2, W, 2, B, S_1) \\
& =_{WA} \;\; (P_1, L_2, W, 2, B, S_2) \\
& <_{CWW} \;\; (P_2, L_1, W, 1, B, S_2) \\
& <_{WOS} \;\; (P_2, L_2, W, 2, A, S_2) \\
& =_{WA} \;\; (P_2, L_2, W, 2, A, S_1) \\
& <_{CWW} \;\; (P_1, L_1, W, 1, A, S_1)
\end{array}$$

Under architecture A(CMP, WOS) there is an element of the graph set for the execution which is circuit-free (though not WA).

$$\begin{array}{ll}
P_1 & P_2 \\
(L_1, R, 1, 1, S_1) & \\
(L_2, R, 2, 2, S_1) & \\
& (L_1, R, 1, 1, S_2) \\
& (L_2, R, 2, 2, S_2) \\
& (L_2, W, 2, A, S_1) \\
(L_1, W, 1, A, S_1) & \\
(L_2, W, 2, B, S) & \\
& (L_1, W, 1, B, S) \\
& (L_2, W, 2, A, S_2) \\
(L_1, W, 1, A, S_2) &
\end{array}$$

Theorem A29. A(CMP, RO) $\neg \Rightarrow$ A(CMP, RO, WA).

Proof. Consider the following execution.

$$\text{Initially, } A = B = X = Y = 0.$$

$$\begin{array}{lll} P_1 & P_2 & P_3 \\ L_1\colon A := 1; & L_1\colon B := A; & L_1\colon X := B; \\ & & L_2\colon Y := A; \end{array}$$

$$\text{Terminally, } A = B = X = 1, Y = 0.$$

Under architecture A(CMP, RO, WA) every member of the graph set for the execution contains the following circuit:

$$(P_1, L_1, W, 1, A, S_2) <_{CWR} (P_2, L_1, R, 1, A, S_2)$$
$$<_{SRW} (P_2, L_1, W, 1, B, S_3)$$
$$<_{CWR} (P_3, L_1, R, 1, B, S_3)$$
$$<_{RO} (P_3, L_2, R, 0, A, S_3)$$
$$<_{CRW} (P_1, L_1, W, 1, A, S_3)$$
$$=_{WA} (P_1, L_1, W, 1, A, S_2)$$

Under architecture A(CMP, RO) there is an element of the graph set for the execution which is circuit-free (though not WA).

$$
\begin{array}{lll}
P_1 & P_2 & P_3 \\
(L_1, R, 1, 1, S_1) & & \\
(L_1, W, 1, A, S_1) & & \\
(L_1, W, 1, A, S_2) & & \\
& (L_1, R, 1, A, S_2) & \\
& (L_1, W, 1, B, S) & \\
& & (L_1, R, 1, B, S_3) \\
& & (L_1, W, 1, X, S) \\
& & (L_2, R, 0, A, S_3) \\
& & (L_2, W, 0, Y, S) \\
(L_1, W, 1, A, S_3) & &
\end{array}
$$

Theorem A30. A(CMP, RA) $\neg \Rightarrow$ A(CMP, RA, WA).

Proof. Consider the following execution.

Initially, A = B = X = 0.

$$
\begin{array}{lll}
P_1 & P_2 & P_3 \\
L_1\colon A := 1; & L_1\colon B := A + 1; & L_1\colon X := A + B;
\end{array}
$$

Terminally, A = 1, B = 2, X = 2.

Under architecture A(CMP, RA, WA) every member of the graph set for the execution contains the following circuit:

$$(P_1, L_1, W, 1, A, S_2) <_{CWR} (P_2, L_1, R, 1, A, S_2)$$
$$<_{SRW} (P_2, L_1, W, 2, B, S_3)$$
$$<_{CWR} (P_3, L_1, R, 2, B, S_3)$$
$$=_{RA} (P_3, L_1, R, 0, A, S_3)$$
$$<_{CRW} (P_1, L_1, W, 1, A, S_3)$$
$$=_{WA} (P_1, L_1, W, 1, A, S_2)$$

Appendix A

Under architecture A(CMP, RA) there is an element of the graph set for the execution which is circuit-free (though not WA).

P_1	P_2	P_3
$(L_1,R,1,1,S_1)$		
$(L_1,W,1,A,S_1)$		
$(L_1,W,1,A,S_2)$		
	$(L_1,R,1,A,S_2)$	
	$(L_1,R,1,1,S_2)$	
	$(L_1,W,2,B,S)$	
		$(L_1,R,0,A,S_3)$
		$(L_1,R,2,B,S_3)$
$(L_1,W,1,A,S_3)$		
		$(L_1,W,2,X,S)$

Corollary. A(CMP, RA, AWC) $\neg \Rightarrow$ A(CMP, RA, WA).

Theorem A31. A(CMP, RS) $\neg \Rightarrow$ A(CMP, RS, WA).

Proof. Consider the following execution.

Initially, A = B = C = D = 0.

P_1	P_2	P_3	P_4
L_1: A:= 1;	L_1: X:= A + B;	L_1: Y:= A + B;	L_1: B:= 2;

Terminally, A = 1, B = 2, X = 1, and Y = 2.

Under architecture A(RS) every element of the graph set for the execution contains one of the following two pairs of paths:

$(P_2,L_1,R,1,A,S_2)$ $<_{RS}$ $(P_3,L_1,R,0,A,S_3)$
$(P_2,L_1,R,0,B,S_2)$ $<_{RS}$ $(P_3,L_1,R,2,B,S_3)$

$(P_3,L_1,R,0,A,S_3)$ $<_{RS}$ $(P_2,L_1,R,1,A,S_2)$
$(P_3,L_1,R,2,B,S_3)$ $<_{RS}$ $(P_2,L_1,R,0,B,S_2)$

Consequently, under architecture A(CMP, RS, WA) every member of the graph set for the execution contains one of the following two circuits:

$(P_2,L_1,R,1,A,S_2)$ $<_{RS}$ $(P_3,L_1,R,0,A,S_3)$
$<_{CRW}$ $(P_1,L_1,W,1,A,S_3)$
$=_{WA}$ $(P_1,L_1,W,1,A,S_2)$
$<_{CWR}$ $(P_2,L_1,R,1,A,S_2)$

$(P_3, L_1, R, 2, B, S_3)$ $<_{RS}$ $(P_2, L_1, R, 0, B, S_2)$
$<_{CRW}$ $(P_4, L_1, W, 2, B, S_2)$
$=_{WA}$ $(P_4, L_1, W, 2, B, S_3)$
$<_{CWR}$ $(P_3, L_1, R, 2, B, S_3)$

Under architecture A(CMP, RS) there is an element of the graph set for the execution which is circuit-free (though not WA).

P_1	P_2	P_3	P_4
$(L_1, R, 1, 1, S_1)$			
			$(L_1, R, 2, 2, S_4)$
$(L_1, W, 1, A, S_1)$			
$(L_1, W, 1, A, S_2)$			
	$(L_1, R, 1, A, S_2)$		
	$(L_1, R, 0, B, S_2)$		
		$(L_1, R, 0, A, S_3)$	
$(L_1, W, 1, A, S_3)$			
$(L_1, W, 1, A, S_4)$			
			$(L_1, W, 2, B, S)$
		$(L_1, R, 2, B, S_3)$	
	$(L_1, W, 1, X, S)$		
		$(L_1, W, 2, Y, S)$	

Corollary. A(CMP, RS, WS) $\neg \Rightarrow$ A(CMP, RS, WA).

Theorem A32. A(CMP, WO) $\neg \Rightarrow$ A(CMP, WO, RA).

Proof. Consider the following execution.

Initially, A = B = X = 0.

P_1	P_2
L_1: X:= A + B;	L_1: A:= 1;
	L_2: B:= 2;

Terminally, A = 1, B = 2, X = 2.

Under architecture A(CMP, RA, WO) every member of the graph set for the execution contains the following circuit:

$(P_1, L_1, R, 2, B, S_1)$ $<_{RA}$ $(P_1, L_1, R, 0, A, S_1)$
$<_{CRW}$ $(P_2, L_1, W, 1, A, S_1)$
$<_{WO}$ $(P_2, L_2, W, 2, B, S_1)$
$<_{CWR}$ $(P_1, L_1, R, 2, B, S_1)$

Appendix A   177

Under architecture A(CMP, WO) there is an element of the graph set for the execution which is circuit-free (though not RA).

```
           P₁                        P₂
                                (L₁,R,1,1,S₂)
      (L₁,R,0,A,S₁)
                                (L₁,W,1,A,S)
                                (L₂,R,2,2,S₂)
                                (L₂,W,2,B,S)
      (L₁,R,2,B,S₁)
      (L₁,W,2,X,S)
```

Theorem A33.   A(CMP, WS) ¬⇒ A(CMP, WS, RA).

Proof. Consider the following execution.

Initially, A = B = C = D = 0.

```
    P₁               P₂                  P₃                  P₄
L₁: A:= 1;    L₁: X:= A + B;    L₁: Y:= A + B;    L₁: B:= 2;
```

Terminally, A = 1, B = 2, X = 1, and Y = 2.

Under architecture A(WS) every element of the graph set for the execution contains one of the following two pairs of paths:

$$(P_1, L_1, W, 1, A, S_2) <_{WS} (P_4, L_1, W, 2, B, S_2)$$
$$(P_1, L_1, W, 1, A, S_3) <_{WS} (P_4, L_1, W, 2, B, S_3)$$

$$(P_4, L_1, W, 2, B, S_2) <_{WS} (P_1, L_1, W, 1, A, S_2)$$
$$(P_4, L_1, W, 2, B, S_3) <_{WS} (P_1, L_1, W, 1, A, S_3)$$

Consequently, under architecture A(CMP, WS, RA) every member of the graph set for the execution contains one of the following two circuits:

$$(P_1, L_1, W, 1, A, S_3) <_{WS} (P_4, L_1, W, 2, B, S_3)$$
$$<_{CWR} (P_3, L_1, R, 2, B, S_3)$$
$$=_{RA} (P_3, L_1, R, 0, A, S_3)$$
$$<_{CRW} (P_1, L_1, W, 1, A, S_3)$$

$$(P_4, L_1, W, 2, B, S_2) <_{WS} (P_1, L_1, W, 1, A, S_2)$$
$$<_{CWR} (P_2, L_1, R, 1, A, S_2)$$
$$=_{RA} (P_2, L_1, R, 0, B, S_2)$$
$$<_{CRW} (P_4, L_1, W, 2, B, S_2)$$

Under architecture A(CMP, WS) there is an element of the graph set for the execution which is circuit-free (though not RA).

```
      P₁                P₂                P₃                P₄
(L₁,R,1,1,S₁)

                                                       (L₁,R,2,2,S₄)
(L₁,W,1,A,S₁)
(L₁,W,1,A,S₂)
                  (L₁,R,1,A,S₂)
                  (L₁,R,0,B,S₂)
                                    (L₁,R,0,A,S₃)

(L₁,W,1,A,S₃)
(L₁,W,1,A,S₄)
                                                       (L₁,W,2,B,S)
                                    (L₁,R,2,B,S₃)
                  (L₁,W,1,X,S)
                                    (L₁,W,2,Y,S)
```

Corollary. $A(CMP, WS, RS) \neg \Rightarrow A(CMP, WS, RA)$.

Theorem A34. $A(CMP, WA) \neg \Rightarrow A(CMP, WA, RA)$.

Proof. Consider the following execution.

```
Initially, A = B = X = 0.

       P₁                P₂                   P₃
L₁: A:= 1;      L₁: B:= A + 1;       L₁: X:= A + B;

Terminally, A = 1, B = 2, X = 2.
```

Under architecture A(CMP, RA, WA) every member of the graph set for the execution contains the following circuit:

$$
\begin{array}{rcl}
(P_1,L_1,W,1,A,S_2) & <_{CWR} & (P_2,L_1,R,1,A,S_2) \\
 & <_{SRW} & (P_2,L_1,W,2,B,S_3) \\
 & <_{CWR} & (P_3,L_1,R,2,B,S_3) \\
 & =_{RA} & (P_3,L_1,R,0,A,S_3) \\
 & <_{CRW} & (P_1,L_1,W,1,A,S_3) \\
 & =_{WA} & (P_1,L_1,W,1,A,S_2)
\end{array}
$$

Under architecture A(CMP, WA) there is an element of the graph set for the execution which is circuit-free (though not RA).

Appendix A

$$P_1 \qquad\qquad P_2 \qquad\qquad P_3$$
$$\qquad\qquad\qquad\qquad\qquad\qquad (L_1,R,0,A,S_3)$$
$$(L_1,R,1,1,S_1)$$
$$(L_1,W,1,A,S)$$
$$\qquad\qquad (L_1,R,1,A,S_2)$$
$$\qquad\qquad (L_1,R,1,1,S_2)$$
$$\qquad\qquad (L_1,W,2,B,S)$$
$$\qquad\qquad\qquad\qquad\qquad\qquad (L_1,R,2,B,S_3)$$
$$\qquad\qquad\qquad\qquad\qquad\qquad (L_1,W,2,X,S)$$

Theorem A35. $A(CMP) \neg \Rightarrow A(CMP, CON)$.

Proof. Consider the following execution.

Initially, A = 0.

$$P_1 \qquad\qquad\qquad P_2$$
L_1: A := 1; $\qquad\qquad L_1$: A := 2;

Terminally, operand A in store S_1 = 2,
and operand A in store S_2 = 1.

Under architecture A(CON) every element of the graph set for the execution contains one of the following two pairs of paths:

$$(P_1,L_1,W,1,A,S_1) \quad <_{CON} \quad (P_2,L_1,W,2,A,S_1)$$
$$(P_1,L_1,W,1,A,S_2) \quad <_{CON} \quad (P_2,L_1,W,2,A,S_2)$$

$$(P_2,L_1,W,2,A,S_1) \quad <_{CON} \quad (P_1,L_1,W,1,A,S_1)$$
$$(P_2,L_1,W,2,A,S_2) \quad <_{CON} \quad (P_1,L_1,W,1,A,S_2)$$

Consequently, under architecture A(CMP, CON) every member of the graph set for the execution contains one of the following two circuits:

$$(P_1,L_1,W,1,A,S_2) \quad <_{CON} \quad (P_2,L_1,W,2,A,S_2)$$
$$\qquad\qquad\qquad\qquad\quad <_{CWW} \quad (P_1,L_1,W,1,A,S_2)$$

$$(P_2,L_1,W,2,A,S_1) \quad <_{CON} \quad (P_1,L_1,W,1,A,S_1)$$
$$\qquad\qquad\qquad\qquad\quad <_{CWW} \quad (P_2,L_1,W,2,A,S_1)$$

Under architecture A(CMP) there is an element of the graph set for the execution which is circuit-free (though not CON).

$$
\begin{array}{ll}
P_1 & P_2 \\
(L_1,R,1,1,S_1) & \\
 & (L_1,R,2,2,S_2) \\
(L_1,W,1,A,S_1) & \\
 & (L_1,W,2,A,S_1) \\
 & (L_1,W,2,A,S_2) \\
(L_1,W,1,A,S_2) &
\end{array}
$$

Theorem A36. $A(\text{CMP, RO}) \neg \Rightarrow A(\text{CMP, RO, CON})$.

Proof. Consider the following execution.

Initially, $A = U = V = X = Y = 0$.

```
    P_1           P_2           P_3           P_4
L_1: A:= 1;   L_1: U:= A;   L_1: X:= A;   L_1: A:= 2;
L_2: A:= 3;   L_2: V:= A;   L_2: Y:= A;
```

Terminally, $A = 3, U = 1, V = 2, X = 2, Y = 1$.

Under architecture $A(\text{CON})$ every element of the graph set for the execution contains one of the following two pairs of paths:

$$
\begin{array}{ll}
(P_1,L_1,W,1,A,S_2) <_{\text{CON}} (P_4,L_1,W,2,A,S_2) \\
(P_1,L_1,W,1,A,S_3) <_{\text{CON}} (P_4,L_1,W,2,A,S_3) \\
\\
(P_4,L_1,W,2,A,S_2) <_{\text{CON}} (P_1,L_1,W,1,A,S_2) \\
(P_4,L_1,W,2,A,S_3) <_{\text{CON}} (P_1,L_1,W,1,A,S_3)
\end{array}
$$

Hence, in every circuit-free element of the graph set for the execution under architecture $A(\text{CMP, CON})$ one of the following two pairs of paths occurs:

$$
\begin{array}{rl}
(P_1,L_1,W,1,A,S_2) & <_{\text{CWR}} (P_2,L_1,R,1,A,S_2) \\
 & <_{\text{CRW}} (P_4,L_1,W,2,A,S_2) \\
 & <_{\text{CWR}} (P_2,L_2,R,2,A,S_2) \\
\\
(P_1,L_1,W,1,A,S_3) & <_{\text{CWR}} (P_3,L_2,R,1,A,S_3) \\
 & <_{\text{CRW}} (P_4,L_1,W,2,A,S_3) \\
 & <_{\text{CWR}} (P_3,L_1,R,2,A,S_3) \\
\\
(P_4,L_1,W,2,A,S_2) & <_{\text{CWR}} (P_2,L_2,R,2,A,S_2) \\
 & <_{\text{CRW}} (P_1,L_1,W,1,A,S_2) \\
 & <_{\text{CWR}} (P_2,L_1,R,1,A,S_2) \\
\\
(P_4,L_1,W,2,A,S_3) & <_{\text{CWR}} (P_3,L_1,R,2,A,S_3) \\
 & <_{\text{CRW}} (P_1,L_1,W,1,A,S_3) \\
 & <_{\text{CWR}} (P_3,L_2,R,1,A,S_3)
\end{array}
$$

Consequently, under architecture A(CMP, RO, CON) every member of the graph set for the execution contains one of the following two circuits:

$$(P_3, L_2, R, 1, A, S_3) \begin{array}{l} <_{CRW} \\ <_{CWR} \\ <_{RO} \end{array} \begin{array}{l} (P_4, L_1, W, 2, A, S_3) \\ (P_3, L_1, R, 2, A, S_3) \\ (P_3, L_2, R, 1, A, S_3) \end{array}$$

$$(P_2, L_2, R, 2, A, S_2) \begin{array}{l} <_{CRW} \\ <_{CWR} \\ <_{RO} \end{array} \begin{array}{l} (P_1, L_1, W, 1, A, S_2) \\ (P_2, L_1, R, 1, A, S_2) \\ (P_2, L_2, R, 2, A, S_2) \end{array}$$

Under architecture A(CMP, RO) there is an element of the graph set for the execution which is circuit-free (though not CON).

P_1	P_2	P_3	P_4
$(L_1, R, 1, 1, S_1)$			
$(L_1, W, 1, A, S_1)$			
$(L_1, W, 1, A, S_2)$			
	$(L_1, R, 1, A, S_2)$		
	$(L_1, W, 1, U, S)$		
			$(L_1, R, 2, 2, S_4)$
			$(L_1, W, 2, A, S)$
		$(L_1, R, 2, A, S_3)$	
		$(L_1, W, 2, X, S)$	
	$(L_2, R, 2, A, S_2)$		
	$(L_2, W, 2, V, S)$		
$(L_1, W, 1, A, S_3)$			
$(L_1, W, 1, A, S_4)$			
		$(L_2, R, 1, A, S_3)$	
		$(L_2, W, 1, Y, S)$	
$(L_2, R, 3, 3, S_1)$			
$(L_2, W, 3, A, S)$			

Theorem A37. A(CMP, POS) $\neg \Rightarrow$ A(CMP, POS, CON).

Proof. Consider the following execution.

Initially, $A = X = Y = 0$.

P_1	P_2
L_1: $A := 1$;	L_1: $A := 2$;
L_2: $X := A$;	L_2: $Y := A$;
L_3: $A := 3$;	

Terminally, $A = 3$, $X = 2$, $Y = 1$.

Under architecture A(CON) every element of the graph set for the execution contains one of the following two pairs of paths:

$$(P_1, L_1, W, 1, A, S_1) <_{CON} (P_2, L_1, W, 2, A, S_1)$$
$$(P_1, L_1, W, 1, A, S_2) <_{CON} (P_2, L_1, W, 2, A, S_2)$$

$$(P_2, L_1, W, 2, A, S_1) <_{CON} (P_1, L_1, W, 1, A, S_1)$$
$$(P_2, L_1, W, 2, A, S_2) <_{CON} (P_1, L_1, W, 1, A, S_2)$$

Hence, in every circuit-free element of the graph set for the execution under architecture A(CMP, CON) one of the following two pairs of paths occurs:

$$(P_1, L_1, W, 1, A, S_2) \begin{array}{l} <_{CWR} (P_2, L_2, R, 1, A, S_2) \\ <_{CRW} (P_2, L_1, W, 2, A, S_2) \end{array}$$

$$(P_2, L_1, W, 2, A, S_1) \begin{array}{l} <_{CWR} (P_1, L_2, R, 2, A, S_1) \\ <_{CRW} (P_1, L_1, W, 1, A, S_1) \end{array}$$

Consequently, under architecture A(CMP, POS, CON) every member of the graph set for the execution contains one of the following two circuits:

$$(P_2, L_2, R, 1, A, S_2) \begin{array}{l} <_{CRW} (P_2, L_1, W, 2, A, S_2) \\ <_{POS} (P_2, L_2, R, 1, A, S_2) \end{array}$$

$$(P_1, L_2, R, 2, A, S_1) \begin{array}{l} <_{CRW} (P_1, L_1, W, 1, A, S_1) \\ <_{POS} (P_1, L_2, R, 2, A, S_1) \end{array}$$

Under architecture A(CMP, POS) there is an element of the graph set for the execution which is circuit-free (though not CON).

P_1	P_2
$(L_1, R, 1, 1, S_1)$	
$(L_1, W, 1, A, S_1)$	
	$(L_1, R, 2, 2, S_2)$
	$(L_1, W, 2, A, S)$
$(L_2, R, 2, A, S_1)$	
$(L_1, W, 1, A, S_2)$	
$(L_2, W, 2, X, S)$	
	$(L_2, R, 1, A, S_2)$
	$(L_2, W, 1, Y, S)$
$(L_3, R, 3, 3, S_1)$	
$(L_3, W, 3, A, S)$	

Theorem A38. A(CMP, RO) $\neg \Rightarrow$ A(CMP, RO, WS).

Appendix A

Proof. Consider the following execution.

Initially, A = B = U = V = X = Y = 0.

```
        P₁              P₂              P₃              P₄
   L₁: A:= 1;      L₁: U:= A;      L₁: X:= B;      L₁: B:= 1;
                   L₂: V:= B;      L₂: Y:= A;
```

Terminally, A = B = U = X = 1, V = Y = 0.

Under architecture A(WS) every element of the graph set for the execution contains one of the following two pairs of paths:

$$(P_1, L_1, W, 1, A, S_2) <_{WS} (P_4, L_1, W, 1, B, S_2)$$
$$(P_1, L_1, W, 1, A, S_3) <_{WS} (P_4, L_1, W, 1, B, S_3)$$

$$(P_4, L_1, W, 1, B, S_2) <_{WS} (P_1, L_1, W, 1, A, S_2)$$
$$(P_4, L_1, W, 1, B, S_3) <_{WS} (P_1, L_1, W, 1, A, S_3)$$

Consequently, under architecture A(CMP, RO, WS) every member of the graph set for the execution contains one of the following two circuits:

$$
\begin{aligned}
(P_1, L_1, W, 1, A, S_3) &<_{WS} (P_4, L_1, W, 1, B, S_3) \\
&<_{CWR} (P_3, L_1, R, 1, B, S_3) \\
&<_{RO} (P_3, L_2, R, 0, A, S_3) \\
&<_{CRW} (P_1, L_1, W, 1, A, S_3)
\end{aligned}
$$

$$
\begin{aligned}
(P_4, L_1, W, 1, B, S_2) &<_{WS} (P_1, L_1, W, 1, A, S_2) \\
&<_{CWR} (P_2, L_1, R, 1, A, S_2) \\
&<_{RO} (P_2, L_2, R, 0, B, S_2) \\
&<_{CRW} (P_4, L_1, W, 1, B, S_2)
\end{aligned}
$$

Under architecture A(CMP, RO) there is an element of the graph set for the execution which is circuit-free (though not WS).

```
        P₁                   P₂                   P₃              P₄
   (L₁, R, 1, 1, S₁)
   (L₁, W, 1, A, S₁)
   (L₁, W, 1, A, S₂)
                        (L₁, R, 1, A, S₂)
                        (L₁, W, 1, U, S)
                        (L₂, R, 0, B, S₂)
                        (L₂, W, 0, V, S)
```

$(L_1, W, 1, A, S_3)$
$(L_1, W, 1, A, S_4)$

$(L_1, R, 1, B, S_3)$
$(L_1, W, 1, X, S)$
$(L_2, R, 0, A, S_3)$
$(L_2, W, 0, Y, S)$

$(L_1, R, 1, 1, S_4)$
$(L_1, W, 1, B, S)$

Corollary. A(CMP, RO, CON) $\neg \Rightarrow$ A(CMP, RO, WS).

Theorem A39. A(CMP, POS) $\neg \Rightarrow$ A(CMP, POS, WS).

Proof. Consider the following execution.

Initially, A = B = X = Y = 0.

$\quad\quad\quad$ P$_1$ $\quad\quad\quad\quad\quad$ P$_2$
L$_1$: A := 1; $\quad\quad$ L$_1$: B := 1;
L$_2$: Y := B; $\quad\quad$ L$_2$: X := A;

Terminally, A = B = 1, X = Y = 0.

Under architecture A(WS) every element of the graph set for the execution contains one of the following two pairs of paths:

$(P_1, L_1, W, 1, A, S_1)$ $<_{WS}$ $(P_2, L_1, W, 1, B, S_1)$
$(P_1, L_1, W, 1, A, S_2)$ $<_{WS}$ $(P_2, L_1, W, 1, B, S_2)$

$(P_2, L_1, W, 1, B, S_1)$ $<_{WS}$ $(P_1, L_1, W, 1, A, S_1)$
$(P_2, L_1, W, 1, B, S_2)$ $<_{WS}$ $(P_1, L_1, W, 1, A, S_2)$

Consequently, under architecture A(CMP, POS, WS) every member of the graph set for the execution contains one of the following two circuits:

$(P_1, L_1, W, 1, A, S_2)$ $<_{WS}$ $(P_2, L_1, W, 1, B, S_2)$
$\quad\quad\quad\quad\quad\quad\quad\quad$ $<_{POS}$ $(P_2, L_2, R, 0, A, S_2)$
$\quad\quad\quad\quad\quad\quad\quad\quad$ $<_{CRW}$ $(P_1, L_1, W, 1, A, S_2)$

$(P_2, L_1, W, 1, B, S_1)$ $<_{WS}$ $(P_1, L_1, W, 1, A, S_1)$
$\quad\quad\quad\quad\quad\quad\quad\quad$ $<_{POS}$ $(P_1, L_2, R, 0, B, S_1)$
$\quad\quad\quad\quad\quad\quad\quad\quad$ $<_{CRW}$ $(P_2, L_1, W, 1, B, S_1)$

Under architecture A(CMP, POS) there is an element of the graph set for the execution which is circuit-free (though not WS).

Appendix A   185

$$
\begin{array}{ll}
P_1 & P_2 \\
& (L_1,R,1,1,S_2) \\
(L_1,R,1,1,S_1) & \\
(L_1,W,1,A,S_1) & \\
(L_2,R,0,B,S_1) & \\
& (L_1,W,1,B,S_1) \\
& (L_1,W,1,B,S_2) \\
& (L_2,R,0,A,S_2) \\
(L_1,W,1,A,S_2) & \\
& (L_2,W,0,X,S_1) \\
& (L_2,W,0,X,S_2) \\
(L_2,W,0,Y,S_1) & \\
(L_2,W,0,Y,S_2) &
\end{array}
$$

Theorem A40. $A(CMP, RA) \neg \Rightarrow A(CMP, RA, WS)$.

Proof. Consider the following execution.

Initially, $A = B = C = D = 0$.

$$
\begin{array}{llll}
P_1 & P_2 & P_3 & P_4 \\
L_1: A:=1; & L_1: X:=A+B; & L_1: Y:=A+B; & L_1: B:=2;
\end{array}
$$

Terminally, $A = 1$, $B = 2$, $X = 1$, and $Y = 2$.

Under architecture $A(WS)$ every element of the graph set for the execution contains one of the following two pairs of paths:

$$
\begin{array}{lll}
(P_1,L_1,W,1,A,S_2) & <_{WS} & (P_4,L_1,W,2,B,S_2) \\
(P_1,L_1,W,1,A,S_3) & <_{WS} & (P_4,L_1,W,2,B,S_3)
\end{array}
$$

$$
\begin{array}{lll}
(P_4,L_1,W,2,B,S_2) & <_{WS} & (P_1,L_1,W,1,A,S_2) \\
(P_4,L_1,W,2,B,S_3) & <_{WS} & (P_1,L_1,W,1,A,S_3)
\end{array}
$$

Consequently, under architecture $A(CMP, RA, WS)$ every member of the graph set for the execution contains one of the following two circuits:

$$
\begin{array}{lll}
(P_1,L_1,W,1,A,S_3) & <_{WS} & (P_4,L_1,W,2,B,S_3) \\
& <_{CWR} & (P_3,L_1,R,2,B,S_3) \\
& =_{RA} & (P_3,L_1,R,0,A,S_3) \\
& <_{CRW} & (P_1,L_1,W,1,A,S_3)
\end{array}
$$

$$
\begin{array}{lll}
(P_4,L_1,W,2,B,S_2) & <_{WS} & (P_1,L_1,W,1,A,S_2) \\
& <_{CWR} & (P_2,L_1,R,1,A,S_2) \\
& =_{RA} & (P_2,L_1,R,0,B,S_2) \\
& <_{CRW} & (P_4,L_1,W,2,B,S_2)
\end{array}
$$

Under architecture A(CMP, RA) there is an element of the graph set for the execution which is circuit-free (though not WS).

$$
\begin{array}{llll}
P_1 & P_2 & P_3 & P_4 \\
(L_1,R,1,1,S_1) & & & \\
(L_1,W,1,A,S_1) & & & \\
 & (L_1,R,1,A,S_2) & & \\
 & (L_1,R,0,B,S_2) & & \\
 & (L_1,W,1,X,S) & & \\
 & & & (L_1,R,2,2,S_4) \\
 & & & (L_1,W,2,B,S) \\
 & & (L_1,R,0,A,S_3) & \\
 & & (L_1,R,2,B,S_3) & \\
 & & (L_1,W,2,Y,S) & \\
(L_1,W,1,A,S_2) & & & \\
(L_1,W,1,A,S_3) & & & \\
(L_1,W,1,A,S_4) & & & \\
\end{array}
$$

Theorem A41. A(CMP, WO) $\neg \Rightarrow$ A(CMP, WO, RS).

Proof. Consider the following execution.

Initially, A = B = X = Y = 0.

$$
\begin{array}{lll}
P_1 & P_2 & P_3 \\
L_1: A:= 1; & L_1: X:= A + B; & L_1: Y:= A + B; \\
L_2: A:= 2; & & \\
L_3: B:= 4; & & \\
L_4: B:= 8; & & \\
\end{array}
$$

Terminally, A = 2, B = 8, X = 8, Y = 2.

Under architecture A(RS) every element of the graph set for the execution contains one of the following two pairs of paths:

$$
\begin{aligned}
(P_2,L_1,R,0,A,S_2) &<_{RS} (P_3,L_1,R,2,A,S_3) \\
(P_2,L_1,R,8,B,S_2) &<_{RS} (P_3,L_1,R,0,B,S_3) \\[6pt]
(P_3,L_1,R,2,A,S_3) &<_{RS} (P_2,L_1,R,0,A,S_2) \\
(P_3,L_1,R,0,B,S_3) &<_{RS} (P_2,L_1,R,8,B,S_2) \\
\end{aligned}
$$

Consequently, under architecture A(CMP, WO, RS) every member of the graph set for the execution contains one of the following two circuits:

$$
\begin{aligned}
(P_2,L_1,R,8,B,S_2) &<_{RS} (P_3,L_1,R,0,B,S_3) \\
&<_{CRW} (P_1,L_3,W,4,B,S_3) \\
&<_{WO} (P_1,L_4,W,8,B,S_2) \\
&<_{CWR} (P_2,L_1,R,8,B,S_2) \\
\end{aligned}
$$

Appendix A

$$(P_3, L_1, R, 2, A, S_3) <_{RS} (P_2, L_1, R, 0, A, S_2)$$
$$<_{CRW} (P_1, L_1, W, 1, A, S_2)$$
$$<_{WO} (P_1, L_2, W, 2, A, S_3)$$
$$<_{CWR} (P_3, L_1, R, 2, A, S_3)$$

Under architecture A(CMP, WO) there is an element of the graph set for the execution which is circuit-free (though not RS).

P_1	P_2	P_3
	$(L_1, R, 0, A, S_2)$	
$(L_1, R, 1, 1, S_1)$		
$(L_1, W, 1, A, S)$		
$(L_2, R, 2, 2, S_1)$		
$(L_2, W, 2, A, S)$		
		$(L_1, R, 2, A, S_3)$
		$(L_1, R, 0, B, S_3)$
$(L_3, R, 4, 4, S_1)$		
$(L_3, W, 4, B, S)$		
$(L_4, R, 8, 8, S_1)$		
$(L_4, W, 8, B, S)$		
	$(L_1, R, 8, B, S_2)$	
	$(L_1, W, 8, X, S)$	
		$(L_1, W, 2, Y, S)$

Theorem A42. A(CMP, WA) $\neg \Rightarrow$ A(CMP, WA, RS).

Proof. Consider the following execution.

Initially, A = B = X = Y = 0.

P_1	P_2	P_3	P_4
L_1: A := 1;	L_1: X := A + B;	L_1: Y := A + B;	L_1: B := 2;

Terminally, A = 1, B = 2, X = 1, and Y = 2.

Under architecture A(RS) every element of the graph set for the execution contains one of the following two pairs of paths:

$$(P_2, L_1, R, 1, A, S_2) <_{RS} (P_3, L_1, R, 0, A, S_3)$$
$$(P_2, L_1, R, 0, B, S_2) <_{RS} (P_3, L_1, R, 2, B, S_3)$$

$$(P_3, L_1, R, 0, A, S_3) <_{RS} (P_2, L_1, R, 1, A, S_2)$$
$$(P_3, L_1, R, 2, B, S_3) <_{RS} (P_2, L_1, R, 0, B, S_2)$$

Consequently, under architecture A(CMP, WA, RS) every member of the graph set for the execution contains one of the following two circuits:

$$(P_2, L_1, R, 1, A, S_2) <_{RS} (P_3, L_1, R, 0, A, S_3)$$
$$<_{CRW} (P_1, L_1, W, 1, A, S_3)$$
$$=_{WA} (P_1, L_1, W, 1, A, S_2)$$
$$<_{CWR} (P_2, L_1, R, 1, A, S_2)$$

$$(P_3, L_1, R, 2, B, S_3) <_{RS} (P_2, L_1, R, 0, B, S_2)$$
$$<_{CRW} (P_4, L_1, W, 2, B, S_2)$$
$$=_{WA} (P_4, L_1, W, 2, B, S_3)$$
$$<_{CWR} (P_3, L_1, R, 2, B, S_3)$$

Under architecture A(CMP, WA) there is an element of the graph set for the execution which is circuit-free (though not RS).

P_1	P_2	P_3	P_4
		$(L_1, R, 0, A, S_3)$	
$(L_1, R, 1, 1, S_1)$			
$(L_1, W, 1, A, S)$			
	$(L_1, R, 1, A, S_2)$		
	$(L_1, R, 0, B, S_2)$		
			$(L_1, R, 2, 2, S_4)$
			$(L_1, W, 2, B, S)$
		$(L_1, R, 2, B, S_3)$	
	$(L_1, W, 1, X, S)$		
		$(L_1, W, 2, Y, S)$	

Theorem A43. A(CMP, RO) $\neg \Rightarrow$ A(CMP, RO, AWC).

Proof. Consider the following execution.

Initially, A = B = X = Y = Z = 0.

P_1	P_2	P_3
L_1: A:= 1;	L_1: X:= B;	L_1: Z:= A;
	L_2: Y:= A;	L_2: B:= 1;

Terminally, A = B = X = 1, Y = 0, Z = 1.

Under architecture A(CMP, RO, AWC) every member of the graph set for the execution contains the following circuit:

Appendix A

$$(P_1,L_1,W,1,A,S_3) \quad <_{CWR} \quad (P_3,L_1,R,1,A,S_3)$$
$$<_{RO} \quad (P_3,L_2,R,1,1,S_3)$$
$$<_{SRW} \quad (P_3,L_2,W,1,B,S_2)$$
$$<_{CWR} \quad (P_2,L_1,R,1,B,S_2)$$
$$<_{RO} \quad (P_2,L_2,R,0,A,S_2)$$
$$<_{CRW} \quad (P_1,L_1,W,1,A,S_2)$$
$$<_{AWC} \quad (P_1,L_1,W,1,A,S_3)$$

Under architecture A(CMP, RO) there is an element of the graph set for the execution which is circuit-free (though not AWC).

P_1	P_2	P_3
$(L_1,R,1,1,S_1)$		
$(L_1,W,1,A,S_1)$		
$(L_1,W,1,A,S_3)$		
		$(L_1,R,1,A,S_3)$
		$(L_1,W,1,Z,S)$
		$(L_2,R,1,1,S_3)$
		$(L_2,W,1,B,S)$
	$(L_1,R,1,B,S_2)$	
	$(L_1,W,1,X,S)$	
	$(L_2,R,0,A,S_2)$	
	$(L_2,W,0,Y,S)$	
$(L_1,W,1,A,S_2)$		

Theorem A44. A(CMP, ARC) $\neg \Rightarrow$ A(CMP, ARC, AWC).

Proof. Consider the following execution.

Initially, A = B = X = 0.

P_1	P_2	P_3
L_1: X:= A + B;	L_1: A:= 1;	L_1: B:= A + 1;

Terminally, A = 1, B = 2, X = 2.

Under architecture A(CMP, ARC, AWC) every member of the graph set for the execution contains the following circuit:

$$(P_1,L_1,R,2,B,S_1) \quad <_{ARC} \quad (P_1,L_1,R,0,A,S_1)$$
$$<_{CRW} \quad (P_2,L_1,W,1,A,S_1)$$
$$<_{AWC} \quad (P_2,L_1,W,1,A,S_3)$$
$$<_{CWR} \quad (P_3,L_1,R,1,A,S_3)$$
$$<_{SRW} \quad (P_3,L_1,W,2,B,S_1)$$
$$<_{CWR} \quad (P_1,L_1,R,2,B,S_1)$$

Under architecture A(CMP, ARC) there is an element of the graph set for the execution which is circuit-free (though not AWC).

```
        P₁                    P₂                    P₃
                        (L₁,R,1,1,S₂)
                        (L₁,W,1,A,S₂)
                        (L₁,W,1,A,S₃)
                                              (L₁,R,1,A,S₃)
                                              (L₁,R,1,1,S₃)
                                              (L₁,W,2,B,S)
  (L₁,R,0,A,S₁)
  (L₁,R,2,B,S₁)
                        (L₁,W,1,A,S₁)
  (L₁,W,2,X,S)
```

Theorem A45. A(CMP, RO) ¬⇒ A(CMP, RO, RWC).

Proof. Consider the following execution.

```
Initially, A = B = C = D = S = T = U = V = X = Y = 0

      P₁              P₂              P₃              P₄
L₁: A:= 1;    L₁: B:= 1;    L₁: U:= A;     L₁: S:= C;
                            L₂: C:= 1;     L₂: V:= A;
                            L₃: T:= D;     L₃: X:= B;
                            L₄: Y:= B;     L₄: D:= 1;

Terminally, A = B = C = D = S = T = U = X = 1,
V = 0, Y = 0.
```

Under architecture A(RWC) every element of the graph set for the execution contains one of the following two pairs of paths:

$$(P_1, L_1, W, 1, A, S_3) <_{RWC} (P_1, L_1, W, 1, A, S_4)$$
$$(P_2, L_1, W, 1, B, S_3) <_{RWC} (P_2, L_1, W, 1, B, S_4)$$

$$(P_1, L_1, W, 1, A, S_4) <_{RWC} (P_1, L_1, W, 1, A, S_3)$$
$$(P_2, L_1, W, 1, B, S_4) <_{RWC} (P_2, L_1, W, 1, B, S_3)$$

Consequently, under architecture A(CMP, RO, RWC) every member of the graph set for the execution contains one of the following two circuits:

$$(P_2, L_1, W, 1, B, S_3) <_{RWC} (P_2, L_1, W, 1, B, S_4)$$
$$<_{CWR} (P_4, L_3, R, 1, B, S_4)$$
$$<_{RO} (P_4, L_4, R, 1, 1, S_4)$$

Appendix A

$$<_{SRW} \ (P_4, L_4, W, 1, D, S_3)$$
$$<_{CWR} \ (P_3, L_3, R, 1, D, S_3)$$
$$<_{RO} \ (P_3, L_4, R, 0, B, S_3)$$
$$<_{CRW} \ (P_2, L_1, W, 1, B, S_3)$$

$$(P_1, L_1, W, 1, A, S_4) \ <_{RWC} \ (P_1, L_1, W, 1, A, S_3)$$
$$<_{CWR} \ (P_3, L_1, R, 1, A, S_3)$$
$$<_{RO} \ (P_3, L_2, R, 1, 1, S_3)$$
$$<_{SRW} \ (P_3, L_2, W, 1, C, S_4)$$
$$<_{CWR} \ (P_4, L_1, R, 1, C, S_4)$$
$$<_{RO} \ (P_4, L_2, R, 0, A, S_4)$$
$$<_{CRW} \ (P_1, L_1, W, 1, A, S_4)$$

Under architecture A(CMP, RO) there is an element of the graph set for the execution which is circuit-free (though not RWC).

P_1	P_2	P_3	P_4
$(L_1, R, 1, 1, S_1)$			
	$(L_1, R, 1, 1, S_2)$		
$(L_1, W, 1, A, S_1)$			
$(L_1, W, 1, A, S_2)$			
$(L_1, W, 1, A, S_3)$			
		$(L_1, R, 1, A, S_3)$	
		$(L_1, W, 1, U, S)$	
		$(L_2, R, 1, 1, S_3)$	
		$(L_2, W, 1, C, S)$	
			$(L_1, R, 1, C, S_4)$
			$(L_1, W, 1, S, S)$
			$(L_2, R, 0, A, S_4)$
			$(L_2, W, 0, V, S)$
$(L_1, W, 1, A, S_4)$			
	$(L_1, W, 1, B, S_1)$		
	$(L_1, W, 1, B, S_2)$		
	$(L_1, W, 1, B, S_4)$		
			$(L_3, R, 1, B, S_4)$
			$(L_3, W, 1, X, S)$
			$(L_4, R, 1, 1, S_4)$
			$(L_4, W, 1, D, S)$
		$(L_3, R, 1, D, S_3)$	
		$(L_3, W, 1, T, S)$	
		$(L_4, R, 0, B, S_3)$	
		$(L_4, W, 0, Y, S)$	
	$(L_1, W, 1, B, S_3)$		

Theorem A46. A(CMP, WO) $\neg \Rightarrow$ A(CMP, WO, ARC).

Proof. Consider the following execution.

Initially, A = B = X = 0.

$$P_1 \qquad\qquad P_2$$
$$L_1: X := A + B; \qquad L_1: B := 2;$$
$$\qquad\qquad\qquad\quad L_2: A := 1;$$

Terminally, A = 1, B = 2, X = 1.

Under architecture A(CMP, WO, ARC) every member of the graph set for the execution contains the following circuit:

$$(P_1, L_1, R, 0, B, S_1) <_{CRW} (P_2, L_1, W, 2, B, S_1)$$
$$\qquad\qquad\qquad\quad <_{WO} (P_2, L_2, W, 1, A, S_1)$$
$$\qquad\qquad\qquad\quad <_{CWR} (P_1, L_1, R, 1, A, S_1)$$
$$\qquad\qquad\qquad\quad <_{ARC} (P_1, L_1, R, 0, B, S_1)$$

Under architecture A(CMP, WO) there is an element of the graph set for the execution which is circuit-free (though not ARC).

$$P_1 \qquad\qquad\qquad P_2$$
$$(L_1, R, 0, B, S_1)$$
$$\qquad\qquad\qquad (L_1, R, 2, 2, S_2)$$
$$\qquad\qquad\qquad (L_1, W, 2, B, S)$$
$$\qquad\qquad\qquad (L_2, R, 1, 1, S_2)$$
$$\qquad\qquad\qquad (L_2, W, 1, A, S)$$
$$(L_1, R, 1, A, S_1)$$
$$(L_1, W, 1, X, S)$$

Theorem A47. A(CMP, AWC) $\neg \Rightarrow$ A(CMP, AWC, ARC).

Proof. Consider the following execution.

Initially, A = B = X = 0.

$$P_1 \qquad\qquad P_2 \qquad\qquad P_3$$
$$L_1: X := A + B; \quad L_1: A := 1; \quad L_1: B := A + 1;$$

Terminally, A = 1, B = 2, X = 2.

Under architecture A(CMP, ARC, AWC) every member of the graph set for the execution contains the following circuit:

$$(P_1, L_1, R, 2, B, S_1) <_{ARC} (P_1, L_1, R, 0, A, S_1)$$
$$\qquad\qquad\qquad\quad <_{CRW} (P_2, L_1, W, 1, A, S_1)$$
$$\qquad\qquad\qquad\quad <_{AWC} (P_2, L_1, W, 1, A, S_3)$$
$$\qquad\qquad\qquad\quad <_{CWR} (P_3, L_1, R, 1, A, S_3)$$
$$\qquad\qquad\qquad\quad <_{SRW} (P_3, L_1, W, 2, B, S_1)$$
$$\qquad\qquad\qquad\quad <_{CWR} (P_1, L_1, R, 2, B, S_1)$$

Under architecture A(CMP, AWC) there is an element of the graph set for the execution which is circuit-free (though not ARC).

P_1 P_2 P_3

$(L_1, R, 0, A, S_1)$

           $(L_1, R, 1, 1, S_2)$
           $(L_1, W, 1, A, S)$

                       $(L_1, R, 1, A, S_3)$
                       $(L_1, R, 1, 1, S_3)$
                       $(L_1, W, 2, B, S)$

$(L_1, R, 2, B, S_1)$
$(L_1, W, 2, X, S)$

Theorem A48. A(CMP, WO) $\neg \Rightarrow$ A(CMP, WO, RRC).

Proof. Consider the following execution.

Initially, A = B = X = Y = 0.

P_1 P_2 P_3 P_4
L_1: A:= 1; L_1: B:= 4; L_1: X:= A + B; L_1: Y:= A + B;
L_2: B:= 2; L_2: A:= 8;

Terminally, A = 8, B = 2, X = 2, Y = 8.

Under architecture A(RRC) every element of the graph set for the execution contains one of the following two pairs of paths:

$(P_3, L_1, R, 0, A, S_3)$ $<_{RRC}$ $(P_3, L_1, R, 2, B, S_3)$
$(P_4, L_1, R, 8, A, S_4)$ $<_{RRC}$ $(P_4, L_1, R, 0, B, S_4)$

$(P_3, L_1, R, 2, B, S_3)$ $<_{RRC}$ $(P_3, L_1, R, 0, A, S_3)$
$(P_4, L_1, R, 0, B, S_4)$ $<_{RRC}$ $(P_4, L_1, R, 8, A, S_4)$

Consequently, under architecture A(CMP, WO, RRC) every member of the graph set for the execution contains one of the following two circuits:

$(P_4, L_1, R, 8, A, S_4)$ $<_{RRC}$ $(P_4, L_1, R, 0, B, S_4)$
                      $<_{CRW}$ $(P_2, L_1, W, 4, B, S_4)$
                      $<_{WO}$ $(P_2, L_2, W, 8, A, S_4)$
                      $<_{CWR}$ $(P_4, L_1, R, 8, A, S_4)$

$(P_3, L_1, R, 2, B, S_3)$ $<_{RRC}$ $(P_3, L_1, R, 0, A, S_3)$
                      $<_{CRW}$ $(P_1, L_1, W, 1, A, S_3)$
                      $<_{WO}$ $(P_1, L_2, W, 2, B, S_3)$
                      $<_{CWR}$ $(P_3, L_1, R, 2, B, S_3)$

Under architecture A(CMP, WO) there is an element of the graph set for the execution which is circuit-free (though not RRC).

P_1	P_2	P_3	P_4
		$(L_1,R,0,A,S_3)$	
			$(L_1,R,0,B,S_4)$
$(L_1,R,1,1,S_1)$			
$(L_1,W,1,A,S)$			
	$(L_1,R,4,4,S_2)$		
	$(L_1,W,4,B,S)$		
	$(L_2,R,8,8,S_2)$		
	$(L_2,W,8,A,S)$		
$(L_2,R,2,2,S_1)$			
$(L_2,W,2,B,S)$			
		$(L_1,R,2,B,S_3)$	
			$(L_1,R,8,A,S_4)$
		$(L_1,W,2,X,S)$	
			$(L_1,W,8,Y,S)$

Appendix B

A Program to Assist with Lemma 12.5

In developing the proof of Lemma 12.5 it was convenient to write a program which accepted the transition templates for the basic model as input and which generated a search tree describing all paths containing three or four or more events, starting from some standard event, represented by (P,L,A,V,O,S). The program handled the tedious, repetitive detail, allowing effort to be placed on finding a minimal set of conditions with which to terminate the search. The program also made it easy to explore variations and alternatives.

The full search tree generated by the program for the proof of Lemma 12.5 is shown below. The program itself is straightforward and of no especial interest.

TRANSITION TEMPLATES

$$(P,L,R,V,O,S) <_{SRW} (=,=,W,-,-,-)$$
$$(P,L,W,V,O,S) <_{CWR} (-,-,R,=,=,=)$$
$$(P,L,R,V,O,S) <_{CRW} (-,-,W,-,=,=)$$
$$(P,L,W,V,O,S) <_{CWW} (-,-,W,-,=,=)$$
$$(P,L,W,V,O,S) <_{UWR} (=,-,R,-,=,=)$$
$$(P,L,R,V,O,S) <_{URW} (=,-,W,-,=,=)$$
$$(P,L,W,V,O,S) <_{UWW} (=,-,W,-,=,=)$$
$$(P,L,R,V,O,S) <_{RO} (=,-,R,-,-,=)$$
$$(P,L,R,V,O,S) <_{ROO} (=,-,R,-,=,=)$$
$$(P,L,W,V,O,S) <_{WO} (=,-,W,-,-,-)$$
$$(P,L,W,V,O,S) <_{WOO} (=,-,W,-,=,-)$$
$$(P,L,W,V,O,S) <_{WOS} (=,-,W,-,-,=)$$

$(P,L,-,V,O,S)$	$<_{PO}$	$(=,-,R,-,-,-)$
$(P,L,-,V,O,S)$	$<_{PO}$	$(=,-,W,-,-,-)$
$(P,L,-,V,O,S)$	$<_{POO}$	$(=,-,R,-,=,-)$
$(P,L,-,V,O,S)$	$<_{POO}$	$(=,-,W,-,=,-)$
$(P,L,-,V,O,S)$	$<_{POS}$	$(=,-,R,-,-,=)$
$(P,L,-,V,O,S)$	$<_{POS}$	$(=,-,W,-,-,=)$
$(P,L,-,V,O,S)$	$<_{RA}$	$(-,-,-,-,-,-)$
(P,L,R,V,O,S)	$=_{RA}$	$(=,=,R,-,-,=)$
$(P,L,-,V,O,S)$	$<_{WA}$	$(-,-,-,-,-,-)$
(P,L,W,V,O,S)	$=_{WA}$	$(=,=,W,=,=,\#)$
$(P,L,-,V,O,S)$	$<_{SA}$	$(-,-,-,-,-,-)$
$(P,L,-,V,O,S)$	$=_{SA}$	$(=,=,R,-,-,-)$
$(P,L,-,V,O,S)$	$=_{SA}$	$(=,=,W,-,-,-)$
(P,L,R,V,O,S)	$<_{RS}$	$(-,-,R,-,=,-)$
(P,L,R,V,O,S)	$<_{ARC}$	$(=,=,R,-,-,=)$
(P,L,R,V,O,S)	$<_{RRC}$	$(=,=,R,-,-,=)$
(P,L,W,V,O,S)	$<_{WS}$	$(-,-,W,-,-,=)$
(P,L,W,V,O,S)	$<_{CON}$	$(-,-,W,-,=,=)$
(P,L,W,V,O,S)	$<_{AWC}$	$(=,=,W,=,=,\#)$
(P,L,W,V,O,S)	$<_{RWC}$	$(=,=,W,=,=,\#)$

THE FULL SEARCH TREE

0		(P,L,W,V,O,S)	
1	$<_{SRW}$	$(-,-,-,-,-,-)$	1. W $<_{SRW}$ $-$.
2	$<_{CWR}$	$(S,-,R,V,O,S)$	6. Not determined.
3	$<_{SRW}$	$(S,-,W,-,-,-)$	5. $E_2 <$ all(E_3).
4	$<_{CWR}$	$(-,-,-,-,-,-)$	1. R $<_{CWR}$ $-$.
5	$<_{CRW}$	$(-,-,W,-,O,S)$	4. $E_1 <_{WS} E_3$.
6	$<_{CWW}$	$(-,-,-,-,-,-)$	1. R $<_{CWW}$ $-$.
7	$<_{UWR}$	$(-,-,-,-,-,-)$	1. R $<_{UWR}$ $-$.
8	$<_{URW}$	$(S,-,W,-,O,S)$	4. $E_1 <_{WS} E_3$.
9	$<_{UWW}$	$(-,-,-,-,-,-)$	1. R $<_{UWW}$ $-$.
10	$<_{RO}$	$(S,-,R,-,-,S)$	3. P–R–P $<$ P–R–P.
11	$<_{ROO}$	$(S,-,R,-,O,S)$	3. P–R–P $<$ P–R–P.
12	$<_{WO}$	$(-,-,-,-,-,-)$	1. R $<_{WO}$ $-$.
13	$<_{WOO}$	$(-,-,-,-,-,-)$	1. R $<_{WOO}$ $-$.
14	$<_{WOS}$	$(-,-,-,-,-,-)$	1. R $<_{WOS}$ $-$.
15	$<_{PO}$	$(S,-,R,-,-,S)$	3. P–R–P $<$ P–R–P.
16	$<_{PO}$	$(S,-,W,-,-,-)$	5. $E_2 <$ all(E_3).
17	$<_{POO}$	$(S,-,R,-,O,S)$	3. P–R–P $<$ P–R–P.
18	$<_{POO}$	$(S,-,W,-,O,-)$	5. $E_2 <$ all(E_3).
19	$<_{POS}$	$(S,-,R,-,-,S)$	3. P–R–P $<$ P–R–P.
20	$<_{POS}$	$(S,-,W,-,-,S)$	4. $E_1 <_{WS} E_3$.
21	$<_{RA}$	$(-,-,-,-,-,-)$	2b. Fail.

Appendix B

22	$=_{RA}$	(S,−,R,−,−,S)	3. P–R–P < P–R–P.
23	$<_{WA}$	(−,−,−,−,−,−)	2b. Fail.
24	$=_{WA}$	(−,−,−,−,−,−)	1. R $=_{WA}$ −.
25	$<_{SA}$	(−,−,−,−,−,−)	2b. Fail.
26	$=_{SA}$	(S,−,R,−,−,S)	3. P–R–P < P–R–P.
27	$=_{SA}$	(S,−,W,−,−,−)	5. E_2 < all(E_3).
28	$<_{RS}$	(−,−,R,−,0,−)	2a. Fail.
29	$<_{ARC}$	(S,−,R,−,−,S)	3. P–R–P < P–R–P.
30	$<_{RRC}$	(S,−,R,−,−,S)	3. P–R–P < P–R–P.
31	$<_{WS}$	(−,−,−,−,−,−)	1. R $<_{WS}$ −.
32	$<_{CON}$	(−,−,−,−,−,−)	1. R $<_{CON}$ −.
33	$<_{AWC}$	(−,−,−,−,−,−)	1. R $<_{AWC}$ −.
34	$<_{RWC}$	(−,−,−,−,−,−)	1. R $<_{RWC}$ −.
35	$<_{CRW}$	(−,−,−,−,−,−)	1. W $<_{CRW}$ −.
36	$<_{CWW}$	(−,−,W,−,0,S)	4. E_1 $<_{WS}$ E_2.
37	$<_{UWR}$	(S,−,R,−,0,S)	6. Not determined.
38	$<_{SRW}$	(S,−,W,−,−,−)	5. E_2 < all(E_3).
39	$<_{CWR}$	(−,−,−,−,−,−)	1. R $<_{CWR}$ −.
40	$<_{CRW}$	(−,−,W,−,0,S)	4. E_1 $<_{WS}$ E_3.
41	$<_{CWW}$	(−,−,−,−,−,−)	1. R $<_{CWW}$ −.
42	$<_{UWR}$	(−,−,−,−,−,−)	1. R $<_{UWR}$ −.
43	$<_{URW}$	(S,−,W,−,0,S)	4. E_1 $<_{WS}$ E_3.
44	$<_{UWW}$	(−,−,−,−,−,−)	1. R $<_{UWW}$ −.
45	$<_{RO}$	(S,−,R,−,−,S)	3. P–R–P < P–R–P.
46	$<_{ROO}$	(S,−,R,−,0,S)	3. P–R–P < P–R–P.
47	$<_{WO}$	(−,−,−,−,−,−)	1. R $<_{WO}$ −.
48	$<_{WOO}$	(−,−,−,−,−,−)	1. R $<_{WOO}$ −.
49	$<_{WOS}$	(−,−,−,−,−,−)	1. R $<_{WOS}$ −.
50	$<_{PO}$	(S,−,R,−,−,S)	3. P–R–P < P–R–P.
51	$<_{PO}$	(S,−,W,−,−,−)	5. E_2 < all(E_3).
52	$<_{POO}$	(S,−,R,−,0,S)	3. P–R–P < P–R–P.
53	$<_{POO}$	(S,−,W,−,0,−)	5. E_2 < all(E_3).
54	$<_{POS}$	(S,−,R,−,−,S)	3. P–R–P < P–R–P.
55	$<_{POS}$	(S,−,W,−,−,S)	4. E_1 $<_{WS}$ E_3.
56	$<_{RA}$	(−,−,−,−,−,−)	2b. Fail.
57	$=_{RA}$	(S,−,R,−,−,S)	3. P–R–P < P–R–P.
58	$<_{WA}$	(−,−,−,−,−,−)	2b. Fail.
59	$=_{WA}$	(−,−,−,−,−,−)	1. R $=_{WA}$ −.
60	$<_{SA}$	(−,−,−,−,−,−)	2b. Fail.
61	$=_{SA}$	(S,−,R,−,−,S)	3. P–R–P < P–R–P.
62	$=_{SA}$	(S,−,W,−,−,−)	5. E_2 < all(E_3).
63	$<_{RS}$	(−,−,R,−,0,−)	2a. Fail.
64	$<_{ARC}$	(S,−,R,−,−,S)	3. P–R–P < P–R–P.
65	$<_{RRC}$	(S,−,R,−,−,S)	3. P–R–P < P–R–P.
66	$<_{WS}$	(−,−,−,−,−,−)	1. R $<_{WS}$ −.
67	$<_{CON}$	(−,−,−,−,−,−)	1. R $<_{CON}$ −.
68	$<_{AWC}$	(−,−,−,−,−,−)	1. R $<_{AWC}$ −.
69	$<_{RWC}$	(−,−,−,−,−,−)	1. R $<_{RWC}$ −.

#	Relation	Tuple	Result
70	$<_{URW}$	$(-,-,-,-,-,-)$	1. W $<_{URW}$ $-$.
71	$<_{UWW}$	$(P,-,W,-,0,S)$	4. $E_1 <_{WS} E_2$.
72	$<_{RO}$	$(-,-,-,-,-,-)$	1. W $<_{RO}$ $-$.
73	$<_{ROO}$	$(-,-,-,-,-,-)$	1. W $<_{ROO}$ $-$.
74	$<_{WO}$	$(P,-,W,-,-,-)$	5. $E_1 < $ all(E_2).
75	$<_{WOO}$	$(P,-,W,-,0,-)$	5. $E_1 < $ all(E_2).
76	$<_{WOS}$	$(P,-,W,-,-,S)$	4. $E_1 <_{WS} E_2$.
77	$<_{PO}$	$(S,-,R,-,-,S)$	6. Not determined.
78	$<_{SRW}$	$(S,-,W,-,-,-)$	5. $E_2 < $ all(E_3).
79	$<_{CWR}$	$(-,-,-,-,-,-)$	1. R $<_{CWR}$ $-$.
80	$<_{CRW}$	$(-,-,W,-,-,S)$	4. $E_1 <_{WS} E_3$.
81	$<_{CWW}$	$(-,-,-,-,-,-)$	1. R $<_{CWW}$ $-$.
82	$<_{UWR}$	$(-,-,-,-,-,-)$	1. R $<_{UWR}$ $-$.
83	$<_{URW}$	$(S,-,W,-,-,S)$	4. $E_1 <_{WS} E_3$.
84	$<_{UWW}$	$(-,-,-,-,-,-)$	1. R $<_{UWW}$ $-$.
85	$<_{RO}$	$(S,-,R,-,-,S)$	3. P–R–P $<$ P–R–P.
86	$<_{ROO}$	$(S,-,R,-,-,S)$	3. P–R–P $<$ P–R–P.
87	$<_{WO}$	$(-,-,-,-,-,-)$	1. R $<_{WO}$ $-$.
88	$<_{WOO}$	$(-,-,-,-,-,-)$	1. R $<_{WOO}$ $-$.
89	$<_{WOS}$	$(-,-,-,-,-,-)$	1. R $<_{WOS}$ $-$.
90	$<_{PO}$	$(S,-,R,-,-,S)$	3. P–R–P $<$ P–R–P.
91	$<_{PO}$	$(S,-,W,-,-,-)$	5. $E_2 < $ all(E_3).
92	$<_{POO}$	$(S,-,R,-,-,S)$	3. P–R–P $<$ P–R–P.
93	$<_{POO}$	$(S,-,W,-,-,-)$	5. $E_2 < $ all(E_3).
94	$<_{POS}$	$(S,-,R,-,-,S)$	3. P–R–P $<$ P–R–P.
95	$<_{POS}$	$(S,-,W,-,-,S)$	4. $E_1 <_{WS} E_3$.
96	$<_{RA}$	$(-,-,-,-,-,-)$	2b. Fail.
97	$=_{RA}$	$(S,-,R,-,-,S)$	3. P–R–P $<$ P–R–P.
98	$<_{WA}$	$(-,-,-,-,-,-)$	2b. Fail.
99	$=_{WA}$	$(-,-,-,-,-,-)$	1. R $=_{WA}$ $-$.
100	$<_{SA}$	$(-,-,-,-,-,-)$	2b. Fail.
101	$=_{SA}$	$(S,-,R,-,-,S)$	3. P–R–P $<$ P–R–P.
102	$=_{SA}$	$(S,-,W,-,-,-)$	5. $E_2 < $ all(E_3).
103	$<_{RS}$	$(-,-,R,-,-,-)$	2a. Fail.
104	$<_{ARC}$	$(S,-,R,-,-,S)$	3. P–R–P $<$ P–R–P.
105	$<_{RRC}$	$(S,-,R,-,-,S)$	3. P–R–P $<$ P–R–P.
106	$<_{WS}$	$(-,-,-,-,-,-)$	1. R $<_{WS}$ $-$.
107	$<_{CON}$	$(-,-,-,-,-,-)$	1. R $<_{CON}$ $-$.
108	$<_{AWC}$	$(-,-,-,-,-,-)$	1. R $<_{AWC}$ $-$.
109	$<_{RWC}$	$(-,-,-,-,-,-)$	1. R $<_{RWC}$ $-$.
110	$<_{PO}$	$(P,-,W,-,-,-)$	5. $E_1 < $ all(E_2).
111	$<_{POO}$	$(S,-,R,-,0,S)$	6. Not determined.
112	$<_{SRW}$	$(S,-,W,-,-,-)$	5. $E_2 < $ all(E_3).
113	$<_{CWR}$	$(-,-,-,-,-,-)$	1. R $<_{CWR}$ $-$.
114	$<_{CRW}$	$(-,-,W,-,0,S)$	4. $E_1 <_{WS} E_3$.
115	$<_{CWW}$	$(-,-,-,-,-,-)$	1. R $<_{CWW}$ $-$.
116	$<_{UWR}$	$(-,-,-,-,-,-)$	1. R $<_{UWR}$ $-$.
117	$<_{URW}$	$(S,-,W,-,0,S)$	4. $E_1 <_{WS} E_3$.

Appendix B

118	$<_{UWW}$	$(-,-,-,-,-,-)$	1. R $<_{UWW}$ $-$.
119	$<_{RO}$	$(S,-,R,-,-,S)$	3. P–R–P $<$ P–R–P.
120	$<_{ROO}$	$(S,-,R,-,0,S)$	3. P–R–P $<$ P–R–P.
121	$<_{WO}$	$(-,-,-,-,-,-)$	1. R $<_{WO}$ $-$.
122	$<_{WOO}$	$(-,-,-,-,-,-)$	1. R $<_{WOO}$ $-$.
123	$<_{WOS}$	$(-,-,-,-,-,-)$	1. R $<_{WOS}$ $-$.
124	$<_{PO}$	$(S,-,R,-,-,S)$	3. P–R–P $<$ P–R–P.
125	$<_{PO}$	$(S,-,W,-,-,-)$	5. $E_2 <$ all(E_3).
126	$<_{POO}$	$(S,-,R,-,0,S)$	3. P–R–P $<$ P–R–P.
127	$<_{POO}$	$(S,-,W,-,0,-)$	5. $E_2 <$ all(E_3).
128	$<_{POS}$	$(S,-,R,-,-,S)$	3. P–R–P $<$ P–R–P.
129	$<_{POS}$	$(S,-,W,-,-,S)$	4. $E_1 <_{WS} E_3$.
130	$<_{RA}$	$(-,-,-,-,-,-)$	2b. Fail.
131	$=_{RA}$	$(S,-,R,-,-,S)$	3. P–R–P $<$ P–R–P.
132	$<_{WA}$	$(-,-,-,-,-,-)$	2b. Fail.
133	$=_{WA}$	$(-,-,-,-,-,-)$	1. R $=_{WA}$ $-$.
134	$<_{SA}$	$(-,-,-,-,-,-)$	2b. Fail.
135	$=_{SA}$	$(S,-,R,-,-,S)$	3. P–R–P $<$ P–R–P.
136	$=_{SA}$	$(S,-,W,-,-,-)$	5. $E_2 <$ all(E_3).
137	$<_{RS}$	$(-,-,R,-,0,-)$	2a. Fail.
138	$<_{ARC}$	$(S,-,R,-,-,S)$	3. P–R–P $<$ P–R–P.
139	$<_{RRC}$	$(S,-,R,-,-,S)$	3. P–R–P $<$ P–R–P.
140	$<_{WS}$	$(-,-,-,-,-,-)$	1. R $<_{WS}$ $-$.
141	$<_{CON}$	$(-,-,-,-,-,-)$	1. R $<_{CON}$ $-$.
142	$<_{AWC}$	$(-,-,-,-,-,-)$	1. R $<_{AWC}$ $-$.
143	$<_{RWC}$	$(-,-,-,-,-,-)$	1. R $<_{RWC}$ $-$.
144	$<_{POO}$	$(P,-,W,-,0,-)$	5. $E_1 <$ all(E_2).
145	$<_{POS}$	$(S,-,R,-,-,S)$	6. Not determined.
146	$<_{SRW}$	$(S,-,W,-,-,-)$	5. $E_2 <$ all(E_3).
147	$<_{CWR}$	$(-,-,-,-,-,-)$	1. R $<_{CWR}$ $-$.
148	$<_{CRW}$	$(-,-,W,-,-,S)$	4. $E_1 <_{WS} E_3$.
149	$<_{CWW}$	$(-,-,-,-,-,-)$	1. R $<_{CWW}$ $-$.
150	$<_{UWR}$	$(-,-,-,-,-,-)$	1. R $<_{UWR}$ $-$.
151	$<_{URW}$	$(S,-,W,-,-,S)$	4. $E_1 <_{WS} E_3$.
152	$<_{UWW}$	$(-,-,-,-,-,-)$	1. R $<_{UWW}$ $-$.
153	$<_{RO}$	$(S,-,R,-,-,S)$	3. P–R–P $<$ P–R–P.
154	$<_{ROO}$	$(S,-,R,-,-,S)$	3. P–R–P $<$ P–R–P.
155	$<_{WO}$	$(-,-,-,-,-,-)$	1. R $<_{WO}$ $-$.
156	$<_{WOO}$	$(-,-,-,-,-,-)$	1. R $<_{WOO}$ $-$.
157	$<_{WOS}$	$(-,-,-,-,-,-)$	1. R $<_{WOS}$ $-$.
158	$<_{PO}$	$(S,-,R,-,-,S)$	3. P–R–P $<$ P–R–P.
159	$<_{PO}$	$(S,-,W,-,-,-)$	5. $E_2 <$ all(E_3).
160	$<_{POO}$	$(S,-,R,-,-,S)$	3. P–R–P $<$ P–R–P.
161	$<_{POO}$	$(S,-,W,-,-,-)$	5. $E_2 <$ all(E_3).
162	$<_{POS}$	$(S,-,R,-,-,S)$	3. P–R–P $<$ P–R–P.
163	$<_{POS}$	$(S,-,W,-,-,S)$	4. $E_1 <_{WS} E_3$.
164	$<_{RA}$	$(-,-,-,-,-,-)$	2b. Fail.
165	$=_{RA}$	$(S,-,R,-,-,S)$	3. P–R–P $<$ P–R–P.

166	$<_{WA}$	$(-,-,-,-,-,-)$	2b. Fail.
167	$=_{WA}$	$(-,-,-,-,-,-)$	1. $R =_{WA} -$.
168	$<_{SA}$	$(-,-,-,-,-,-)$	2b. Fail.
169	$=_{SA}$	$(S,-,R,-,-,S)$	3. P–R–P $<$ P–R–P.
170	$=_{SA}$	$(S,-,W,-,-,-)$	5. $E_2 <$ all(E_3).
171	$<_{RS}$	$(-,-,R,-,-,-)$	2a. Fail.
172	$<_{ARC}$	$(S,-,R,-,-,S)$	3. P–R–P $<$ P–R–P.
173	$<_{RRC}$	$(S,-,R,-,-,S)$	3. P–R–P $<$ P–R–P.
174	$<_{WS}$	$(-,-,-,-,-,-)$	1. $R <_{WS} -$.
175	$<_{CON}$	$(-,-,-,-,-,-)$	1. $R <_{CON} -$.
176	$<_{AWC}$	$(-,-,-,-,-,-)$	1. $R <_{AWC} -$.
177	$<_{RWC}$	$(-,-,-,-,-,-)$	1. $R <_{RWC} -$.
178	$<_{POS}$ $(P,-,W,-,-,S)$		4. $E_1 <_{WS} E_2$.
179	$<_{RA}$	$(-,-,-,-,-,-)$	2b. Fail.
180	$=_{RA}$	$(-,-,-,-,-,-)$	1. $W =_{RA} -$.
181	$<_{WA}$	$(-,-,-,-,-,-)$	2b. Fail.
182	$=_{WA}$	$(P,L,W,V,O,-)$	2c. Fail.
183	$<_{SA}$	$(-,-,-,-,-,-)$	2b. Fail.
184	$=_{SA}$	$(S,L,R,-,-,S)$	6. Not determined.
185	$<_{SRW}$	$(S,L,W,-,-,-)$	5. $E_2 <$ all(E_3).
186	$<_{CWR}$	$(-,-,-,-,-,-)$	1. $R <_{CWR} -$.
187	$<_{CRW}$	$(-,-,W,-,-,S)$	4. $E_1 <_{WS} E_3$.
188	$<_{CWW}$	$(-,-,-,-,-,-)$	1. $R <_{CWW} -$.
189	$<_{UWR}$	$(-,-,-,-,-,-)$	1. $R <_{UWR} -$.
190	$<_{URW}$	$(S,-,W,-,-,-)$	4. $E_1 <_{WS} E_3$.
191	$<_{UWW}$	$(-,-,-,-,-,-)$	1. $R <_{UWW} -$.
192	$<_{RO}$	$(S,-,R,-,-,S)$	3. P–R–P $<$ P–R–P.
193	$<_{ROO}$	$(S,-,R,-,-,S)$	3. P–R–P $<$ P–R–P.
194	$<_{WO}$	$(-,-,-,-,-,-)$	1. $R <_{WO} -$.
195	$<_{WOO}$	$(-,-,-,-,-,-)$	1. $R <_{WOO} -$.
196	$<_{WOS}$	$(-,-,-,-,-,-)$	1. $R <_{WOS} -$.
197	$<_{PO}$	$(S,-,R,-,-,S)$	3. P–R–P $<$ P–R–P.
198	$<_{PO}$	$(S,-,W,-,-,-)$	5. $E_2 <$ all(E_3).
199	$<_{POO}$	$(S,-,R,-,-,S)$	3. P–R–P $<$ P–R–P.
200	$<_{POO}$	$(S,-,W,-,-,-)$	5. $E_2 <$ all(E_3).
201	$<_{POS}$	$(S,-,R,-,-,S)$	3. P–R–P $<$ P–R–P.
202	$<_{POS}$	$(S,-,W,-,-,S)$	4. $E_1 <_{WS} E_3$.
203	$<_{RA}$	$(-,-,-,-,-,-)$	2b. Fail.
204	$=_{RA}$	$(S,L,R,-,-,S)$	3. P–R–P $<$ P–R–P.
205	$<_{WA}$	$(-,-,-,-,-,-)$	2b. Fail.
206	$=_{WA}$	$(-,-,-,-,-,-)$	1. $R =_{WA} -$.
207	$<_{SA}$	$(-,-,-,-,-,-)$	2b. Fail.
208	$=_{SA}$	$(S,L,R,-,-,S)$	3. P–R–P $<$ P–R–P.
209	$=_{SA}$	$(S,L,W,-,-,-)$	5. $E_2 <$ all(E_3).
210	$<_{RS}$	$(-,-,R,-,-,-)$	2a. Fail.
211	$<_{ARC}$	$(S,L,R,-,-,S)$	3. P–R–P $<$ P–R–P.
212	$<_{RRC}$	$(S,L,R,-,-,S)$	3. P–R–P $<$ P–R–P.
213	$<_{WS}$	$(-,-,-,-,-,-)$	1. $R <_{WS} -$.

Appendix B

214	$<_{CON}$	$(-,-,-,-,-,-)$	1. R $<_{CON}$ —.
215	$<_{AWC}$	$(-,-,-,-,-,-)$	1. R $<_{AWC}$ —.
216	$<_{RWC}$	$(-,-,-,-,-,-)$	1. R $<_{RWC}$ —.
217	$=_{SA}$	$(P,L,W,-,-,-)$	2c. Fail.
218	$<_{RS}$	$(-,-,-,-,-,-)$	1. W $<_{RS}$ —.
219	$<_{ARC}$	$(-,-,-,-,-,-)$	1. W $<_{ARC}$ —.
220	$<_{RRC}$	$(-,-,-,-,-,-)$	1. W $<_{RRC}$ —.
221	$<_{WS}$	$(-,-,W,-,-,S)$	4. $E_1 <_{WS} E_2$.
222	$<_{CON}$	$(-,-,W,-,0,S)$	4. $E_1 <_{WS} E_2$.
223	$<_{AWC}$	$(P,L,W,V,0,-)$	2c. Fail.
224	$<_{RWC}$	$(P,L,W,V,0,-)$	2c. Fail.

Explanations

1. R (W) $<$xxx —. A read (write) event cannot have an arc labeled $<$xxx incident out of it.
2a. Fail. The lemma fails irreparably on arcs labeled $<_{RS}$.
2b. Fail. Arcs labeled $<_{RA}$, $<_{WA}$, and $<_{SA}$ are excluded from the lemma.
2c. Fail. Arcs labeled $=_{WA}$, $=_{SA}$, $<_{AWC}$, and $<_{RWC}$ are excluded from the lemma (but see Lemma 12.4).
3. P–R–P $<$ P–R–P. Two read events in sequence in a path have the same process and store components.
4. $E_1 <_{WS} E_i$. There is a path from E_1 to E_i. The two write events have the same store component. Since the execution is write synchronized and circuit-free, there is also an arc labeled $<_{WS}$ from E_1 to E_i. Hence, $E_1 <_{WS} X(E_i, E_1)$.
5. $E_i <$xxx all(E_j). By the definition of $<$xxx if $E_i <$xxx E_j, then $E_i <$xxx E_k, where E_k is any other write event in the statement containing E_j. In particular, $E_i <_{WS} X(E_i, E_j)$.
6. Not Determined. There is insufficient information in the event either to prove or to disprove the lemma at this event in the path. Therefore, continue the search at the next level down in the tree.

Appendix C

Problems and Solutions

1.1. Consider each sequence of X values below (for $k = 5$) as the result of executing Program 1.
  (a) If the sequence obeys both Condition 1 and Condition 2, then show an arrangement of events (statements will do) that computes the X sequence.
  (b) If the sequence violates Condition 1, say how.
  (c) If the sequence obeys Condition 1, but violates Condition 2, then show an arrangement of statements that computes the X sequence, but violates the rule of write order. Do the same for read order.
  (a) 1, 2, 2, 3, 5.
  (b) 1, 2, 97, 3, 5.
  (c) 1, 2, 4, 3, 5.

  [Ans. Obeys Conditions 1 and 2. Violates Condition 1. Obeys Condition 1, but violates Condition 2.]

1.2. Assume four runs were made using Program 2 (with $k = 5$) to see if a machine obeyed the architecture consisting of the rules of computation, write order, read order, and write atomicity. For each set of output data shown below, say what rule, if any, the data shows the machine not to obey.

  a.

U	V	X	Y
1	0	0	4
2	1	3	4
2	1	4	5
4	1	7	5
5	1	7	5

  [Ans. X[4] > 5 and X[5] > 5 imply that the execution does not obey the rule of computation.]

Appendix C

b.

U	V	X	Y
0	1	1	4
2	1	2	5
4	1	4	5
3	2	4	5
5	2	4	5

[Ans. U[3] > U[4] implies that the execution does not obey the rules of computation, write order, or read order.]

c.

U	V	X	Y
2	0	1	2
5	1	1	3
5	4	3	4
5	5	3	5
5	5	4	5

[Ans. V[2] < X[3] and Y[3] < U[2] implies that the execution does not obey the rules of computation, write order, read order, or write atomicity.]

d.

U	V	X	Y
0	2	0	1
3	2	0	1
3	2	0	3
4	2	5	4
4	3	5	5

[Ans. Does not visibly disobey the rules of computation, write order, read order, and write atomicity.]

1.3. A failure to be write atomic means that two write events in the same statement can be shown not to have happened at the same time. Use the "happens before" relations in the section on atomicity to show that $(P_4, L_n, W, B, S_3) < \ldots < (P_4, L_n, W, B, S_2)$ in Program 2.

[Ans.
$$
\begin{aligned}
(P_4, L_n, W, B, S_3) &< (P_3, L_{BJ}, R, B, S_3) \\
&< (P_3, L_{AJ}, R, A, S_3) \\
&< (P_1, L_m, W, A, S_2) \\
&< (P_2, L_{AI}, R, A, S_2) \\
&< (P_2, L_{BI}, R, B, S_2) \\
&< (P_4, L_n, W, B, S_2)]
\end{aligned}
$$

1.4. A straightforward search for a violation of Condition 3 involves $2 * k ** 2$ tests: test for V[I] < X[J] and test for Y[J] < U[I] at each point (I,J) on the grid that follows.

```
k • • • • • •     •
  • • • • • •     •
  • • • • • •     •
  • • • • • •     •
5 • • • • • •     •
4 • • • • • •     •
3 • • • • • •     •
2 • • • • • •     •
1 • • • • • •     •
  1 2 3 4 5       k
```

Assume that the values in the U, V, X, and Y sequences are monotonically increasing and find a search that requires only $2 * k$ tests. (Hint. If $V[I] \geq X[J]$, then what is known about $V[I+D]$ and $X[J]$, for $D > 0$?)

[Ans. If $V[I] \geq X[J]$, then $V[I+D] \geq X[J]$ since $V[I+D] \geq V[I]$. Consequently, the cases for $I + D$ and J, for $D > 0$, can be ignored and the search can continue with an incremented value of J. Similarly, if $Y[J] \geq U[I]$, then the search can continue with an incremented value of [I].]

1.5. Consider the following variation on Program 1 in Fig. 1.6. If the program is executed on a machine that obeys the rules of computation, read order, and write order, then what will the values of the A's be? What will the values of the X's be? What can be determined from a suitable pattern of X values?

P_1

L_1: A[1]: = 1;
L_2: A[2]: = 2;
L_3: A[3]: = 3;
. . .
Lk: A[$\underline{k}$]: = $\underline{k}$;

P_2

L_1: X[1]: = A[1];
L_2: X[2]: = A[2];
L_3: X[3]: = A[3];
. . .
Lk: X[$\underline{k}$]: = A[$\underline{k}$]; **Figure 1.6** Program 3.

[Ans. A[i] = i. The nonzero X values will be monotonically increasing. If not, then, as before, the X values reveal a failure of the machine executing the program to be read ordered or write ordered.]

1.6. The execution in Fig. 1.7 occurs on a machine that is reputed to obey the rules of computation, read order, and write atomicity. Identify the circuit which shows this not to be the case.

Initially, $A = B = C = R = S = U = V = X = Y = 0$.

P_1	P_2	P_3	P_4	P_5	P_6
L_1:A:=1;	L_1:R:=A;	L_1:B:=1;	L_1:U:=B;	L_1:C:=1;	L_1:X:=C;
	L_2:S:=B;		L_2:V:=C		L_2:Y:=A;

Terminally, $A = B = C = R = U = X = 1$, $S = V = Y = 0$.

Figure 1.7 Program 4.

[Ans. Since statement L_2 in process P_2 reads a zero value from B in S_2 before statement L_1 in process P_3 writes a one value into B in S_2, it must be that $(P_2,L_2,R,0,B,S_2) < (P_3,L_1,W,1,B,S_2)$. But since the program is write atomic, $(P_2,L_2,R,0,B,S_2) < (P_3,L_1,W,1,B,S_3)$ also. Similarly, it must be that $(P_4,L_2,R,0,C,S_4) < (P5,L_1,W,1,C,S_4)$ and $(P6,L_2,R,0,A,S6) < (P_1,L_1,W,1,A,S_2)$.

Consequently, the following circuit exists and demonstrates a failure of the machine running the execution to obey the rules of computation, read order, and/or write atomicity

Appendix C

$$
\begin{aligned}
(P_1,L_1,W,1,A,S_2) &< (P_2,L_1,R,1,A,S_2) \\
&< (P_2,L_2,R,0,B,S_2) \\
&< (P_3,L_1,W,1,B,S_3) \\
&< (P_4,L_1,R,1,B,S_4) \\
&< (P_4,L_2,R,0,C,S_4) \\
&< (P_5,L_1,W,1,C,S_4) \\
&< (P_6,L_1,R,1,C,S_6) \\
&< (P_6,L_2,R,0,A,S_6) \\
&< (P_1,L_1,W,1,A,S_2)]
\end{aligned}
$$

2.1. In Chap. 1 the analysis of Program 2 showed that when a program failed to obey the architecture rules of computation, read order, write order, and write atomicity, then a circuit existed among the events. Problem 1.3 required that a part of this circuit could be construed as a path which demonstrates a failure to be write atomic. Now select a part of this path to show that Program 2 did not obey CF.
[Ans. An old value is read after a new value is written.

$$
\begin{aligned}
(P_4,L_n,W,B,S_3) &< (P_3,L_{BJ},R,B,S_3) \\
&< (P_3,L_{AJ},R,A,S_3) \\
&< (P_1,L_m,W,A,S_2) \\
&< (P_2,L_{AI},R,A,S_2) \\
&< (P_2,L_{BI},R,B,S_2)]
\end{aligned}
$$

3.3. What is the smallest value of k for which fact(k) > 10 ** k? (Hint: use a calculator.)
[Ans. Fact(24) = 6.2045 * 10**23. Fact(25) = 1.5511 * 10**25.]

3.4. The product of two simple graphs can be a compound graph. Explain.
[Ans. The simple graphs have different colored arcs.]

3.5. A graph set is a set of graphs, but a set of graphs may fail to be a graph set. Explain.
[Ans. Not all of the graphs in the set of graphs need have the same set of nodes.]

3.6. Even though G * G = G, it is not generally true that for a graph set product GS_1, $GS_1 * GS_1 = GS_1$. Explain.
[Ans. {(S,A),(S,B)} * {(S,A),(S,B)} = {(S,A),(S,B),(S,A+B)} which is not equal to {(S,A),(S,B)} unless A is contained in B or B is contained in A.]

3.7. Let GS_1 and GS_2 be simple graph sets with distinct colors. Let GS_1 have n_1 elements and GS_2 have n_2 elements. How many elements are there in $GS_1 * GS_2$?
[Ans. $n_1 * n_2$.]

3.8. Let GS_1 and GS_2 be simple graph sets, both with the same color and let S = {a,b,c}. Let GS_1 = {(S,{(a<b),(b<c)}),(S,{(a<b)})} and GS_2 = {(S,{(b<c)})}. Find the product of GS_1 and GS_2 and so conclude that no general result holds as with the preceding problem.
[Ans. $GS_1 * GS_2$ = {(S,{(a<b),(b<c)}).]

3.9. Show that the product of two partly circuit-free graph sets may result in circuit-full graph set.
[Ans. {({a,b},{(a<b)})} and {({a,b},{(b<a)})} are circuit-free graph sets (each consisting of a single graph). Their product {({a,b},{(a<b),(b,a)})} is circuit-full.]

3.10. Let S be a set of k points. Let G = {$G_1, G_2, \ldots, G_n$} be the largest possible simple graph set on S. How many elements are there in G, that is, what is the value of n in terms of k? Calculate n for $k = 5$.

[Ans. Between any two points a, b there can be zero arcs, one arc from a to b, one arc from b to a, or two arcs, one from a to b and one from b to a. There are $k(k - 1)/2$ pairs of points. Since there are four choices for each pair of points, there are $4 ** (k(k - 1)/2) = 2 ** k(k-1)$ graphs. For $k = 5$, $n = 4 ** 10 = 1,048,576$.]

3.11. Let S be a set of n elements. Let GS_1 be the graph set consisting of all of the complete graphs of S.

  a. How many elements does GS_1 have?

  (Hint. Construct a simple graph set $\{G_1, G_2, \ldots, G_m\}$ as follows. For each pair of points a,b in S construct the graph set $\{(S,\{(a<b)\}),(S,\{(b<a)\})\}$. How many such graph sets are there? Take the product of all these graph sets. How many graphs are there in the graph set product? What does this procedure construct?)

  [Ans. There are $n(n - 1)/2$ pairs of points, and therefore, $n(n - 1)/2$ graph sets, each containing two graphs. The number of elements in the product graph set is $2 * 2 * \ldots * 2$, $n(n - 1)/2$ times, or $2 ** (n(n - 1)/2)$ elements. The graph set product is the set of complete graphs for S.]

  b. How many elements of GS_1 are circuit-free?

  [Ans. From Lemma 3.6 each circuit-free complete graph has a unique complete path. Each complete path is equivalent to a linear ordering of the nodes of the graphs. There are fact(n) linear orderings of n elements. From the construction of GS_1 all possible linear orderings must occur among the elements of GS_1. Therefore, there are fact(n) circuit-free elements of GS_1.]

  c. How many elements of GS_1 contain a circuit?

  [Ans. $2 ** (n(n - 1)/2) - $ fact(n).]

  d. Calculate the answers to a., b., and c. for $n = 4$.

  [Ans. 64, 24, 40.]

4.1. Write down the events for the following execution.

$$\text{Initially, A = B = 0.}$$

$$
\begin{array}{ll}
P_1 & P_2 \\
L_1: A := 1; & L_1: B := 1; \\
L_2: B := 2; & L_2: A := 2;
\end{array}
$$

$$\text{Terminally, A = B = 1.}$$

[Ans.] $(P_1, L_1, R, 1, 1, S_1)$ $(P_2, L_1, R, 1, 1, S_2)$
          $(P_1, L_1, W, 1, A, S_1)$ $(P_2, L_1, W, 1, B, S_1)$
          $(P_1, L_1, W, 1, A, S_2)$ $(P_2, L_1, W, 1, B, S_2)$

          $(P_1, L_2, R, 2, 2, S_1)$ $(P_2, L_2, R, 2, 2, S_2)$
          $(P_1, L_2, W, 2, B, S_1)$ $(P_2, L_2, W, 2, A, S_1)$
          $(P_1, L_2, W, 2, B, S_2)$ $(P_2, L_2, W, 2, A, S_2)$]

4.2. For some execution E with set of events $S = \{a,b,c\}$, rule R_1 defines the graph set $\{(S,\{a<b,c<a\}),(S,\{c<b\})\}$ and rule R_2 defines the graph set $\{(S,\{b<c\})\}$. Does E obey $A(R_1)$? $A(R_2)$? $A(R_1,R_2)$?

Appendix C   207

[Ans. Under $A(R_1)$ the graph set for E is not circuit-full. Therefore, E obeys $A(R_1)$. The same is true with $A(R_2)$. However, the graph for E under $A(R_1,R_2)$ is circuit-full, and so E does not obey $A(R_1,R_2)$.]

4.3. Rule R_1 defines the graph set $\{(S,\{(a<b)\})\}$ for execution E and $\emptyset$ for all other executions. Rule R_2 defines the graph set $\{(S,\{(b<a)\})\}$ for execution E and $\emptyset$ for all other executions. Then $A(R_1) \Leftrightarrow A(R_2)$. Explain.

[Ans. Both graph sets are partially circuit-free. Therefore, whenever any execution obeys one architecture, it obeys the other.]

5.1. If the following execution obeys A(CMP), what label appears on the arc from $(P_1,L_1,W,1,A,S_1)$ to $(P_1,L_2,R,1,A,S_1)$?

Initially, A = B = 0.

P_1
L_1: A:= 1;
L_2: B:= A;

Terminally, A = B = 1.

[Ans. $<_{CWR}$.]

5.2. If the following execution obeys A(CMP), what label appears on the arc from $(P_1,L_1,R,0,A,S_1)$ to $(P_1,L_2,W,1,A,S_1)$?

Initially, A = B = 0.

P_1
L_1: B:= A;
L_2: A:= 1;

Terminally, A = 1, B = 0.

[Ans. $<_{CRW}$.]

5.3. If the following execution obeys A(CMP), what label appears on the arc from $(P_1,L_1,W,1,A,S_1)$ to $(P_1,L_2,W,2,A,S_1)$?

Initially, A = 0.

P_1
L_1: A:= 1;
L_2: A:= 2;

Terminally, A = 2.

[Ans. $<_{CWW}$.]

5.4. If the following execution obeys A(CMP), what labels appear on the arcs from $(P_1,L_2,W,1,A,S_2)$ to $(P_2,L_1,R,1,A,S_2)$ and from $(P_2,L_2,W,1,B,S_1)$ to $(P_1,L_1,R,1,B,S_1)$?

Initially, $A = B = X = Y = 0$.

P_1 P_2
L_1: $Y := B$; L_1: $X := A$;
L_2: $A := 1$; L_2: $B := 1$;

Terminally, $A = B = X = Y = 1$.

[Ans. $<_{CWR}$, $<_{CWR}$.]

5.5. If the following execution obeys A(CMP), what labels appear on the arcs from $(P_2, L_2, R, 0, A, S_2)$ to $(P_1, L_1, W, 1, A, S_2)$ and from $(P_1, L_1, W, 1, A, S_2)$ to $(P_2, L_1, R, 1, A, S_2)$?

Initially, $A = X = Y = 0$.

P_1 P_2
L_1: $A := 1$; L_1: $X := A$;
                    L_2: $Y := A$;

Terminally, $A = X = 1$, $Y = 0$.

[Ans. $<_{CRW}$, $<_{CWR}$.]

5.6. If the following execution obeys A(CMP), what labels appear on the arc from $(P_1, L_2, W, 2, B, S_1)$ to $(P_2, L_1, W, 1, B, S_1)$ and from $(P_2, L_2, W, 2, A, S_1)$ to $(P_1, L_1, W, 1, A, S_1)$?

Initially, $A = B = 0$.

P_1 P_2
L_1: $A := 1$; L_1: $B := 1$;
L_2: $B := 2$; L_2: $A := 2$;

Terminally, $A = B = 1$.

[Ans. $<_{CWW}$, $<_{CWW}$.]

5.7. If the following execution obeys A(CMP), what labels appear on the arc from $(P_1, L_2, R, 0, B, S_1)$ to $(P_2, L_1, W, 1, B, S_1)$ and from $(P_2, L_2, W, 2, A, S_1)$ to $(P_1, L_1, W, 1, A, S_1)$?

Initially, $A = B = X = 0$.

P_1 P_2
L_1: $A := 1$; L_1: $B := 1$;
L_2: $X := B$; L_2: $A := 2$;

Terminally, $A = B = 1$, $X = 0$.

[Ans. $<_{CRW}$, $<_{CWW}$.]

5.8. Under A(CMP) the following execution can compute a terminal value of either 3 or 7 for X. Explain.

Appendix C

Initially, X = 0.

P_1
L_1: X:= 3;
L_2: X:= 7;

Terminally, X = ?.

[Ans. Under A(CMP) statements are not required to occur in program order.]

5.9. What terminal values can C have if the following execution obeys A(CMP)? A(CMP,PO)?

Initially, A = B = C = 0.

P_1 P_2
L_1: A:= 1; L_1: C:= A + B;
L_2: B:= 2;

Terminally, A = 1, B = 2, C = ?

[Ans. 0,1,2,3; 0,1,3]

5.10. Answer the following questions for this execution.

Initially, A = 0.

P_1
L_1: A:= 1;

Terminally, A = 7.

(a) What are the SOSS sets?
(b) Display the computation tree for A in S_1.
(c) At which of the five steps in forming the graph set for CMP does the execution fail to compute?

[Ans.
(a) There are two. One for the literal source operand in S_1, and one for A in S_1.
(b) $(P_1, L_1, R, 1, 1, S_1) <_{SRW} (P_1, L_1, W, 1, A, S_1)$.
(c) At Step 5: the computed value, 1, is not equal to the terminal value, 7, for A in S_1.]

5.11. How many elements are there in GS_1 for the following execution?

Initially, A = B = X = 0.

P_1 P_2 P_3
L_1: A:= 3; L_1: B:= 4; L_1: X:= A + B:

Terminally, A = 3, B = 4, X = 7.

[Ans. All the SOSS sets have only one element except those for operand A in store S_3 and operand B in store S_3, each of which have two elements. The number of elements of GS_1 is fact(2) * fact(2) * fact(1) * . . . * fact(1) = 4.]

5.12. Assume the execution in Problem 5.11 obeys A(CMP). Label the arcs and fill in the values of the events in the graph which shows how X obtains the value 7.

$$(P_1,L_1,R,\_,3,S_1) \qquad\qquad (P_2,L_1,R,\_,4,S_2)$$
$$|\qquad\qquad\qquad\qquad\qquad |$$
$$(P_1,L_1,W,\_,A,S_3) \qquad\qquad (P_2,L_1,W,\_,B,S_3)$$
$$|\qquad\qquad\qquad\qquad\qquad |$$
$$(P_3,L_1,R,\_,A,S_3) \qquad\qquad (P_3,L_1,R,\_,B,S_3)$$
$$\qquad |\qquad\qquad\qquad |$$
$$(P_3,L_1,W,\_,X,S_3)$$

[Ans.
$$(P_1,L_1,R,3,3,S_1) \qquad\qquad (P_2,L_1,R,4,4,S_2)$$
$$|<_{SRW} \qquad\qquad\qquad\qquad |<_{SRW}$$
$$(P_1,L_1,W,3,A,S_3) \qquad\qquad (P_2,L_1,W,4,B,S_3)$$
$$|<_{CWR} \qquad\qquad\qquad\qquad |<_{CWR}$$
$$(P_3,L_1,R,3,A,S_3) \qquad\qquad (P_3,L_1,R,4,B,S_3)$$
$$|<_{SRW} \qquad\qquad |<_{SRW}$$
$$(P_3,L_1,W,X,7,S_3)]$$

5.13. What is the source of the duplicates which are eliminated in Step 3?

[Ans. Two read events can occur between two write events in one order in one SOSS sequence and in the other order in a second SOSS sequence. Both SOSS sequences translate to the same element of GS_2.]

5.14. Show the elements of GS_1, GS_2, and GS_3 for the following execution. In particular show how there are fewer elements of GS_3 than of GS_2 due to circuits being created when $<_{SRW}$ arcs are added to the elements of GS_2.

$$\text{Initially, } A = 1, B = 2.$$
$$\qquad P_1 \qquad\qquad P_2$$
$$L_1: A := B; \qquad L_1: B := A;$$

$$\text{Terminally, } A = 2, B = 1.$$

[Ans. The four elements of GS_1 each consist of two paths of two events each (plus the events $(P_1,L_1,W,-,A,S_1)$ and $(P_2,L_1,W,-,B,S_2)$):

$$(P_1,L_1,R,-,B,S_1) \quad <sos \quad (P_2,L_1,W,-,B,S_1)$$
$$(P_1,L_1,W,-,A,S_2) \quad <sos \quad (P_2,L_1,R,-,A,S_2)$$

$$(P_2,L_1,W,-,B,S_1) \quad <sos \quad (P_1,L_1,R,-,B,S_1)$$
$$(P_1,L_1,W,-,A,S_2) \quad <sos \quad (P_2,L_1,R,-,A,S_2)$$

$$(P_1,L_1,R,-,B,S_1) \quad <sos \quad (P_2,L_1,W,-,B,S_1)$$
$$(P_2,L_1,R,-,A,S_2) \quad <sos \quad (P_1,L_1,W,-,A,S_2)$$

$$(P_2,L_1,W,-,B,S_1) \quad <sos \quad (P_1,L_1,R,-,B,S_1)$$
$$(P_2,L_1,R,-,A,S_2) \quad <sos \quad (P_1,L_1,W,-,A,S_2)$$

The four elements of GS_2 are the same as the elements of GS_1 with $<_{CWR}$ or $<_{CRW}$ substituted for $<sos$ in the obvious places.

Appendix C

There are only three elements of GS_3, because when $<_{SRW}$ arcs are added to the second pair of GS_2, the following circuit results:

$$(P_2,L_1,W,-,B,S_1) \begin{array}{l} <_{CWR} \\ <_{SRW} \\ <_{CWR} \\ <_{SRW} \end{array} \begin{array}{l} (P_1,L_1,R,-,B,S_1) \\ (P_1,L_1,W,-,A,S_2) \\ (P_2,L_1,R,-,A,S_2) \\ (P_2,L_1,W,-,B,S_1) \end{array}]$$

5.15. The elements of GS_2 are circuit-free. Prove.

[Ans. The elements of GS_2 are sets of linear sequences of events. Each linear sequence is for a distinct SOSS set. Therefore, there cannot be an arc from an element of one linear sequence to an element of another linear sequence. Therefore, there can be no circuit.]

6.1. Prove
   (a) UPO $\Rightarrow$ URW.
   (b) UPO $\Rightarrow$ UWW.
   (c) PO $\Rightarrow$ WO.
   (d) PO $\Rightarrow$ RO.
   (e) PO $\Rightarrow$ POS.
   (f) WO $\Rightarrow$ WOS.
   (g) POS $\Rightarrow$ RO.
   (h) POS $\Rightarrow$ WOS.

   [Ans. Mimic the proofs of Theorems 6.1 and 6.4.]

6.2. Argue for or against the position that a datum which is only read from, never written into, should be considered a local datum, not a global datum, even though it may be referenced by many different processes.

   [Ans. For: References to such a datum can be replaced by references to literal operands or to local operands with the same initial value without making any observable difference. Against: While no rule exists currently which would enable the above cases to be distinguished, there is no guarantee that such a rule will never be defined.]

In the next several problems the phrase "rule set" refers to a set consisting of the following rules.

CWR	CRW	CWW	SRW	
UWR	URW	UWW		
PO	WO	RO	POS	WOS

6.3. In the graph set for the execution

    Initially, X = 0.

              P_1
         L_1: X:= 3;
         L_2: X:= 7;

    Terminally, X = 7.

which rules in the rule set require that an arc occur from $(P_1,L_1,W,3,X,S_1)$ to $(P_1,L_2,W,7,X,S_1)$?

   [Ans. CWW,UWW,PO,WO,POS]

6.4. In the graph set for the execution

$$\text{Initially, } X = Y = 0.$$

$$P_1$$
$$L_1: X := 1;$$
$$L_2: Y := X;$$

$$\text{Terminally, } X = Y = 1.$$

which rules in the rule set require that an arc occur from $(P_1, L_1, W, 1, X, S_1)$ to $(P_1, L_2, R, 1, X, S_1)$?

[Ans. CWR, UWR, PO, POS]

6.5. In the graph set for the execution

$$\text{Initially, } X = Y = 0.$$

$$P_1$$
$$L_1: Y := X;$$
$$L_2: X := 1;$$

$$\text{Terminally, } X = 1, Y = 0.$$

which rules in the rule set require that an arc occur from $(P_1, L_1, R, 0, X, S_1)$ to $(P_1, L_2, W, 1, X, S_1)$?

[Ans. CRW, URW, PO, POS]

6.6. In the graph set for the execution

$$\text{Initially, } X = Y = Z = 0.$$

$$P_1$$
$$L_1: Y := X;$$
$$L_2: Z := X;$$

$$\text{Terminally, } X = Y = Z = 0.$$

which rules in the rule set require that an arc occur from $(P_1, L_1, R, 0, X, S_1)$ to $(P_1, L_2, R, 0, X, S_1)$?

[Ans. PO, RO, POS]

6.7. While POS $\Rightarrow$ UPO, it is not true that UPO $\Rightarrow$ POS. Explain why not.

[Ans. UPO allows two read events to the same operand and same store to be out of program order so long as there is no intervening write event to the same operand and store. POS doesn't.]

6.8. In the discussion of the execution exhibiting a failure to be program ordered, the statement was made that the only possible SOSS sequence for B in S_2 is

$$(P_2, L_1, W, 1, B, S_1) <_{\text{CWR}} (P_1, L_2, R, 1, B, S_1)$$

Explain why.

[Ans. Mimic the prose leading up to $(P_1, L_2, W, 1, A, S_2) <_{\text{CWR}} (P_2, L_1, R, 1, A, S_2)$.]

Appendix C   **213**

6.9. For rule PO there is rule POS. For WO there is WOS. There is a rule named RO, but none named ROS. Why not?

[Ans. POS and WOS link events whose store is that for the process containing the events. Read events are defined always to reference the store for the process containing the events.]

6.10. Use the execution in Fig. 6.3 that was used to show a failure to obey the rule of UWW to show a failure to obey the rule of WOS.

[Ans. $(P_1,L_1,W,2,X,S_1) <_{CWW} (P_1,L_2,W,1,X,S_1)$ shows that the execution does not obey the rule of WOS.]

*6.11. The theorem underlying the design of uniprocessors is that $A(CMP,UPO) \Leftrightarrow A(CMP,PO)$. Or, more generally, let A be any set of rules that does not contain either UPO or PO. Let $A_1 = A * A(UPO)$ and $A_2 = A * A(PO)$. Then $A_1 \Leftrightarrow A_2$.

Even though the methods for proving architectures to be indistinguishable are not demonstrated until Chap. 11, try now to prove that $A(CMP,UPO) \Leftrightarrow A(CMP,PO)$ on a system consisting of only a single process.

(Hint. Proof of $\Leftarrow$. PO $\Rightarrow$ UPO.

Proof of $\Rightarrow$. Assume the contrary. Then there is an execution E which obeys $A(CMP,UPO)$, but does not obey $A(CMP,PO)$. Let GS_1 be the graph set for E under $A(CMP,UPO)$. Let GS_2 be the graph set for E under $A(CMP,PO)$. Let GS_3 be the graph set for E under $A(CMP,UPO,PO)$.

Choose some circuit-free graph G_1 in the graph set GS_1 for E under $A(CMP,UPO)$.

Consider the element G_3 of GS_3 formed from the product of G_1 and the graph set of E under $A(PO)$.

G_3 contains a circuit C_3 since all members of GS_2 contain a circuit, and G_3 is obtained from some member of GS_2 by adding arcs labeled $<_{UPO}$. Further, C_3 contains an arc labeled $<_{PO}$, since G_1 is circuit-free.

Complete the proof of the theorem by inventing another circuit C_4 which does not have an arc labeled $<_{PO}$ and which must occur also in G_1, contrary to assumption.)

[Ans. It is not possible to have only arcs labeled $<_{PO}, <_{SRW}, <_{UWR}, <_{URW}$, and $<_{UWW}$ in C_1. (A more general form of this fact is given in Theorem 10.4.) If C_1 contains an arc labeled $<_{CMP}$ from event x to event y, then (since x and y must be in different statements in the same process) either $x <_{PO} y$ or $y <_{PO} x$. It cannot be that the first case holds for all arcs since then C_1 could not exist. Therefore, there is a circuit C_2 consisting of $x <_{CMP} y <_{PO} x$, where $<_{CMP}$ is either $<_{CWR}, <_{CRW}$, or $<_{CWW}$. If $x <_{CWR} y$ and $y <_{PO} x$, then it must be that $y <_{URW} x$ and so the circuit $x <_{CWR} y <_{URW} x$ exists in G_2. But then this circuit exists also in G_1, contrary to assumption. Similarly if $x <_{CRW} y$ or $x <_{CWW} y$.]

7.1. Prove: if there are n statements in an execution which obeys $A(SA)$, then there are fact(n) circuit-free elements of the graph set for the execution under $A(SA)$.

[Ans. For each element of GS_1 create the subgraph consisting of the write events for store S_1. From the way the elements of GS_1 are constructed, the new graphs are complete. By Lemma 3.6 there is a path in each new graph which visits each node once and only once. This imposes a linear order on the elements of the new graph and therefore on the atomic sets in the corresponding element of the graph set. From the construction of GS_1 all possible linear orders are represented in GS_1.

The number of distinct linear orders of n atomic sets is fact(n). Therefore, there are fact(n) circuit-free elements of GS_1. ∎]

7.2. Prove SA ⇒ RA (Theorem 7.2).
[Ans. Mimic the proof of Theorem 7.1.]

7.3. If an execution fails to be statement atomic, then for some events e_1 and e_2 in the same statement there is another event e_3 (or path), not in the statement, such that $e_1 < e_3 < e_2$. In the example showing a failure to be statement atomic, what event can be shown to occur between $(P_1, L_1, R, 1, B, S_1)$ and $(P_1, L_1, W, 1, A, S_2)$? (Fill in the blanks.)

$$(P_1, L_1, R, 1, B, S_1) \begin{array}{l} <_{CRW} \\ =_{SA} \\ <_{CRW} \end{array} \begin{array}{l} (P\_, L\_, \_, \_, \_, S\_) \\ (P\_, L\_, \_, \_, \_, S\_) \\ (P_1, L_1, W, 1, A, S_2) \end{array}$$

[Ans: $(P_1, L_1, R, 1, B, S_1)$ $\begin{array}{l}<_{CRW} \\ =_{SA} \\ <_{CRW}\end{array}$ $\begin{array}{l}(P_2, L_1, W, 0, B, S_1) \\ (P_2, L_1, R, 0, A, S_2) \\ (P_1, L_1, W, 1, A, S_2)\end{array}$]

7.4. Same question for the write atomic example.

$$(P_1, L_1, W, 1, A, S_2) \begin{array}{l} <_{CWR} \\ <_{RO} \\ <_{CRW} \\ =_{WA} \\ <_{CWR} \\ <_{RO} \\ <_{CRW} \end{array} \begin{array}{l} (P\_, L\_, \_, \_, \_, S\_) \\ (P\_, L\_, \_, \_, \_, S\_) \\ (P\_, L\_, \_, \_, \_, S\_) \\ (P\_, L\_, \_, \_, \_, S\_) \\ (P\_, L\_, \_, \_, \_, S\_) \\ (P\_, L\_, \_, \_, \_, S\_) \\ (P_1, L_1, W, 1, A, S_3) \end{array}$$

[Ans: $(P_1, L_1, W, 1, A, S_2)$ $\begin{array}{l}<_{CWR} \\ <_{RO} \\ <_{CRW} \\ =_{WA} \\ <_{CWR} \\ <_{RO} \\ <_{CRW}\end{array}$ $\begin{array}{l}(P_2, L_1, R, 1, A, S_2) \\ (P_2, L_2, R, 0, B, S_2) \\ (P_4, L_1, W, 1, B, S_2) \\ (P_4, L_1, W, 1, B, S_3) \\ (P_3, L_1, R, 1, B, S_3) \\ (P_3, L_2, R, 0, A, S_3) \\ (P_1, L_1, W, 1, A, S_3)\end{array}$]

7.5. Same question for the read atomic example.

$$(P_1, L_1, R, 0, A, S_1) \begin{array}{l} <\_\_\_ \\ <\_\_\_ \\ <\_\_\_ \end{array} \begin{array}{l} (P\_, L\_, \_, \_, \_, S\_) \\ (P\_, L\_, \_, \_, \_, S\_) \\ (P_1, L_1, R, 2, B, S_1) \end{array}$$

[Ans: $(P_1, L_1, R, 0, A, S_1)$ $\begin{array}{l}<_{CRW} \\ <_{WO} \\ <_{CWR}\end{array}$ $\begin{array}{l}(P_2, L_1, W, 1, A, S_1) \\ (P_2, L_2, W, 2, B, S_1) \\ (P_1, L_1, R, 2, B, S_1)\end{array}$]

Appendix C

7.6. Consider the following execution under A(SA).

$$P_1 \qquad\qquad P_2$$
$$L_1: A := B; \qquad L_1: X := Y;$$
$$L_2: C := B;$$

It contains nine events. How many nodes does each element of the graph set contain? How many statement atomic sets are there? How many elements of the graph set are there before the elements with circuits are thrown away? After the elements with circuits are thrown away? How many arcs are there in each element of the graph set?

[Ans: Each element of the graph set contains nine nodes, one node for each event. There are three statement atomic sets, one set for each statement. There are six events outside each statement atomic set. For each event outside a statement atomic set there are a pair of graphs, one with three arcs from the event to the set, the other with three arcs from the set to the event. There is a total of 3 * 6 pairs of graphs. The graph set for the execution formed from the product of the 18 pairs of graphs contains 2 ** 18 graphs. Of these, only fact(3) = 6 are circuit-free. Each graph contains three arcs from each of the 18 graphs of which it is the product; thus, each graph contains 54 arcs.]

7.7. Consider the following execution and its events.

$$\text{Initially, } A = 0, B = 1.$$

$$P_1 \qquad\qquad P_2$$
$$L_1: A := B; \qquad L_1: B := A;$$

$$\text{Terminally, } A = 1 \text{ and } B = 0.$$

Consider the graph of these events with the following arcs:

$$(P_1, L_1, R, -, B, S_1) <_{WA} (P_2, L_1, W, -, B, S_1)$$
$$(P_1, L_1, R, -, B, S_1) <_{WA} (P_2, L_1, W, -, B, S_2)$$
$$(P_1, L_1, W, -, A, S_1) <_{WA} (P_2, L_1, W, -, B, S_1)$$
$$(P_1, L_1, W, -, A, S_1) <_{WA} (P_2, L_1, W, -, B, S_2)$$
$$(P_1, L_1, W, -, A, S_2) <_{WA} (P_2, L_1, W, -, B, S_1)$$
$$(P_1, L_1, W, -, A, S_2) <_{WA} (P_2, L_1, W, -, B, S_2)$$
$$(P_2, L_1, R, -, A, S_2) <_{WA} (P_2, L_1, W, -, B, S_1)$$
$$(P_2, L_1, R, -, A, S_2) <_{WA} (P_2, L_1, W, -, B, S_2)$$

$$(P_2, L_1, R, -, A, S_2) <_{WA} (P_1, L_1, W, -, A, S_1)$$
$$(P_2, L_1, R, -, A, S_2) <_{WA} (P_1, L_1, W, -, A, S_2)$$
$$(P_2, L_1, W, -, B, S_1) <_{WA} (P_1, L_1, W, -, A, S_1)$$
$$(P_2, L_1, W, -, B, S_1) <_{WA} (P_1, L_1, W, -, A, S_2)$$
$$(P_2, L_1, W, -, B, S_2) <_{WA} (P_1, L_1, W, -, A, S_1)$$
$$(P_2, L_1, W, -, B, S_2) <_{WA} (P_1, L_1, W, -, A, S_2)$$
$$(P_1, L_1, R, -, B, S_1) <_{WA} (P_1, L_1, W, -, A, S_1)$$
$$(P_1, L_1, R, -, B, S_1) <_{WA} (P_1, L_1, W, -, A, S_2)$$

Does this graph occur in the graph set for the execution under A(WA) before the graphs with circuits have been thrown away?

[Ans: Yes. The graph set for the execution under A(WA) contains all graphs such

7.8. The events for the SOSS set for A and S_2 in the execution that follows are $(P_1,L_1,W,1,A,S_2)$, $(P_2,L_1,R,0,A,S_2)$, and $(P_2,L_1,W,0,A,S_2)$. Show the order in which the events occur in the SOSS sequence to compute the terminal value of 0 for A.

$$\text{Initially, } A = 0.$$

$$
\begin{array}{ll}
P_1 & P_2 \\
L_1: A := 1; & L_1: A := A;
\end{array}
$$

$$\text{Terminally, } A = 0.$$

From this conclude that the execution does not obey A(CMP,SA).
[Ans: $\quad (P_2,L_1,R,0,A,S_2) \; <_{CRW} \; (P_1,L_1,W,1,A,S_2)$
$\qquad\qquad\qquad\qquad\quad <_{CWW} \; (P_2,L_1,W,0,A,S_2) \;]$

7.9. Under the example of a failure to be statement atomic it was stated that the only possible SOSS sequence for B in S_1 is

$$(P_1,L_1,R,1,B,S_1) \; <_{CRW} \; (P_2,L_1,W,0,B,S_1)$$

Derive this statement in the same way as was done for A in S_2.
[Ans. There are two events in the SOSS set for operand B in Store S_1.

$$
\begin{array}{l}
(P_1,L_1,R,-,B,S_1) \\
(P_2,L_1,W,-,B,S_1)
\end{array}
$$

The two events can be arranged in one of two orders

$$
\begin{array}{llll}
(P_1,L_1,R,-,B,S_1) & <_{CRW} & (P_2,L_1,W,-,B,S_1) \\
(P_2,L_1,W,-,B,S_1) & <_{CWR} & (P_1,L_1,R,-,B,S_1)
\end{array}
$$

Once values are assigned, the events are

$$
\begin{array}{llll}
(P_1,L_1,R,0,B,S_1) & <_{CRW} & (P_2,L_1,W,1,B,S_1) \\
(P_2,L_1,W,1,B,S_1) & <_{CWR} & (P_1,L_1,R,0,B,S_1)
\end{array}
$$

The terminal value of A requires that the SOSS sequence for B in S_1 be

$$(P_1,L_1,R,0,B,S_1) \; <_{CRW} \; (P_2,L_1,W,1,B,S_1) \;]$$

8.1. Prove:
  (a) WS $\Rightarrow$ CON (Theorem 8.3).
  (b) RA $\Rightarrow$ RS (Theorem 8.4).
     [Ans. Mimic the proof of Theorem 8.1.]

8.2. How many elements does the graph set for the following execution have under A(RS)?

```
        P₁              P₂                  P₃                      P₄
L₁: A:= 1;      L₁: B:= 4;      L₁: C:= A + B;      L₁: D:= A + B;
L₂: B:= 2;      L₂: A:= 8;
```

[Ans. Two. Only one pair of statements share operands.]

9.1. Prove:
  (a) RA $\Rightarrow$ ARC (Theorem 9.2).
  (b) AWC $\Rightarrow$ RWC (Theorem 9.3).
  (c) ARC $\Rightarrow$ RRC (Theorem 9.4).
  [Ans. Mimic the proof for Theorem 9.1.]

10.1. Carry out the proof of Theorem 10.1.
  [Ans.
  1. The set of executions that obey A is the same as the set of executions that obey A. Hence, A $\Leftrightarrow$ A.
  2. If the set of executions that obey A is the same as the set of executions that obey B, then the set of executions that obey B is the same as the set of executions that obey A.
  3. If the set of executions that obey A is the same as the set of executions that obey B, and if the set of executions that obey B is the same as the set of executions that obey C, then the set of executions that obey A is the same as the set of executions that obey C.]

11.1. Prove A(CMP, WO, SA) $\Leftrightarrow$ A(CMP, PO, SA).
  [Ans. Mimic the proof of Theorem 11.1, changing RO to WO.]

11.2. Prove A(CMP, RO, SA) $\Leftrightarrow$ A(CMP, WO, SA). Hint: Use the results of Prob. 11.1 and Theorem 11.1.
  [Ans. A(CMP, RO, SA) $\Leftrightarrow$ A(CMP, PO, SA) by Theorem 11.1.
  $\Leftrightarrow$ A(CMP, WO, SA) by Prob. 11.1.]

11.3. Let A be any architecture not containing RO, PO, or SA. Let $A_1 = A * A(RO) * A(SA)$ and $A_2 = A * A(PO) * A(SA)$. Then $A_1 \Leftrightarrow A_2$. Prove.
  [Ans. Define $A3 = A * A(RO) * A(PO) * A(SA)$ and mimic the proof of Theorem 11.1.]

Prove the following facts regarding architectures A_1, A_2, A_3, and A_4 used in the proof of Frey's Theorem.

11.4. $A_2 \Rightarrow A_1$.
  [Ans. By Lemma 3.4.]

11.5. $A_2 \Leftrightarrow A_3$.
  [Ans. If GS_2 is circuit-full, then so is GS_3. If GS_2 is partly circuit-free, then there is a circuit-free graph G_2 in GS_2. The elements of G_2 can be extended to a linear ordering, thereby linearly ordering the read events of E. Label the arcs between read events $<_{RUF}$. Then this circuit-free graph can be found in GS_3. Hence, GS_2 and GS_3 are either both circuit-full or both partly circuit-free, that is, $A_2 \Leftrightarrow A_3$.]

11.6. Prove $A_1 \Rightarrow A_4$ in the first half of Frey's Theorem.)
  [Ans. Let E be an execution which obeys A_1. Then there is a circuit-free graph in the graph set for E under A_1. The same graph occurs in the graph set of E under A_3 (with $<_{RO}$ replaced by $<_{RUF}$ since the graph set for A_3 contains all possible orderings

of the read events). Since $R_1 <_{RO} R_2$ in G_1 and $R_1 <_{RUF} R_2$ in G_3, the G_3 graph does not meet the criterion for exclusion from GS_4 and so occurs also in GS_4. Hence if E obeys A_1, then it also obeys A_4.]

11.7. $A_3 \Rightarrow A_4$.

[Ans. $A_3 \Leftrightarrow A_2 \Rightarrow A_1 \Leftrightarrow A_4$.]

12.1. Let W_1 and W_2 be write events in an execution that is write synchronized. Prove each of the following statements.

(a) $X(W_1,W_1) = W_1$.

[Ans. The write event in the statement containing event W_1 which has the same store component as W_1 is just W_1.]

(b) If W_1 and W_2 are in the same statement, then $X(W_2,W_1) = W_1$.

[Ans. The write event in the statement containing write event W_2 which has the same store component as W_1 is just W_1.]

(c) W_1 and $X(W_2,W_1)$ have the same store components.

[Ans. $X(W_2,W_1)$ is defined to have the same store component as W_1.]

(d) If W_1 and W_2 have the same store components, then $X(W_2,W_1) = W_2$.

[Ans. The function of W_1 is solely to designate a store component. Since W_1 and W_2 have the same store component, the role of W_1 could as well be performed by W_2. Thus, $X(W_2,W_1) = X(W_2,W_2)$ which by Prob. 12.1a is equal to W_2.]

12.2. Let W_1 and W_2 be write events in distinct statements in an execution which obeys WS. Prove that if $W_1 <_{WS} X(W_2,W_1)$, then $X(W_1,W_2) <_{WS} W_2$.

[Ans. By Lemma 12.5 and Prob. 12.1a $W_1 <_{WS} X(W_2,W_1) \Rightarrow X(W_1,W_1) <_{WS} X(W_2,W_1) \Rightarrow X(W_1,W_2) <_{WS} X(W_2,W_2) \Rightarrow X(W_1,W_2) <_{WS} W_2$.]

12.3. Prove: $X(X(W_1,W_2),W_3) = X(W_1,W_3)$.

[Ans. $X(W_1,W_2)$ is an event in the same statement as W_1.]

12.4. Prove $X[W_1,X(W_2,W_3)] = X(W_1,W_3)$.

[Ans. $X(W_2,W_3)$ is an event with the same store component as W_3.]

12.5. Theorem 12.1 says that an architecture which includes write synchronization but not read synchronization is indistinguishable from an architecture which is write atomic. Is there a corresponding theorem that an architecture which includes read synchronization but not write synchronization is indistinguishable from an architecture which is read atomic? (Hint. Ask what an execution which is vacuously read synchronized would look like and then examine the proof of Theorem A32.)

[Ans. No. The proof of Theorem A32 displays an execution which is (vacuously) read synchronized, but which is not read atomic.]

12.6. Theorem 12.1 says that a write synchronized system appears to be write atomic, no matter how many processes are in the system. If the number of processes is restricted, then can a system appear to be write atomic by obeying a weaker rule than write synchronization? For example, suppose a machine has only two processors and obeys the rule of consistency. Will the machine appear to be write atomic?

(Hint. Use the following execution adapted from Theorem A29 to show that A(CMP,RO,CON) $\neg\Rightarrow$ A(CMP,RO,WA), even on a system consisting of only two processes.

Appendix C 219

$$\text{Initially, } A = B = X = Y = 0.$$

P_1	P_2
$L_1: A := 1;$	$L_1: X := B;$
$L_2: B := A;$	$L_2: Y := A;$

$$\text{Terminally, } A = B = X = 1, Y = 0.)$$

[Ans. The following path in every graph for the execution shows that the execution is not write atomic.

$$(P_1, L_1, W, 1, A, S_1) <_{CWR} (P_1, L_2, R, 1, A, S_1)$$
$$<_{SRW} (P_1, L_2, W, 1, B, S_2)$$
$$<_{CWR} (P_2, L_1, R, 1, B, S_2)$$
$$<_{RO} (P_2, L_2, R, 0, A, S_2)$$
$$<_{CRW} (P_1, L_1, W, 1, A, S_2)\,]$$

13.2. Theorems A24 and A28 are based on the same execution, presented in both proofs in the process format. Rewrite the executions in both proofs in the store format. Draw a line connecting every pair of write events from the same statement. What is different about the connecting lines in the two cases? What does the difference reveal?

[Ans. None of the lines cross in the first case. Some do in the second case. The difference shows that the first execution is write synchronized; the second is not.]

13.3. Dijkstra [DIJK74] described a set of processes arranged in a ring, but interacting in quite a different way from that described in this chapter. For each process there is a separate store. Each variable occurs in only one store. Each process writes only into its own store, but can read variables in its own store and in the stores of each of its two neighbors. How is write atomicity achieved in this system?

[Ans. There is only one copy of any variable, so there is no opportunity for different processors to see a variable have different values at the same time.]

15.1. The PTUI Computer Company's newest machine generates only write atomic answers. However, the architecture for the machine says that the machine does not obey the rule of write atomicity. Can any program detect that the machine does not obey its architecture?

[Ans. No, since no number of WA answers ensures that all answers will be WA.]

Appendix D

Programs to Test a Machine for a Failure To Obey Its Architecture

Here are seven programs that can be used to test for the failure of a machine to obey basic architectural rules. Test 1 and Test 6 were discussed in Chapter 1. There are also five variations which can be applied to the test programs.

Each test consists of three parts: a program, a set of conditions which the output from the program should meet, and an explanation of the reasoning behind the conclusion that a failure to meet the conditions implies a failure of the machine to obey the architectural rules. Each program and its associated conditions can be understood with no background. The analysis of the failure cases relies on rules that are defined in Chapters 5 through 7.

Each test should obey either two, three, or four conditions. Two of the conditions should be obeyed (except where noted) by all of the tests. Therefore, they are stated here once, rather than separately for each test.

Condition 1. Range.
The elements of each result vector X should obey
$0 \leq X[i] \leq k$, for $1 \leq i \leq k$.

If the results of a test should obey Condition 1, but do not, then the test reveals a failure of the machine to obey the rule of computation.

Condition 2. Monotonicity.
The elements of each result vector should obey
$X[i] \leq X[i + 1]$, for $0 \leq i \leq k - 1$.

If the results of a test should obey Condition 2, but do not, then the test reveals a failure of the machine to obey the rules of computation, read order, and/or write order.

Appendix D

Except where stated otherwise, each operand is assumed to be initialized to zero.

Test 1. First Test of A(CMP, RO, WO)

The test in Figure D.1 was discussed in Chapter 1.

	P_1	P_2
	L_1: A := 1;	L_1: X[1] := A;
	L_2: A := 2;	L_2: X[2] := A;
	. . .	. . .
	L_k: A := k;	L_k: X[k] := A;

Figure D.1 Test for a violation of A(CMP, RO, WO).

Variation 1. Multiple, Logically Independent Tests.

Two or more logically independent tests can be combined into one test, as in Figure D.2 where two separate copies of Test 1 are interleaved in two processes. While the tests are logically independent, a machine on which they run may erroneously allow some form of interaction between the tests. The purpose of the variation is to see if any such interaction is visible.

	P_1	P_2
	L_{11}: A := 1;	L_{11}: X[1] := A;
	L_{12}: Y[1] := B;	L_{12}: B := 1,
	L_{21}: A := 2;	L_{21}: X[3] := A;
	L_{22}: Y[2] := B;	L_{22}: B := 3,
	L_{31}: A := 3;	L_{31}: X[3] := A;
	L_{32}: Y[3] := B;	L_{32}: B := 3,
	. . .	. . .

Figure D.2 Two logically independent tests.

Variation 2. Multiple Observers.

Another variation, shown in Figure D.3, is due to an observation by Heimbach [HEIM91] that the number of observing processes can be increased arbitrarily. As with the previous variation, there should be no visible interaction due to the additional process(es) in the test.

P_1	P_2	P_3
L_1: A := 1;	L_1: X[1] := A;	L_1: Y[1] := A;
L_2: A := 2;	L_2: X[2] := A;	L_2: Y[2] := A;
L_3: A := 3;	L_3: X[3] := A;	L_3: Y[3] := A;
. . .	. . .	. . .

Figure D.3 Multiple, independent observers.

Variation 3. Multiple Operands Modified.

Instead of changing one operand repeatedly, a test may change multiple operands each only once. The result of applying this variation to Figure D.1 is shown in Figure D.4. Condition 2 then becomes
$X[i] \le X[j]$ for $0 < i < j \le k$ and $X[i] \neg = 0 \neg = X[j]$.

```
        P₁                    P₂
L₁: A[1]:= 1;        L₁: X[1]:= A[1];
L₂: A[2]:= 2;        L₂: X[2]:= A[2];
    . . .                . . .
Lₖ: A[k]:= k;        Lₖ: X[k]:= A[k];
```

Figure D.4 A test yielding nonmonotonic results.

If the condition is not obeyed, then $X[i] = a > X[j] = b > 0$, and so one of two circuits exists among the events of the execution. If $b + 1 = a$, then

$$(P_1, L_a, W, a, A[a], S_2) \quad <_{CWR} \quad (P_2, L_i, \quad R, a, \quad A[a], \quad S_2)$$
$$<_{RO} \quad (P_2, L_j, \quad R, b, \quad A[b], \quad S_2)$$
$$<_{CRW} \quad (P_1, L_{b+1}, W, b+1, A[b+1], S_2)$$

If $b + 1 < a$, then

$$(P_1, L_a, W, a, A[a], S_2) \quad <_{CWR} \quad (P_2, L_i, \quad R, a, \quad A[a], \quad S_2)$$
$$<_{RO} \quad (P_2, L_j, \quad R, b, \quad A[b], \quad S_2)$$
$$<_{CRW} \quad (P_1, L_{b+1}, W, b+1, A[b+1], S_2)$$
$$<_{WO} \quad (P_1, L_a, \quad W, a, \quad A[a], \quad S_2)$$

Variation 4. Stressing the Storage Hierarchy.

To stress variously the processor, the cache, or the paging mechanism, the offset (n in Figure D.5) between write addresses in Variation 3 can be adjusted to address a sequence of words, of cache lines, or of pages.

```
         P₁                      P₂
L₁: A[1*n]:= 1;          L₁: X[1]:= A[1*n];
L₂: A[2*n]:= 2;          L₂: X[2]:= A[2*n];
    . . .                    . . .
Lₖ: A[k*n]:= k;          Lₖ: X[k]:= A[k*n];
```

Figure D.5 Variable write stride.

Test 2. Second Test of A(CMP, RO, WO)

Since the execution in Figure D.6 is write ordered, the values of A and B always differ by exactly one. Since the execution is read ordered, a value fetched from A is never more than one greater than the previous value fetched from B, and

never more than one greater than the previous value values of the X and Y vectors meet
$Y[i] + 1 \leq X[i + 1] + 2$.
n Theorem A7 in Appendix A.
rly subscripts on statement numbers, Condition 1 must
t values to occur over the range from -1 to k.)

Initially, $A = -1, B = 0$.

P_1	P_2
L_1: A:= 1;	L_{11}: X[1]:= A;
L_2: B:= 2;	L_{12}: Y[1]:= B;
L_3: A:= 3;	L_{21}: X[2]:= A;
L_4: B:= 4;	L_{22}: Y[2]:= B;
L_5: A:= 5;	L_{31}: X[3]:= A;
L_6: B:= 6;	L_{32}: Y[3]:= B;
...	...

n of A(CMP,

ndition 3 takes the form of either $X[i] > Y[i] + 1$, or
.et $X[i] = a > Y[i] + 1 = b + 1$. Since $a > b + 1$, a is odd, and b is even, it must be that $a > b + 2$. Under this condition a circuit exists among the events of an execution of the program.

$$(P_2, L_{i1}, R, a, A, S_2) <_{RO} (P_2, L_{i2}, R, b, B, S_2)$$
$$<_{CRW} (P_1, L_{b+2}, W, b+2, B, S_2)$$
$$<_{WO} (P_1, L_a, W, a, A, S_2)$$
$$<_{CWR} (P_2, L_{i1}, R, a, A, S_2)$$

Let $Y[i] = b > X[i + 1] + 1 = a + 1$. Since $b > a + 1$, b is even, and a is odd, it must be that $b > a + 2$. Then a different circuit exists among the events of an execution of the program.

$$(P_2, L_{i2}, R, b, B, S_2) <_{RO} (P_2, L_{i+1,1}, R, a, A, S_2)$$
$$<_{CRW} (P_1, L_{a+2}, W, a+2, A, S_2)$$
$$<_{WO} (P_1, L_b, W, b, B, S_2)$$
$$<_{CWR} (P_2, L_{i2}, R, b, B, S_2)$$

Test 3. Third Test for A(CMP, RO, WO).

The program in Figure D.7 is based on Theorem A6 in Appendix A.

If the values in the X and Y vectors are monotonic in an execution of the program in Figure D.7, then no error is detectable. Therefore, assume that there is a failure to be monotonic. Let $i+$ be greater than i and $j+$ greater than j. If $X[i+] = a < Y[j] = b < Y[j+] = c < X[i] = d$, and if a, b, c, d are odd, even, odd, even, respectively, then a circuit exists among the events of the execution.

```
        P₁              P₂              P₃              P₄
L₁: A:= 1;      L₁: B:= 1;      L₁: X[1]:= A;   L₁: Y[1]:= B;
L₂: B:= 2;      L₂: A:= 2;      L₂: X[2]:= A;   L₂: Y[2]:= B;
L₃: A:= 3;      L₃: B:= 3;      L₃: X[3]:= A;   L₃: Y[3]:= B;
L₄: B:= 4;      L₄: A:= 4;      L₄: X[4]:= A;   L₄: Y[4]:= B;
L₅: A:= 5;      L₅: B:= 5;      L₅: X[5]:= A;   L₅: Y[5]:= B;
L₆: B:= 6;      L₆: A:= 6;      L₆: X[6]:= A;   L₆: Y[6]:= B;
 . . .           . . .           . . .           . . .
```

Figure D.7 Test for a violation of A(CMP, RO, WO).

Since the events of the execution obey $(P_3, L_i, R, d, A, S_3) <_{RO} (P_3, L_{i+}, R, a, A, S_3)$, it must be that

$$
\begin{aligned}
(P_2, L_d, W, d, A, S_3) &<_{CWR} (P_3, L_i, R, d, A, S_3) \\
&<_{CRW} (P_1, L_a, W, a, A, S_3) \\
&<_{CWR} (P_3, L_{i+}, R, a, A, S_3)
\end{aligned}
$$

Consequently, $(P_2, L_d, W, d, A, S_3) <_{CWW} (P_1, L_a, W, a, A, S_3)$. Similarly, $(P_1, L_b, W, b, B, S_4) <_{CWW} (P_2, L_c, W, c, B, S_4)$. Therefore,

$$
\begin{aligned}
(P_1, L_a, W, a, A, S_3) &<_{WO} (P_1, L_b, W, b, B, S_4) \\
&<_{CWW} (P_2, L_c, W, c, B, S_4) \\
&<_{WO} (P_2, L_d, W, d, A, S_3) \\
&<_{CWW} (P_1, L_a, W, a, A, S_3)
\end{aligned}
$$

Another circuit exists (1) if $Y[j+] = a < X[i] = b < X[i+] = c < Y[j] = d$, and (2) if a, b, c, d are even, odd, even, odd, respectively,

$$
\begin{aligned}
(P_1, L_c, W, c, B, S_3) &<_{WO} (P_1, L_d, W, d, A, S_4) \\
&<_{CWW} (P_2, L_a, W, a, A, S_4) \\
&<_{WO} (P_2, L_b, W, b, B, S_3) \\
&<_{CWW} (P_1, L_c, W, c, B, S_3)
\end{aligned}
$$

Test 4. Test of A(CMP, PO).

The program in Figure D.8 is based on Theorem A7 in Appendix A.

```
        P₁                      P₂
L₁₁: A:= 1;             L₁₁: B:= 1;
L₁₂: Y[1]:= B;          L₁₂: X[1]:= A;
L₂₁: A:= 2;             L₂₁: B:= 2;
L₂₂: Y[2]:= B;          L₂₂: X[2]:= A;
 . . .                   . . .
Lₖ₁: A:= k;             Lₖ₁: B:= k;
Lₖ₂: Y[k]:= B;          Lₖ₂: X[k]:= A;
```

Figure D.8 A Test for a Violation of PO.

Appendix D

Condition 3 is complex and offers no insight into the essential form the results must fit. It is easier simply to state the tests that indicate that a circuit exists. Note that Test 4 and Variation 2 differ only trivially.

If $X[i] = a < j$ and $Y[j] = b < i$, then

$$
\begin{aligned}
(P_1, L_{j2}, R, b, B, S_1) &<_{CRW} (P_2, L_{i1}, W, i, B, S_1) \\
&<_{PO} (P_2, L_{i2}, R, a, A, S_2) \\
&<_{CRW} (P_1, L_{j1}, W, j, A, S_2) \\
&<_{PO} (P_1, L_{j2}, R, b, B, S_1)
\end{aligned}
$$

If $X[i] = a > j$ and $Y[j] = b > i$, then

$$
\begin{aligned}
(P_1, L_{a1}, W, a, A, S_2) &<_{CWR} (P_2, L_{i2}, R, a, A, S_2) \\
&<_{PO} (P_2, L_{b1}, W, b, B, S_1) \\
&<_{CWR} (P_1, L_{j2}, R, b, B, S_1) \\
&<_{PO} (P_1, L_{a1}, W, a, A, S_2)
\end{aligned}
$$

Test 5. First Test of A(CMP, RO, WO, WA).

The simplest test for a failure to be write atomic, shown in Fig. D.9, is due to Dubois, Scheurich, and Briggs [DUBO86, cited in Chapter 1]. See also Theorem A29 in Appendix A.

Condition 3. $X[i] \leq Y[i]$, $1 \leq i \leq k$.

	P_1		P_2		P_3
L_1:	A:= 1;	L_1:	B:= A;	L_{11}:	X[1]:= B;
L_2:	A:= 2;	L_2:	B:= A;	L_{12}:	Y[1]:= A;
L_3:	A:= 3;	L_3:	B:= A;	L_{21}:	X[2]:= B;
L_4:	A:= 4;	L_4:	B:= A;	L_{22}:	Y[2]:= A;
L_5:	A:= 5;	L_5:	B:= A;	L_{31}:	X[3]:= B;
L_6:	A:= 6;	L_6:	B:= A;	L_{32}:	Y[3]:= A;

Figure D.9 The DSB test for a violation of A(CMP, RO, WO, WA).

If $X[i] = b > Y[i] = a$ for any i, then a circuit exists among the events of the execution. (The statement numbers of process 2 cannot be known and so are represented by a dash (–).)

$$
\begin{aligned}
(P_1, L_b, W, b, A, S_2) &<_{CWR} (P_2, L_-, R, b, A, S_2) \\
&<_{SRW} (P_2, L_-, W, b, B, S_3) \\
&<_{CWR} (P_3, L_{i1}, R, b, B, S_3) \\
&<_{RO} (P_3, L_{i2}, R, a, A, S_3) \\
&<_{CRW} (P_1, L_b, W, b, A, S_3) \\
&=_{WA} (P_1, L_b, W, b, A, S_2)
\end{aligned}
$$

Test 6. Second Test of A(CMP, RO, WO, WA).

The program in Figure D.10 is based on Theorem A38 in Appendix A. It was discussed in Chapter 1.

P_1	P_2	P_3	P_4
L_1: A:= 1;	L_{11}: U[1]:= A;	L_{11}: X[1]:= B;	L_1: B:= 1;
L_2: A:= 2;	L_{12}: V[1]:= B;	L_{12}: Y[1]:= A;	L_2: B:= 2;
L_3: A:= 3;	L_{21}: U[2]:= A;	L_{21}: X[2]:= B;	L_3: B:= 3;
L_4: A:= 4;	L_{22}: V[2]:= B;	L_{22}: Y[2]:= A;	L_4: B:= 4;
L_5: A:= 5;	L_{31}: U[3]:= A;	L_{31}: X[3]:= B;	L_5: B:= 5;
L_6: A:= 6;	L_{32}: V[3]:= B;	L_{32}: Y[3]:= A;	L_6: B:= 6;
...	...	...	...

Figure D.10 The ABUVXY test for a violation of A(CMP, RO, WO, WA).

Condition 3. $V[i] \geq X[j]$ or $Y[j] \geq U[i]$ for $1 \leq i, j \leq k$.

If $V[i] = b < X[j] = c$ and $Y[j] = d < U[i] = a$ for some i and j, then a circuit exists among the events of an execution of the test program.

$$
\begin{aligned}
(P_1, L_a, W, a, A, S_2) &<_{CWR} (P_2, L_{i1}, R, a, A, S_2) \\
&<_{RO} (P_2, L_{i2}, R, b, B, S_2) \\
&<_{CRW} (P_4, L_c, W, c, B, S_2) \\
&=_{WA} (P_4, L_c, W, c, B, S_3) \\
&<_{CWR} (P_3, L_{j1}, R, c, B, S_3) \\
&<_{RO} (P_3, L_{j2}, R, d, A, S_3) \\
&<_{CRW} (P_1, L_a, W, a, A, S_3) \\
&=_{WA} (P_1, L_a, W, a, A, S_2)
\end{aligned}
$$

It was in this context that Heimbach originally saw the value of additional pairs of observing processes. If there are $2 * k$ observing processes, then there are $k(k - 1)/2$ pairs of vectors to analyze.

Variation 5. Tests for More Complex Conditions.

Test 6 can be extended in the manner shown in Figure D.11 in order to detect a more complex condition. The test will fail if the machine has been correctly implemented, or if the more complex condition simply does not occur. It will succeed where Test 6 failed to find any problem if the machine has been correctly implemented to handle the simple case, but not the more complex case.

Appendix D

P_1	P_2	P_3	P_4	P_5	P_6
L_1:A:=1;	L_1:R[1]:=A;	L_1:B:=1;	L_1:U[1]:=B;	L_1:C:=1;	L_1:X[1]:=C;
L_2:A:=2;	L_2:S[1]:=B;	L_2:B:=2;	L_2:V[1]:=C;	L_2:C:=2;	L_2:Y[1]:=A;
L_3:A:=3;	L_3:R[2]:=A;	L_3:B:=3;	L_3:U[2]:=B;	L_3:C:=3;	L_3:X[2]:=C;
L_4:A:=4;	L_4:S[2]:=B;	L_4:B:=4;	L_4:V[2]:=C;	L_4:C:=4;	L_4:Y[2]:=A;
L_5:A:=5;	L_5:R[3]:=A;	L_5:B:=5;	L_5:U[3]:=B;	L_5:C:=5;	L_5:X[3]:=C;
L_6:A:=6;	L_6:S[3]:=B;	L_6:B:=6;	L_6:V[3]:=C;	L_6:C:=6;	L_6:Y[3]:=A;
...	...	...	...	...	...

Figure D.11 Test for a more complex violation of A(CMP, RO, WO, WA).

Test 7. Test of A(CMP, RO, WO, WA, UPO).

Test 6 can be collapsed onto two processes, as shown in Figure D.12. The three conditions for Test 6 apply also to Test 7. But Test 7 can be subjected to a fourth test, namely, a test to detect a failure to obey UPO [SMIT84].

Condition 4. $V[i] \geq j$ or $Y[j] \geq i$ for $0 \leq i, j \leq k$.

P_1	P_2
L_{11}: A:= 1;	L_{11}: B:= 1;
L_{12}: —:= A;	L_{12}: —:= B;
L_{13}: V[1]:= B;	L_{13}: Y[1]:= A;
L_{21}: A:= 2;	L_{21}: B:= 2;
L_{22}: —:= A;	L_{22}: —:= B;
L_{23}: V[2]:= B;	L_{23}: Y[2]:= A;
...	...
L_{k1}: A:= k;	L_{k1}: B:= k;
L_{k2}: —:= A;	L_{k2}: —:= B;
L_{k3}: V[k]:= B;	L_{k3}: Y[k]:= A;

Figure D.12 Test for a violation of A(CMP, RO, WO, UPO).

If $V[i] = b < j$ and $Y[j] = a < i$, then a circuit exists among the events of an execution of the test program.

$$
\begin{aligned}
(P_1, L_{i3}, R, b, B, S_1) &<_{CRW} (P_2, L_{j1}, W, j, B, S_1) \\
&=_{WA} (P_2, L_{j1}, W, j, B, S_2) \\
&<_{UPO} (P_2, L_{j2}, R, j, B, S_2) \\
&<_{RO} (P_2, L_{j3}, R, a, A, S_2) \\
&<_{CRW} (P_1, L_{i1}, W, i, A, S_2) \\
&=_{WA} (P_1, L_{i1}, W, i, A, S_1) \\
&<_{UPO} (P_1, L_{i2}, R, i, A, S_1) \\
&<_{RO} (P_1, L_{i3}, R, b, B, S_1)
\end{aligned}
$$

REFERENCES.

[HEIM91]   ROY C. HEIMBACH. Private communication, 1991.

[SMIT84]   RONALD M. SMITH. Private communication, 1984.

Index

$\Leftrightarrow$, 36
$<_{ARC}$, 93
$<_{AWC}$, 91
$<_{CON}$, 85
$<_{CWA}$, 144
$<_{CWS}$, 145
$<_o$, 52
$<_{RA}$, 72
$<_{RRC}$, 97
$<_{RS}$, 87
$<_{RUF}$, 108
$<_{RWC}$, 95
$<_{SA}$, 72
$<_{SRW}$, 40
$<_{SRW1}$, 133
$<_{SRW2}$, 133
$<_{SWR}$, 133
$<_{WA}$, 72
$<_{WS}$, 83
$<_{XA}$, 73
$\Rightarrow$, 36
$=_{RA}$, 72
$=_{SA}$, 72
$=_{WA}$, 72
$=_{XA}$, 72
$\neg \Rightarrow$, 36

A

Absolute read canonical order rule (*see* ARC)
Absolute write canonical order rule (*see* AWC)
Adjacent paths, 26
Adve, S. V., 20, 21, 23
Anderson, D. W., 14, 23
Applications, 19, 103–4, 119, 121–28, 129–42
ARC, 92–94
Archibald, J. K., 19, 23
Architectures, 1, 35
 distinguishable, 13, 21, 32, 36
 indistinguishable, 13, 15, 19, 20, 21, 22, 32, 36, 103
 product of, 102
 warp, 107
Arcs, 26
 determined, 78
 incident into a node, 26
 incident out of a node, 26
 nondetermined, 78
Atomicity, 1
 general rule of, 71

Atomicity (*cont.*)
  multiple copy, 17
  notation, 72–73
  rules, 15–16
  single copy, 16–17
  violation of?, 91
AWC, 90–92

B

Berge, C., 30
Briggs, F. A., 20, 24, 149, 225

C

Cache coherence, 19
Caches, 15–16, 129–32
Censier, L. M., 18, 23, 138
CF, 18, 19, 23, 138
Circuit, 4, 26
CMP, 1, 4, 39–42
  creating the graph set for, 42–47
  importance of rule of, 101–2
Collier, W. W., 19, 23, 128, 149
Compare and Swap, 21
Computation rule (*see* CMP)
Compute-read-write subrule (*see* CRW)
Compute-write-read subrule (*see* CWR)
Compute-write-write subrule (*see* CWW)
CON, 82, 85–86
Concatenation, 146
Conditional rules, 73, 144
Conditional Write Atomicity (*see* CWA)
Conditional Write Synchronization (*see* CWS)
Consistency (*see* CON)
Corollaries, 148
Correctness, 20, 21, 100
Critical section routines, 1–2, 21
CRW, 41–42
CWA, 144
CWR, 40–41
CWS, 145
CWW, 42

D

Data base systems, 22, 100
Data:
  local, 32, 33, 145
  global, 32–33, 145
  shared, 1, 9, 17, 21
Deadlock, 136
DeBruijn, N. G., 1, 11
Dijkstra, E. W., 1, 11, 128
Distinguishability, 13
Distinguishable architectures (*see* architectures)
Dubois, M., 20, 24, 149, 225

E

Edler, J., 21, 24
Eisenberg, M. A., 1, 11
Events, 4, 34
  global, 145
  local, 145
  phantom, 137
  read, 34
  value of, 34–35, 133
  write, 34
Exclusive flag, 130
Executions, 33
  sets of, 101
  that do not obey an architecture, 36, 100
  that obey an architecture, 36, 100

F

Factorials, 25–26
Failure of events to occur instantaneously, 70–71
Failure to obey:
  A(CMP, WO, RO), 2
  A(CMP, WO, RO, WA), 6
  ARC, 93–94
  AWC, 91–92
  CON, 86
  PO, 58–60

Index

POS, 64–66
RA, 77–78
RO, 63
RRC, 97–98
RS, 87–88
RWC, 95–96
SA, 73–75
URW, 55
UWR, 53–54
UWW, 56–57
WA, 7, 75–77
WO, 61–62
WS, 84
Feautrier, P., 18, 23, 138
Fetch and Op, 21
Flag:
  exclusive, 130
  not here, 130
  read only, 130
Frey, B. G., 15, 24, 104, 109
Frey's theorem, 20, 23, 108, 144

G

Gelenbe, E., 19, 24
Global events, 145
Gottlieb, A., 21, 24
Graph of rules, 101, 148
Graph sets, 26–27
  circuit-full, 26
  compound, 26
  partly circuit-free, 26
  product of, 26
  simple, 26
Graphs, 26–29
  complete, 28
  compound, 26
  simple, 26
  sum of, 26

H

"Happens before" rule, 4
Heimbach, R. C., 221, 226, 227

Hill, M. D., 20, 21, 23
Hofri, M., 1, 12

I

IBM System 370 Principles of Operation, 16, 21, 24
IBM System 370, 16, 21
Indistinguishability, 13
Indistinguishable architectures (see Architectures)
Instantaneous operations, 16–17, 70–71
Interstatement rules, 82–89
Interstitial function, 132
Intrastatement rules, 90–98

J

Jefferson, D. R., 109

K

Knuth, D. E., 1, 12
Kruskal, C. P., 21, 24
Kuck, D. J., 14, 24
Kuhn, R. H., 14, 24

L

Lamport, L., 1, 12, 19, 20, 24, 37
Leasure, B., 14, 24
Livelock, 136
Locality of spatial reference, 16
Locality of temporal reference, 15
Logical correctness (see Correctness)

M

McAuliffe, K. P., 21, 24
McGuire, M. R., 1, 11

Model of a multiprocessing system, 33–37, 129–42
Model of time, 37–38
Models, building, 31
Models, goals, 31
Monotonic sequence, 3, 8
Multiprocessing system:
 essence of, 32
 model of, 33, 129–42

N

Nicholas, K. E., 19, 21, 24
Node, 26
Nondeterminism, reification of, 108
Not here flag, 130

O

Operands:
 local, 33
 global, 33
 see also Values
Operating system, 22
Operator:
 addition, 33
 concatenation, 146
 noncommutative, 146–47
 commutative, 146–47
Order, 1
Order rules, 13–15
 uniprocessor, 52, 53–57
 multiprocessor, 52, 57–66
Ordering, strong, 20
Ordering, weak, 20
Out-of-order reads, 15, 103–9

P

Papadimitriou, C. H., 22, 24
Path, 26
 adjacent, 26
 complete, 28

Pederson, R. J., 109
Performance improvement, 119
Phantom events, 137
PO, 57–60
POO, 68
POS, 64–66
Processes, 32, 33
Program order by store rule (*see* POS)
Program order rule (*see* PO)
PTUI computer, 143, 146

R

RA, 72, 77–78
Range, values in, 3, 8
Raynal, M., 1, 12
Read atomicity rule (*see* RA)
Read only flag, 130
Read order rule (*see* RO)
Read order obeyed, but not write order, 4–5
Read, out-of-order (*see* Out-of-order reads)
Read synchronization, problem with, 19, 118
Read synchronization rule (*see* RS)
Read-unordered-factorially rule (*see* RUF)
Relative read canonical order rule (*see* RRC)
Relative write canonical order rule (*see* RWC)
Ring architectures, 121–28
 Program ordered by store, 127–28
 Write atomic, 124–25
 Write synchronized, 125–27
RO, 4, 6, 62–63
ROO, 69
RRC, 96–98
RS, 19, 82, 87–88
Rudolph, L., 21, 24
RUF, 108
Rules, 4, 26, 32
 conditional, 73, 144
 graph of, 148

Index

233

limits on disobeying, 143
sets of, 101
RWC, 94–96

S

SA, 71, 73–75
Same-order-same-store (*see* SOSS)
Scheurich, C., 20, 24, 149, 225
Section, critical (*see* Critical section)
Sequential consistency, 20, 21, 100
Set, SOSS (*see* SOSS)
Sets, 25
Sevcik, K., 19, 24
Shared data, (*see* Data, shared)
Smith, R. M., 14, 24, 149, 227
Snir, M., 21, 24
SOSS set, 42–44
SOSS sequence, 146
Sparacio, F. J., 14, 23
Spatial reference, locality of, 16
SRW, 40
Statement atomicity rule (*see* SA)
Statement-read-write subrule (*see* SRW)
Synchronization (*see* Read synchronization, write synchronization)

T

Teller, P. J., 21, 24
Templates (*see* Transition templates)
Temporal reference, locality of, 15
Test and Set instruction, 2
Theorem:
 A1, 53
 A2, 55
 A3, 56
 A4, 14, 47, 58
 A5, 15
 A6, 15, 61, 223
 A7, 9, 223, 224
 A13, 63
 A21, 64
 A24, 128, 149
 A25, 22, 73
 A28, 128, 148, 149
 A29, 20, 148, 149, 225
 A30, 148
 A31, 148
 A32, 77
 A35, 86
 A38, 9, 75, 226
 A39, 84
 A41, 87
 A43, 91–92
 A45, 95
 A46, 93
 A48, 97
Time, model of, 37–38
Tomasulo, R. M., 14, 23, 24
Transition templates, 36–37, 104–5
Triplet, 26

U

Uniprocessor order rule (*see* UPO)
Uniprocessor-read-write rule (*see* URW)
Uniprocessor-write-read rule (*see* UWR)
Uniprocessor-write-write rule (*see* UWW)
UPO, 57
URW, 14, 54–55
UWR, 14, 53–54
UWW, 14, 55–57

V

Values:
 in range, 3, 8, 220
 initial, 33
 monotonic, 3, 220
 terminal, 33

W

WA, 7–8, 19, 72, 75–77, 139
Warp architectures, 107

Wegner, P., 21, 24
Wilson, J., 21, 24
WO, 4, 6, 60–62
WOO, 69
Wolfe, M., 14, 24
WOS, 66
Write atomicity rule (*see* WA)
Write order by store rule (*see* WOS)
Write order obeyed, but not read order, 5
Write order rule (*see* WO)
Write set, 132
Write synchronization rule (*see* WS)
WS, 18, 82, 83–84, 139
WSISWA Theorem, 19, 20, 23, 110–20, 143

X

X function, 111
XA, 73, 78